# Your Complete Guide to Transition Planning and Services

# Your Complete Guide to Transition Planning and Services

by

**Mary E. Morningstar, Ph.D.**
University of Kansas
Lawrence

and

**Beth Clavenna-Deane, Ph.D.**
Keystone Learning Services
Ozawkie, Kansas

*with invited contributors*

·P A U L·H·
BROOKES
PUBLISHING C⁰ ®

Baltimore • London • Sydney

**Paul H. Brookes Publishing Co.**
Post Office Box 10624
Baltimore, Maryland 21285-0624
USA

www.brookespublishing.com

Typeset by Progressive Publishing Services, York, Pennsylvania.
Manufactured in the United States of America by
Sheridan Books, Chelsea, Michigan.

**Library of Congress Cataloging-in-Publication Data**

Names: Morningstar, Mary E., author.
Title: Your complete guide to transition planning and services / Mary E. Morningstar, University of
    Kansas Lawrence, and Beth Clavenna-Deane, Ph.D., Keystone Learning Services; with invited
    contributors.
Description: 1 | Baltimore : Paul H. Brookes Publishing Co., [2017] | Includes bibliographical references
    and index.
Identifiers: LCCN 2017017695 | ISBN 9781598573114 (paperback)
Subjects: LCSH: Children with disabilities—Education (Secondary)—United States. | Students with
    disabilities—Services for—United States. | High school students—Counseling of—United States. |
    School-to-work transition—United States. | BISAC: EDUCATION / Special Education / General. |
    EDUCATION / Special Education / Social Disabilities.
Classification: LCC LC4031 .M649 2017 | DDC 371.9—dc23
LC record available at https://lccn.loc.gov/2017017695

British Library Cataloguing in Publication data are available from the British Library.

2021   2020   2019   2018   2017

10    9    8    7    6    5    4    3    2    1

# Contents

# About the Forms

Purchasers of this book may download, print, and/or photocopy the blank forms for professional or educational use. These blank forms are included with the print book and are also available at **www.brookespublishing.com/morningstar/materials** for both print and e-book buyers.

# About the Authors

**Mary E. Morningstar, Ph.D.,** University of Kansas, Department of Special Education, 1122 W. Campus Road, Lawrence, Kansas 66045

Dr. Mary E. Morningstar is an associate professor in the Department of Special Education at the University of Kansas (KU), Codirector of the National Assistance Center on Transition, and Director of the Transition Coalition, which offers online, hybrid, and in-person professional development and resources for secondary special educators and transition practitioners. Her research agenda includes evaluating how secondary teacher quality and professional development have an impact on transition practices and student outcomes, transition planning with culturally diverse families, and facilitating interagency collaboration for improved outcomes. Dr. Morningstar coordinates the online transition master's program and the teacher education program for teachers of students with significant disabilities, working to transform special education coursework to support inclusive practices in schools and the community. She is the principal investigator for the fully inclusive KU-Transition to Postsecondary Education program that supports Kansas University students with intellectual disabilities.

**Beth Clavenna-Deane, Ph.D.,** Keystone Learning Services, 500 E. Sunflower Boulevard, Ozawkie, Kansas 66070

Dr. Beth Clavenna-Deane has worked with secondary students with disabilities for over 25 years; she began her career as a secondary special education teacher before spending almost 10 years as a transition coordinator. She has provided special education services to students with varying levels of disability ranging from mild to significant. Over the past decade, Dr. Clavenna-Deane has focused her expertise and research on autism, behavior, and social-emotional learning, and on the impact of related characteristics and skills upon the transition to adulthood. She currently provides technical assistance and training to multiple Kansas school districts on making universal, targeted, and intensive supports available for all students needing assistance through the Kansas MTSS framework.

# About the Contributors

**Megan Heidrich, BSW, MSW,** works as the program coordinator for an inclusive postsecondary education program for students with intellectual disabilities at the University of Kansas.

**Ryan Kellems, M.Ed., Ph.D.,** is an assistant professor in the counseling psychology and special education department at Brigham Young University. His primary research interests are video modeling, transition, and using the latest technology to assist students with disabilities as they transition to life after school.

**Dawn Rowe, Ph.D.,** is an assistant research professor in the secondary special education and transition (SSET) unit at the University of Oregon where she works as a researcher and technical assistance provider for the National Technical Assistance Center on Transition (NTACT).

**Monica L. Simonsen, MSE, Ph.D.,** is the program director for the special education online graduate programs at the University of Kansas (KU). Prior to her current role, she worked as the program coordinator for the online transition graduate program at KU.

*To all of the secondary special educators and transition coordinators who have inspired students and families to be successful*

# 1

# I'm Responsible for Transition Planning … Now What Do I Do?

Michael, a newly hired transition coordinator in a medium-sized suburban school district, is excited yet overwhelmed. Having worked for several years as a special educator in one of the district's two high schools, he has the background, passion, and drive for supporting youth with special needs, and he is familiar with transition services and requirements. Two years ago, Michael completed his master's degree in special education and took a course in his program focused on transition education and services. He applied what he learned from this class and started facilitating a more student-directed planning approach to transition, using an evidence-based curriculum he had learned about to support his students. He also helped some of his graduating students prepare to attend postsecondary educational settings, sharing information about postsecondary disability services with students and families. Yet the transition coordinator role is new to him. The school district created the transition coordinator position after examining the past 3 years of data associated with the transition requirements, in which the district was found to need improvement. Michael is now expected to coordinate transition services for two high schools and support all secondary special educators and students age 16 and older who are involved in transition planning and services.

The transition-related activities Michael implemented as a special educator were helpful to his students, but he cannot possibly work directly with all the students across the two high schools. He will need to shift his focus to coordinating transition planning and services for the district, and sharing information and resources with secondary teachers. In addition, he will need to start collaborating with community agencies to ensure seamless transitions to adulthood for students exiting school. His new responsibility is great, but he is unsure where to begin. What first steps should Michael take to improve transition planning and services in his district?

Whether you are a transition coordinator (also called transition specialist, facilitator, and administrator) like Michael, or a secondary special educator preparing your students for life after school, this book will support you in embracing and navigating your challenging role in supporting all students to succeed, achieve, and realize a successful future. This important work, though rewarding, may sometimes give us pause, especially if new responsibilities are thrust upon us when we have had little preparation or training. Like Michael, we too may find ourselves asking, "*Now* what do I do?" This book can be helpful in answering this question and getting you "unstuck" when your role in helping students transition to adulthood seems overwhelming or when you need concrete solutions for next steps. It will provide you with a set of skills, tips, strategies, and evidence-based interventions to support your students in achieving positive post-school outcomes.

Michael's situation is very common among transition coordinators, who are often promoted from within a district and may have little training in coordinating transition services. In addition, many special educators (maybe even yourself) have had little formal training other than perhaps a single introductory course in transition planning, with most special educators learning about transition on the job (Morningstar & Benitez, 2013). That's why this chapter starts with the basics, helping you understand the importance of transition planning in the lives of students with disabilities and explaining the roles of various professionals in implementing a quality transition program.

## GETTING STARTED:
## Learning the Basics of Transition Planning and Services

For the past 25 years, transition planning and services have been required by the Individuals with Disabilities Education Act (IDEA; PL 108-446). This legislation has been a strong impetus for professionals to develop a coordinated approach to facilitate their students' transition from school to postsecondary settings, including integrated employment, postsecondary education and training, and independent living. This chapter, as well as the rest of this book, will describe specialized skills, activities, and tasks required of professionals like Michael, and provide strategies for tackling daily responsibilities. However, if you are a secondary special educator, the resources and information in this book are equally relevant to your role during transition. Not every school district has created a transition coordinator role, and this may mean that as a special educator you will be responsible for ensuring that your students' transition is coordinated.

Special education teachers are responsible for planning and providing transition services for the students on their caseload. Despite these requirements, students with disabilities continue to be less prepared for adulthood than their peers without disabilities (Newman, Wagner, Cameto, & Knokey, 2009). Over the years, secondary special education teachers have reported being unprepared to plan and deliver transition services (Li, Bassett, & Hutchinson, 2009; Wolfe, Boone, & Blanchett, 1998). Studies have revealed that special education teachers who lack specific transition competencies are less likely to implement effective transition services (Benitez, Morningstar, & Frey, 2009). Consequently, teachers who are unprepared to plan and deliver transition services may be contributing to poor outcomes for students with disabilities.

Preparing for transition planning can be a formidable task for special educators, who must juggle a multitude of shifting priorities and responsibilities. Many secondary special educators have reported increased pressure to support students with disabilities to fully access the general education curriculum to meet high-stakes testing requirements. In addition, they may be experiencing challenges associated with meeting the compliance requirements of the individualized education program (IEP), as well as increased data-based decision making and other administrative tasks. Yet despite these competing tasks, it is still crucial for special educators to support their students in achieving successful post-school outcomes. If you are a special educator, this book provides ideas and strategies so you can embed transition practices into your daily work and meet some of these challenges. To begin, let's start by examining the role of the special education teacher versus the transition coordinator.

## Key School Personnel: The Secondary Special Educator and Transition Coordinator

Two types of school personnel are most often involved with transition planning and services: 1) secondary special education teachers engaged in IEP transition planning and instruction, and 2) transition coordinators who ensure a coordinated set of activities as specified in the transition requirements of the IDEA. The IDEA has determined that all special educators who are serving students with disabilities are responsible for transition planning, but this is typically at the student level (i.e., the students on each special educator's caseload). What we know is that the most effective programs have designated personnel (i.e., transition coordinators) who coordinate all in-school services and supports affecting students, families, and teachers, as well as coordinate with outside agencies involved in transition (Morningstar & Benitez, 2013). Figure 1.1 is helpful in understanding the differences between the two primary professionals involved in transition. Depending on your role, you can use the checklist provided in the figure to review your transition responsibilities. What are you currently doing, and what might you add to your daily practice?

***The Role of the Secondary Special Educator***    Secondary special educators are responsible for individual student skill development and planning activities rather than program development or service coordination. In fact, identifying secondary special educators who work in classrooms for most of their day as transition "coordinators" misrepresents the complexity of the transition process. In working with individual students, special educators teach specific skills using evidence-based practices related to transition outcomes (e.g., self-determination, interpersonal engagement, learning processes, core academics, career development and preparation). They also help identify and provide accommodations students will need in school and in the community (Blalock, Kleinhammer-Tramill, Morningstar, & Wehmeyer, 2003).

In most middle and high school settings, secondary special educators provide necessary curricula and instruction addressing students' academic and functional IEP goals. As IEP case managers, teachers are also required to ensure that students receive transition planning and appropriate transition services beginning in middle school and extending throughout the student's high school career. For these reasons, we know that secondary special education teachers are most comfortable with transition competencies related to planning and developing transition IEPs. However, a wider range of knowledge and skills is needed to create transition programs for students with disabilities that lead to improved postsecondary outcomes. In fact, preparing qualified school personnel is recognized as one of the critical factors in improving the outcomes of students with disabilities (Blalock et al., 2003; Kohler & Greene, 2004). However, this knowledge and these skills extend well beyond what many teachers receive as far as training and professional development, as was the case for Michael, the new transition coordinator (Anderson et al., 2003; Hu, 2001).

***The Role of the Transition Coordinator***    The position of transition coordinator emerged with the inclusion of transition planning and services in the IDEA. This specialized position focuses primarily on coordinating transition services rather than providing direct services to students (Morningstar & Clavenna-Deane, 2014). Transition coordinators ensure that teachers are informed of current transition-related information and methods for facilitating transition planning (e.g., identifying students' post-school interests, preferences, strengths, needs). In this respect, transition coordinators often provide important professional development to teachers throughout a high school(s) or district(s). Furthermore, transition coordinators work as liaisons between students, parents, administrators,

# Special Educator/Transition Coordinator Checklist

Think about the transition-related activities you engage in on an ongoing basis. Depending on your role, check off which activities you are doing and think about what practices you might start implementing.

| Secondary special educators | ✓ | Transition coordinator/Transition specialist | ✓ |
|---|---|---|---|
| Prepare individualized education programs (IEP)s during transition planning. | | Train teachers to develop compliant and high quality transition IEPs and monitor IEPs to ensure compliance. | |
| Support students by teaching skills needed to fully participate in their transition planning. | | Support teachers to know about and use evidence-based strategies for student involvement in IEPs. | |
| Collaborate with families about upcoming transition planning meetings and gather input ahead of time. | | Provide resources and materials to teachers to help them engage with their families before, during, and after transition planning meetings. | |
| Teach students with disabilities the skills they need to be successful post-high school, focusing on integrated employment, postsecondary education and training, and adult roles and responsibilities. | | Share information, resources, and training with school staff related to student engagement and effective strategies to ensure post-school success. | |
| Collaborate with general education teachers to ensure students have access to general education curriculum and context. | | Collaborate with all school staff to provide resources and training related to improving access to general education and meeting the transition needs of students. | |
| Ensure students understand their support needs and help them identify the accommodations they need to be successful. | | Provide information, training, and resources to school personnel, families, and students about post-school accommodations and services. | |
| Collect data and progress monitor to ensure students are achieving identified skills, IEP goals, and objectives to facilitate movement toward post-school success. | | Collect and monitor post-school outcomes data to evaluate student outcomes and make improvements to services. | |
| Advocate for individual students and families when needed related to transition skills, experiences, and opportunities. | | Advocate for improvements to transition services with school and district administrators; take on a leadership role with community agencies providing programs and services needed by students. | |
| Provide information and resources to families and students about outside agencies and services and share information about family and student trainings. | | Provide information, resources, and training events about outside agencies to school staff and case managers to share with families and students. | |
| Support families and students with the referral process to be eligible for community agencies and receive needed adult supports. | | Collaborate regularly with outside community agencies and other critical transition stakeholders to ensure seamless transitions to adult services. | |
| Participate in professional development associated with transition planning and services. | | Develop, coordinate, and provide professional development for school staff related to evidence-based practices. | |

**Figure 1.1.** Which role do you play? Transition coordinator versus special educator checklist.

and staff to connect postsecondary goals with the curriculum decisions that drive course content. According to Blalock and colleagues (2003), transition coordinators support

1. Student development by developing and coordinating career preparation programs

2. Student planning by assisting to identify postsecondary options, coordinating with community agencies and services, and monitoring the IEP transition services

3. Interagency collaboration by encouraging collaboration with community services and developing information and training about community resources

4. Program evaluation by evaluating school and student transition-related data, and facilitating strategic planning for transition program improvements

Transition coordinators are expected to possess certain knowledge and skills as reflected in the *Council for Exceptional Children's Advanced Specialty Set: Special Education Transition Specialist* (Council for Exceptional Children [CEC], 2015.) There are seven advanced preparation standards for a transition coordinator (i.e., transition specialist), each with an associated set of knowledge and skills:

1. Assessment: Transition specialists use valid and reliable assessment procedures to evaluate students' interests, strengths, and preferences for development of postsecondary goals and transition services, and monitor the effectiveness of transition practices and programs. They are familiar with both formal and informal assessments, and can use the results of transition assessments to develop measurable postsecondary goals and supports.

2. Curricular content knowledge: Transition specialists know about evidence-based instruction and curricula that are instrumental in developing and improving transition programs, supports, and services. They continuously cultivate and expand their expertise on teaching strategies, instructional methods, curricula, and assistive technologies that allow students with special needs to access academic and transition-related content. This often includes sharing curricular resources related to self-determination, career awareness, postsecondary education, and community participation.

3. Programs, services, and outcomes: Transition specialists advocate for, develop, evaluate, and help improve general and special education programs, supports, and services for students with special needs. They must support and coordinate services across classrooms, schools, and district-level systems. This means knowing about available community- and school-based transition services; understanding the skills needed for success in employment and other postsecondary settings; and promoting transition strategies, models, and curricula.

4. Research and inquiry: Transition specialists conduct and evaluate research and collect data on effective transition practices. They keep abreast of the transition practices that result in positive post-school outcomes and emerging evidence-based models of transition programs and services. They are often responsible for ensuring compliance with federal and state transition regulations.

5. Leadership and policy: Transition specialists assume leadership in overseeing transition programs. They are responsible for upholding professional and ethical expectations; advocating for policies and practices that improve transition planning, services,

and outcomes; and promoting a collaborative and collegial work environment. They need to be knowledgeable about current and upcoming transition policies and laws affecting teachers and students.

6. Professional and ethical practice: Transition specialists display professionalism, respect, and ethical behavior, with the goal of supporting the success of their colleagues and the students they serve. They continually engage in lifelong learning and professional development, keeping informed of important organizations in the field of transition and the latest publications and research. They are knowledgeable about their roles and responsibilities, as well as the responsibilities of other key stakeholders in the transition process

7. Collaboration: Transition specialists collaborate with a variety of school professionals, as well as community agency staff to coordinate and provide transition services and supports to students and families. They are knowledgeable about teamwork, conflict resolution, and the communication strategies and skills needed for working with a variety of stakeholders, including educators, employers, and families. They often lead community-wide transition teams and coordinate out-of-school experiences, such as work-based learning.

The standards can be used to develop a job description for what transition coordinators can and should do, and some districts use them in this way. The impact of transition coordinators extends beyond the scope of the classroom, as they are instrumental in improving transition planning and services for students and families while in school, and also ensuring appropriate supports are in place when students exit special education. Transition coordinators must be knowledgeable about transition assessment, planning, and evaluation, as well as curricular and instructional practices that affect post-school environments (see the Chapter 1 Appendix for a checklist closely adapted from the CEC Advanced Specialty Set and associated skills). Transition coordinators play a critical and meaningful role in promoting successful post-school outcomes for youth with disabilities. Their knowledge and skills focus on systems coordination, and they are instrumental in ensuring that secondary special educators are providing effective transition planning.

## MAKING IT HAPPEN:
### Implementing Effective Transition Programs and Services

Effective transition programs can be designed to address a wide range of transition services for students with disabilities. Because of the complexity of transition, no one professional can sufficiently provide the variety of needed services and supports. Your role in transition may focus on elements of the bigger process, depending on whether you are a secondary special educator, transition coordinator, educational or adult agency professional, or transition stakeholder (e.g., family members). Understanding all the critical features of high-quality transition programs may seem daunting. To break down what makes a transition program effective, let's describe an approach to identifying quality indicators of transition programs and clarify who is best suited to coordinate and implement each critical component. A recently validated measure of transition programs, the *Quality Indicators of Exemplary Transition Programs Needs Assessment-2* QI-2 (Morningstar, Lee, Lattin, & Murray, 2015), looks at seven indicators of a quality transition program and the associated actions school professionals should take to ensure progress toward quality transition practices. Figure 1.2 illustrates the seven indicators.

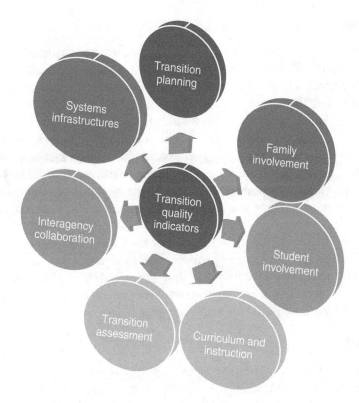

**Figure 1.2.** Quality indicators of effective transition programs. (From Morningstar, M. E., Lee, H., Lattin, D. L., & Murray, A. K. *Career Development and Transition for Exceptional Individuals* [Vol 39, Issue 4] pp. 227–236. Copyright © 2016 by SAGE Publications, Inc. Reprinted by permission of SAGE Publications, Inc.)

Few existing program evaluation measures sufficiently or comprehensively address the IDEA transition regulations, emerging evidence-based practices research, and predictors of post-school success (Test, Fowler et al., 2009; Test, Mazzotti et al., 2009). In addition, critical contextual issues such as cultural diversity, assistive technology, and statewide accountability measures, while not yet established as predictive of transition outcomes, are essential to consider when developing quality secondary transition programs. The seven indicators of quality transition programs, to be discussed individually in this chapter, take these factors into account and provide a framework for understanding how well-run transition programs operate.

## Transition Assessment

Assessment is a first step to transition planning and involves identifying the student's strengths, preferences, interests, and specific transition needs in order to prepare for a successful future. Note that transition assessment should be ongoing throughout the school year, not just completed once, as the student's interests and vision for the future may change over time. The results of the transition assessment should directly inform the development of the student's postsecondary goals and should be communicated and discussed with the student and family (Morningstar et al., 2015). For more on transition assessment, see Chapter 5.

## Transition Planning

Transition planning is at the center of a high-quality transition program and focuses on identifying measurable postsecondary goals for youth with disabilities based on a student's interests, strengths, and preferences, as well as aligning services to facilitate students meeting their goals. Transition planning is in line with the IDEA transition requirements, which mandate that annual IEP goals be aligned with anticipated outcomes that address academics and transition needs (2004). The measurable postsecondary goals identified during transition planning must target education/training, employment, and when appropriate, independent living. In addition, effective transition planning is student- and family-centered, acknowledging the diversity of families and taking the student's culture into account. By putting students and families at the center of planning, transition becomes individualized, comprehensive, and collaborative (Bui & Turnbull, 2003; Keyes & Owens-Johnson, 2003; Michaels & Ferrara, 2005). For the most part, secondary special educators implement the transition planning process with individual students. However, transition coordinators play a role in ensuring that first, transition planning meets the requirements of the IDEA, and second, that educators have the resources and strategies needed to ensure quality student-centered planning approaches.

## Family Involvement

Family members play a critical role throughout a student's life (Geenen, Powers, & Lopez-Vasquez, 2005; Hetherington et al., 2010; Morningstar, Turnbull, & Turnbull, 1995). Teachers and transition coordinators should jointly promote family involvement in the transition process. For example, transition coordinators should take the lead on developing family-friendly transition information and resources, and share these with teachers, who can then directly distribute to families. Teaching parents about the major concepts associated with transition planning has been shown to be an effective practice (Boone, 1992), and transition coordinators should guide educators and professionals (e.g., teachers, social workers, related service providers) on providing support and information to families. The National Technical Assistance Center on Transition (NTACT, 2015) suggests practices for parent-professional collaboration, including 1) creating a family mentoring program, 2) developing a survey to ask families how they would like to be involved, and 3) working with culturally specific community organizations that already have established relationships with families. Because of the system-wide scope of these strategies, transition coordinators, in conjunction with teachers, take the lead. Transition coordinators identify approaches such as family- and student-centered IEP meetings and then train teachers to use these strategies during transition planning (Cho & Gannotti, 2005; Geenen et al., 2005).

## Student Involvement

Students with higher levels of self-determination are more likely to be engaged in employment and independent living after graduation (Morningstar et al., 2010; Wehmeyer & Schwartz, 1997). Therefore, quality transition programs must use practices that teach students skills in decision making, goal setting, problem solving, and self-advocacy. Curricula that help teach and enhance self-determination skills are many and varied, including 1) curricula teaching academic, social, and job-specific skills (Moore, Cartledge, &

Heckaman, 1995; Wolgemuth, Cobb, & Dugan, 2007); 2) curricula teaching self-monitoring for functional life skills (Bullock & Mahon, 1992; Todd & Reid, 2006); and 3) the *Self-Determined Learning Model of Instruction* (Wehmeyer et al., 2012). These curricula help students acquire the skills they need to be as independent, active, and involved as possible in the transition process.

To further support student involvement, opportunities for making real-life choices should be provided to students while in school (Brewer, 2006) and at home (Morningstar, 2006). Teaching students to direct their own IEP meetings using evidence-based curricula is an indicator of quality. Transition coordinators and teachers can share in identifying and implementing evidence-based curricula such as the *Self-Directed IEP* (Martin, Marshall, Maxson, & Jerman, 1996), the *Self-Advocacy Strategy* (Van Reusen, Bos, Schumaker, & Deshler, 1994), and *Whose Future Is It Anyway?* (Wehmeyer et al., 2004), all of which are further described in Chapter 3. Transition coordinators might take the lead on identifying the curricula best suited to their district, and then teachers implement these curricula directly with students. Oftentimes, transition coordinators assist with or teach a class in which these skills are taught.

## Transition-Focused Curriculum and Instruction

Specific transition-related knowledge and skills are established predictors leading to successful adult roles (Test, Mazzotti et al., 2009). Research has shown that students who are included in general education academic courses were more likely to be engaged in postsecondary education, employment, and independent living (Baer et al., 2003). To ensure that students are included in the general education curriculum, quality programs incorporate effective instructional methods when teaching academics. This primarily is the responsibility of the secondary special educator—to collaborate with general education teachers to ensure students with disabilities are fully supported with appropriate accommodations and modifications.

Balancing academics and transition-specific content has also been recognized as an indicator of quality. It is important that content essential to adult independence (e.g., career development, independent living skills) is taught and incorporated in the classroom, and this is often the responsibility of transition coordinators, who share ideas with secondary educators on how to make transition a part of the learning process and academic instruction. We know that enrollment in occupational and vocational coursework and work-based learning experiences are strong predictors of employment (Carter, Cushing, & Kennedy, 2009; Migliore, Mank, Grossi, & Rogan, 2007). Transition coordinators are the leaders in developing, implementing, and evaluating career development and employment approaches taught in school- and work-based settings (Walker & Bartholomew, 2012). In addition, developing social and interpersonal skills should likewise be included in comprehensive transition programs. This area of transition is most appropriate for secondary educators to lead through both direct instruction, as well as embedding the training and practice of critical social skills across academic content. Teaching adult roles and responsibilities (e.g., independent living) is also an important aspect of transition, and secondary teachers typically lead such efforts. Direct skill instruction is the purview of teachers, whereas transition coordinators influence quality by developing essential programs and ensuring that teachers have up-to-date knowledge and resources.

**TIP FOR TRANSITION: Use a College and Career Readiness Framework**

While college and career ready (CCR) initiatives (U.S. Department of Education, 2010) have been instrumental in reforming educational practices, have you thought about what you should consider to prepare your students to be college and career ready? Researchers now suggest college and career readiness goes well beyond core academics, such as those identified in state academic standards. It is equally important to teach students nonacademic skills to ensure students develop the attitudes and behaviors that lead to improved academic knowledge and skills (Conley, 2010; Farrington et al., 2012). Morningstar and colleagues (2015) have developed a helpful framework of six domains that should be considered by special educators to ensure students with disabilities are college and career ready. You can use this list to plan for how to provide opportunities to increase your students' college and career readiness:

1. Academic Engagement
   - Acquiring cognitive and content knowledge (core academics, career and technical education content)
   - Understanding critical knowledge structures (facts, linking ideas, organizing concepts)
   - Performing essential academic behaviors (attendance, productivity, work habits, class participation, adaptability, and flexibility)

2. Mindsets
   - Developing a sense of belonging (trusting relationships, extracurricular engagement)
   - Ensuring growth mindsets (opportunities to practice, learning from mistakes)
   - Taking ownership for learning (advocating, self-awareness, self-efficacy, self-regulation, goal setting)
   - Persevering through challenges (persistence, effort, motivation, seeing value in work, grit)

3. Learning Processes
   - Using skills to access academic content (test-taking skills, note-taking skills, time management, organizational skills, technology, metacognition)
   - Engaging in learning (group/team engagement, listening and speaking skills)

4. Critical Thinking
   - Problem solving
   - Researching
   - Interpreting
   - Communicating
   - Working toward precision and accuracy

5. Interpersonal Engagement
   - Developing skills within self (responsibility, adaptability)
   - Learning to engage with others (asserting self, accountability, leadership, collaboration)
   - Understanding others (social awareness, empathy, respect for diversity)

6. Transition Competencies
   - Early planning for adulthood
   - Understanding career cultures

- Understanding college cultures
- Developing adult roles and responsibilities

## Interagency Collaboration and Community Services

Interagency collaboration is a critical indicator of post-school success (Kohler, 1996; Test, Mazzotti et al., 2009). School-business partnerships are recognized as an essential factor in student career development (Carter, Cushing, & Kennedy, 2009). Access to community agencies leads to stronger postsecondary education and employment outcomes (Bullis, Davis, Bull, & Johnson, 1995). Therefore, establishing a process for communicating and coordinating with outside agencies is a critical responsibility of transition coordinators. This includes establishing procedures for referring students to agencies prior to exiting school, discussing anticipated service needs of students, and developing interagency agreements related to information exchanged, resources shared, and services coordinated. Quality programs provide parents and students with accurate and timely resources about services, which can be a shared responsibility of both educators and transition coordinators.

## Systems-Level Infrastructure

Supporting effective delivery of transition planning and services requires systems-level thinking (Kohler & Rusch, 1996). As you might expect, school districts that hire professionals responsible for coordinating transition programs and services significantly enhance the effectiveness of transition programs (Morningstar & Clavenna-Deane, 2014). Program infrastructures must be in place to maintain support for effective transition programs and policies (Stodden & Leake, 1994). Typically, transition coordinators, along with other school and community officials, lead infrastructure efforts. These efforts address emerging issues such as inclusive education, dropout prevention, and supporting culturally diverse families and students. Evaluating the impact of transition programs on students' learning also requires systems-level infrastructure. Transition coordinators and other central office administration should be managing data systems for academic outcomes, as well as behavioral, nonacademic, and transition competencies. It is important to collect data to monitor whether transition programs result in positive outcomes so they can be modified if needed.

There is much to think about when deciding where to concentrate your focus for transition improvements. When you do identify an area that you believe needs improvement, whether it be to improve the skills and behaviors of your student or to strengthen school and transition programs, you should turn first to the research related to effective transition practices. The National Technical Assistance Center on Transition (NTACT, 2015) has carefully identified a range of evidence-based practices for transition. Table 1.1 clarifies the difference between evidence-based practices, research-based practices, promising practices, and unestablished practices as classified by the NTACT.

**Table 1.1.** Distinguishing evidence-based transition practices

| Evidence-based practices | Research-based practices | Promising practices | Unestablished practices |
|---|---|---|---|
| Based on group experimental, single-case, and correlational research that | Based on group experimental, single-case, and correlational research that | Based on group experimental, single-case, correlational, or qualitative research that | Based on anecdotal evidence or professional judgment that |
| • Used rigorous research designs.<br>• Demonstrated a strong record of success for improving outcomes.<br>• Have undergone a systematic review process.<br>• Adhered to quality indicators related to specific research design. | • Used rigorous research designs.<br>• Demonstrated a sufficient record of success for improving outcomes.<br>• May or may not have undergone a systematic review process.<br>• May or may not adhere to quality indicators related to specific research design. | • Demonstrated limited success for improving outcomes.<br>• May or may not have undergone a systematic review process.<br>• May or may not adhere to quality indicators related to specific research design. | • Could include evidence from rigorous research studies which demonstrate negative effects. |

From the National Technical Assistance Center on Transition (NTACT) (2015). *Effective practices and predictors*. Retrieved from www.transitionta .org/effectivepractices.

## WHAT YOU CAN DO RIGHT NOW:
### Putting Ideas Into Action

Now that you have an overview of some of the basic skills and competencies needed for working with secondary students, coordinating transition services, and the essential characteristics of a quality transition program, it's time to apply that knowledge to your own work with transitioning youth. As you look through the CEC advanced preparation standards for qualified, well-prepared transition coordinators found in the Chapter 1 Appendix, jot down what you already know about transition, which skills you are proficient in, and which skills you need to further develop. The checklist can be a helpful first step in evaluating your skills and knowledge in implementing transition programs. You can consider your own skill level and evaluate your school or district transition program using the seven quality indicators of transition programs. You might also consider accessing the full QI-2 survey online through the Transition Coalition web site (www.transitioncoalition .org) to share with colleagues in your school or district to complete.

Regardless of your role in the transition process (e.g., secondary educator, transition coordinator), an informal assessment of what you know about transition, as well as what you still need to learn, can be an important first step in professional development and improvement. It can also serve as a springboard for how to use this book. As you evaluate your own skills and program quality, you can jump to the chapters in this book that are most likely to support you in implementing new strategies, as well as enhancing existing programs. Armed with the guidance from this book and its plethora of resources, you will be well equipped to launch into this exciting and important endeavor of helping students transition into adulthood.

# Skills and Knowledge Checklist for the Transition Specialist

| CEC Advanced Preparation Standard 1: Assessment | | |
|---|---|---|
| **Skills** | **✓** | **How can I improve in this area? What do I still need to learn?** |
| Utilize a variety of transition assessments on an ongoing basis to develop appropriate transition plans. | | |
| Modify transition assessments to meet individual student needs. | | |
| Interpret results of transition assessments for students, families, and professionals. | | |
| Develop measurable postsecondary goals based on transition assessment results. | | |
| Match student preferences and interests with assessment results with skills and demands of post-school environments. | | |
| Apply transition assessment results to develop natural support systems in post-school settings. | | |
| Assess student progress in work-based experiences. | | |

**Additional notes/professional goals:**

| CEC Advanced Preparation Standard 2: Curricular Content Knowledge | | |
|---|---|---|
| **Skills** | **✓** | **How can I improve in this area? What do I still need to learn?** |
| Provide teachers with instructional practices and related activities to embed transition content within general academic courses. | | |
| Offer instructional, related activities, and curricular resources related to transition planning. | | |
| Deliver self-advocacy and self-determination information and resources. | | |
| Provide instructional resources and related activities addressing career awareness leading to employment preparation and postsecondary education. | | |
| Develop school-based employment experiences and curricula in preparation for postsecondary education and community integration. | | |
| Ensure that student instructional and related activities facilitate movement toward identified postsecondary goals. | | |
| Evaluate evidence-based transition practices and curricula to ensure postschool outcomes. | | |
| Facilitate student-centered transition planning approaches. | | |

**Additional notes/professional goals:**

| CEC Advanced Preparation Standard 3: Programs, Services, and Outcomes | | |
|---|---|---|
| **Skills** | **✓** | **How can I improve in this area? What do I still need to learn?** |
| Develop annual goals and objectives related to measurable postsecondary goals. | | |
| Select relevant transition services and course of study to achieve postsecondary goals and objectives. | | |
| Align instructional activities and related activities with postsecondary goals and objectives. | | |
| Identify and facilitate modifications within work and community environments. | | |
| Evaluate instructional and related activities in relation to postsecondary goals. | | |
| Develop educational experiences that correspond with IEP postsecondary goals. | | |
| **Additional notes/professional goals:** | | |

| CEC Advanced Preparation Standard 4: Research & Inquiry | | |
|---|---|---|
| Skills | ✓ | How can I improve in this area? What do I still need to learn? |
| Collect post-school outcomes data for youth exiting school to identify relevant variables to improve transition services and programs. | | |
| Analyze data of individual transition plans to address federal and state compliance requirements. | | |
| Use evidence-based practices and research to develop transition programs and services. | | |

**Additional notes/professional goals:**

| CEC Advanced Preparation Standard 5: Leadership and Policy | | |
|---|---|---|
| **Skills** | **✓** | **How can I improve in this area? What do I still need to learn?** |
| Advocate for transition program and policy changes to improve transition services. | | |
| Engage in individual student advocacy to obtain transition planning and services. | | |
| Train district professionals, community agency personnel, and other transition stakeholders about transition for individuals with exceptionalities. | | |
| Provide leadership to ensure that individuals with exceptionalities experience the same opportunities and resources as those without exceptionalities. | | |
| Include and prepare students, families, teams, and other related-agency members for the transition planning process. | | |
| Coordinate and facilitate ongoing transition planning during and after IEP meetings. | | |
| Ensure same career and vocational opportunities as peers without disabilities. | | |

**Additional notes/professional goals:**

| CEC Advanced Preparation Standard 6: Professional and Ethical Practice | | |
|---|---|---|
| **Skills** | **✓** | **How can I improve in this area? What do I still need to learn?** |
| Develop and maintain professional transition-related ethics in working with community and related agency personnel. | | |
| Participate in activities of professional organizations in the field of transition. | | |

**Additional notes/professional goals:**

| CEC Advanced Preparation Standard 7: Collaboration | | |
|---|---|---|
| **Skills** | **✓** | **How can I improve in this area?** **What do I still need to learn?** |
| Promote active involvement of families, especially those who are culturally and linguistically diverse, throughout the transition decision-making and implementation process. | | |
| Coordinate interagency agreements and partnerships to use and share data to achieve postsecondary outcomes. | | |
| Communicate with employers and other professionals to develop and monitor natural support networks. | | |
| Disseminate transition information and resources to stakeholders. | | |
| Participate in community-level transition teams. | | |
| Ensure compliance with federal and state policies regarding transition (e.g., Americans with Disabilities Act, Fair Labor Standards Act, Vocational Rehabilitation Act). | | |
| Provide referrals for individuals with exceptionalities and their families to postsecondary and community services. | | |
| Coordinate work-based programs (e.g., work-study, paid work experiences, internships). | | |
| Coordinate regularly with employers, businesses, and worksite personnel. | | |
| Plan accommodations and modifications in postsecondary, educational, and training settings. | | |
| Develop job placements within the community and coordinate placement activities with relevant agencies. | | |
| **Additional notes/professional goals:** | | |

# 2

# Transition Planning
# From Compliance to Quality

When Bryce first started high school, he wasn't thinking about his goals for the future. He was only concerned about the courses he needed to graduate—especially the number of math classes he had to take—because he hated math and found it very difficult. Bryce has a learning disability that makes academics challenging for him, and he sometimes becomes frustrated and discouraged. He has a passion for carpentry and woodworking, and has helped his father build furniture in the workshop behind their farmhouse. Bryce loves his rural lifestyle, and he particularly enjoys spending time outdoors tending the small plot of land his family owns. The educational team wants to get a head start on planning for Bryce's life after high school. How can they help Bryce realize and achieve his goals? What would the transition planning process entail?

You are most likely working with or will be working with a student like Bryce who is in need of transition planning. Do you know what is required of you? Transition planning and services were first mandated by the IDEA in 1990 (and then amended in 1997 and 2004). Understanding the requirements of a transition-focused IEP is important, so this chapter's first purpose is to provide you with working knowledge of the IDEA transition requirements. However, to ensure positive adult outcomes for your students, it is essential to use evidence-based strategies and interventions for student-focused transition planning, and this involves more than just memorizing what the law says about transition. You'll need to know about approaches to assist students and their families to connect with transition services both within and outside of the school system. In this chapter, you will learn about many strategies for transition planning that capture the spirit and intent of IDEA, which means ensuring that you support and facilitate proactive, person-centered planning (PCP) for life after high school. The end goal is to implement compliant, high-quality transition planning that leads to positive outcomes for every student.

## GETTING STARTED:
### Understanding the IDEA Requirements for Transition

Where did the transition requirements of IDEA come from? In 1984, Madeline Will, the Assistant to the Secretary of Education for the Office of Special Education and Rehabilitation Programs (OSERS), and mother of Jonathon, then just an adolescent with disabilities, was concerned by the lack of progress students with disabilities had made since the authorization of the law, PL 94-142, which guaranteed a free and appropriate education for all students with disabilities. She defined transition as the bridge to employment, and directed the OSERS to support transition grant initiatives to improve transition services.

A few years after Madeline Will first introduced the concept of transition to adulthood as a federal policy, IDEA was passed in 1990, outlining specific federal provisions for transition services. However, early research on post-school outcomes (Haring & Lovett, 1990; Hasazi, Johnson, Hasazi, Gordon, & Hull, 1989) showed that the first generation of students with disabilities who had gone through school under special education were not making successful transitions to adulthood. Today, students with disabilities have been making slow progress toward achieving their post-school goals (Blackorby & Wagner, 1996), yet their outcomes are still lower than those of their peers without disabilities (Carter, Austin, & Trainor, 2012; Newman, Wagner, Cameto, Knokey, & Shaver, 2010). IDEA has been reauthorized since its inception in 1990, and the requirements related to transition planning and services have evolved more recently in response to the aforementioned research. Understanding the requirements of the IDEA for transition planning and services is a critical first step toward preparing your students for adulthood. The most recent reauthorization of IDEA occurred in 2004, and its requirements for transition planning address:

- When transition planning must start

- Who is involved in transition planning

- How to write transition IEPs

- How to improve interagency linkages

- What is meant by the age of majority and transfer of rights

- How to provide a summary of performance when a student exits high school

### TIP FOR TRANSITION: Understand the Spirit and Intent of IDEA When Transition Planning

Understanding the IDEA transition regulations can be complicated. Be sure to read up on the law and know exactly what is required, and encourage educational team members to collaborate and converse on ways to make the law come alive in transition planning practices. The IDEA Partnership web site (www.ideapartnership.org) provides links to the *IDEA Dialogue Guides*, tools to bridge the gap between what IDEA requires and how we actually implement the law in our schools and communities (The IDEA Partnership, n.d.). Be sure to read the *Topical Dialogue Guide on Secondary Transition*, which contains a set of dialogue starters, including reaction questions and application questions, for the team.

## When Transition Planning Starts

It is critical to ensure that a sufficient amount of time and energy be given to developing the transition component of the IEP and to guarantee that it is guided by quality transition planning. In 2004, IDEA mandated that transition planning must start no later than the first IEP to be in effect when the child is 16. To most teachers, this often refers to the IEP that is developed when the student is 15 years old, depending on when the IEP meeting occurs. To maintain compliance with IDEA, it is important to pay attention to when the IEP meeting will be held and not wait until the student is 16 years old to start thinking about transition planning.

The mandate that transition planning should begin at age 16 was disappointing to those who advocated that transition planning should begin when students are younger, especially for those who are at risk of dropping out of school. However, many states have opted to keep transition planning at 14 years old, so you should check your state special education laws to make sure you know when transition starts for your students. Remember, even if you are in a state in which transition planning doesn't officially start until 16 years old, you can still begin sooner, as the law only tells you when you *must* have started transition planning. It's never too early to start planning for the future!

## Who Is Involved in Transition Planning

IDEA is clear on who is required to participate in IEP meetings for transition planning. Required participants include the parents, at least one regular and special educator, a representative of the district (usually an administrator), someone to interpret evaluation results (usually the school psychologist), others the family would like to invite, and the student (if appropriate) [34 CFR 300.321(b)] [20 U.S.C. 1414(d)(1)(B)]. Two of the most critical stakeholders during transition IEPs are the student and his or her family.

*Students*     IDEA mandates that if a purpose of an IEP team meeting is to consider a student's postsecondary goals and transition services, then the student must be invited to attend the meeting. While IDEA does not require that the student attend his or her meeting, it does make it clear that whenever appropriate, the student should be a member of the IEP team. If a student cannot attend the IEP meeting, it is preferable that the meeting be rescheduled to accommodate him or her. At a minimum, it is essential that the student's needs, strengths, preferences, and interests are considered during the IEP planning.

Because the IEP is based upon a student's needs, strengths, preferences, and interests, it makes sense for the student to be present at transition meetings. In the most ideal situation, the student actually runs his or her own IEP meeting, or what is called a student-run (or self-directed) IEP. Using this approach, the student prepares ahead of time for his or her IEP by 1) identifying his or her strengths, preferences, and interests, as well as needs related to postsecondary goals; 2) practicing leading the IEP meeting; and 3) developing goals to include in the IEP. More information about this approach can be found in Chapter 3.

*Parents*     According to IDEA, parents are to be active members of IEP teams. When you send notification to families of an upcoming IEP transition meeting, you can provide a brochure on transition (see Figure 2.1) along with required written parental notification. This helps parents have more information about transition prior to the meeting. It is recommended that the parent notice include information indicating that the student will be invited to the meeting. In addition, parents should be notified of any other agency that will be invited to send a representative, and schools must seek consent from parents prior to inviting outside agency representatives [34 CFR 300.321(b)(3)]. Remember that parents are allowed to bring or invite other people to the meeting to participate on the IEP team.

If parents cannot attend the IEP meeting, you can use other methods to ensure parent participation, including individual or conference telephone calls. Whether parents attend the IEP meeting or not, they are still entitled to copies of the completed IEP. Of course,

## There's a world of opportunity out there... if you dream and prepare!

**Students** and **families** are **vital** to the transition planning process

\*\*\*\*\*\*\*\*\*\*\*\*\*\*\*\*\*\*\*\*\*\*\*\*\*\*\*\*\*\*\*\*\*\*\*\*\*\*\*\*\*\*\*\*\*\*\*\*\*\*\*\*\*\*\*\*\*\*\*\*

For information about transition in your school:

## What path will your child take *after* High School?

## Transition Planning

can **help** you

with the **answers**...

**Figure 2.1.** Transition planning brochure to share with families. (From the Transition Coalition [2015]. *Transition Planning Brochure*. Lawrence: Transition Coalition, The University of Kansas. Retrieved from http://transitioncoalition .org/blog/tc-materials/transition-planning/; adapted by permission.)

# Do you have questions about how your child will learn, work, have friends and a good life after high school?

Transition services help students and families establish a vision for the future about where students will live and work, and how they will participate in their community

## Transition planning focuses on:

- Future Education & Training
- Future Careers & Employment
- Community Involvement
- Connections with Agencies & Services

## *Students, families, schools, and agencies work as a team to support the student's plans for the future.*

*(continued)*

**Figure 2.1.** *(continued)*

# Transition Planning consists of… curriculum, services and supports to help students move successfully to life after high school.

- Transition planning must begin by the IEP in effect when a student turns 16.

- Transition planning can begin earlier, if needed.

- Some states start transition planning when the student turns 14.

- ALL students with IEPs must receive transition planning and services.

- Each year, the student and IEP team identify what the student wants to do after high school for employment, education/training, and independent living.

- The IEP must include coursework, annual goals and transition services to work toward the student's future plans.

### You and your son or daughter will help identify:

- A vision for the future

- High School courses to take

- College and other future learning & training options

- Employment options and experiences

- Extracurricular activities to participate in

- Community experiences, and

- Agencies or services

***It's never too early to start preparing for a successful future.***

involving families in transition planning requires more than just having them at the IEP meeting. Communicating regularly with families so they are up to date on current issues about transition is an important practice. More information about involving families in transition planning can be found in Chapter 4.

## Writing Transition Individualized Education Programs

The first step in writing transition IEPs is to consider the student's future goals and aspirations. After brainstorming, Bryce was able to come up with some dreams for the future: "I'd like to have my own carpentry company and I'd like to have my own farm. I'm not talking about a real big farm; a couple of heads of cattle, my own garden. Of course, I'll be married." The IEP can be considered a road map for reaching the final destination: the student and family's vision for a future adult life. All information written into the IEP should facilitate this vision for the future (which may change several times while the student is in school). The transition requirements of the IDEA focus on developing measurable postsecondary goals (MPGs) in the IEP based on the student's and family's aspirations. Bryce's MPGs described his plans to go to trade school to study carpentry, work within the building trades industry, live on a farm, and get married. His MPGs supported his dreams for the future and helped direct the transition and educational services he would need while in high school to facilitate his movement toward his goals.

The transition planning process is an ongoing review of postsecondary goals, services, and activities, with the focus remaining on the interests, preferences, and strengths of the student. When writing the transition IEP, assessment of the student's strengths, interests, and preferences for the future helps guide the development of the MPGs, with transition services, course of study, and annual IEP goals designed to facilitate the student to achieve his or her measurable postsecondary goals. Because of the critical role MPGs play during transition planning, best practice places them at the beginning of the IEP, because they lay the foundation for everything else that is to be included in the document. Even if the format of the IEP doesn't start with measurable postsecondary goals, you can still run your transition IEP meetings by discussing these goals first. You can use an agenda for your meeting that starts with the discussion of the student's goals for the future and the development of the measurable postsecondary goals.

### TIP FOR TRANSITION: Use an Individualized Education Program Agenda Flip Chart

If your school's IEP is set up and the MPGs are not at the beginning of the IEP, you can still start your meeting by focusing on the student's postsecondary goals. Here is a tip from one transition coordinator: "The use of an IEP agenda flip chart helps the team cover the transition information that is important and focuses on the process, not just the paperwork. I personally attend several hundred IEPs a year and have used the tool to help provide a better understanding for all team members" (Kellems & Morningstar, 2009, p. 6). If discussing transition is a critical element of your next IEP, be sure to develop an agenda so all of the critical components you have learned about are discussed. Visit the Transition Coalition web site (www.transitioncoalition.org) to find more Tips for Transition and get many more ideas.

***Transition Assessments***     The measurable postsecondary goals in the IEP must be developed based upon age-appropriate transition assessments. Transition assessments are not a new idea; in fact, even before they were included in IDEA, Sitlington, Neubert, and Leconte (1997) defined transition assessment as,

> The ongoing process of collecting data on the individual's needs, preferences, and interests as they relate to the demands of current and future working, educational, living, and personal and social environments. Assessment data serve as the common thread in the transition process and form the basis for defining goals and services to be included in the IEP. (pp. 70–71)

The requirements for using transition assessments as an element of IEP planning were mandated in 2004.

Keep in mind that age-appropriate transition assessments refer to a student's chronological age, not developmental age. For example, if a student is 17 years old and reads at a fifth grade level, you should use assessments that are appropriate for high school students and make appropriate accommodations for the student, rather than have the student complete an assessment for younger children. Transition assessment serves many purposes, including:

- Identifying a student's strengths, interests, preferences, and needs

- Developing measurable postsecondary goals

- Determining relevant academic and functional skills instruction

- Identifying appropriate transition services

- Identifying necessary interagency supports and linkages

- Evaluating instruction and supports already in place (Noonan, Morningstar, & Clark, 2009)

Transition assessment is an ongoing process, not a single form that you fill out right before the transition IEP. Age-appropriate transition assessments must be planned and completed over the course of the student's school career. They are used to identify measurable postsecondary goals, and also to track progress toward the student's goals. Therefore, using transition assessments is a dynamic process and should be incorporated throughout a school year.

Typically, results from transition assessments are reported in the student's present levels of academic and functional performance on the IEP and are discussed before the measurable postsecondary goals are developed. During transition planning, the section of the IEP that addresses present level of educational and functional performance should also include transition-specific information about:

- Strengths of the student

- How the student's disability affects performance in the general education setting

- Parents' current concerns about the education of their child

- Changes in functioning since the last IEP

- Summary of the most recent evaluation or reevaluation results

- Summary of performance on formal or informal transition assessments

More information and some examples of transition assessments can be found in Chapter 5.

***Measurable Postsecondary Goals***    IEP teams must develop and specify MPGs in the areas of employment, education and/or training, and where appropriate, independent living. This requires IEP teams to focus on long-term goals that are measurable, and the team must be able to demonstrate how they helped to facilitate the student to achieve his or her postsecondary goals. It can be hard for some IEP teams to decide if an independent living goal is needed. Independent living includes the skills and knowledge needed to be independent in the home and in the community. The Independent Living Postsecondary Goal IEP Team Decision Assistance form (Figure 2.2) can help the IEP team decide if an independent living postsecondary goal is necessary for a student.

Writing measurable postsecondary goals requires that you pay attention to three important characteristics:

1.  Write the goal so anyone can measure the extent to which the goal was achieved.

2.  Include a time element that makes it clear that the goal will occur after the student exits secondary school.

3.  Make sure that the goal reflects the student's and family's desired outcomes.

To be measurable, the goal must be "observable." For example, stating that Bryce "would *like to be* a carpenter" is not an example of an observable goal. A measurable way to write this goal would be "Bryce *will work* as a carpenter." A good way to determine whether a goal is measurable is to ask yourself, "A year from now, if I asked Bryce where he is working, would I be able to answer yes or no to the question: 'Did he meet his employment measurable postsecondary goal?'"

Postsecondary goals should also be written so it is clear they are future plans. The postsecondary goals are not what the student is currently doing while in high school. Instead, they reflect what the student wants to do after graduating or exiting high school, as does this sample postsecondary goal for Bryce: "After graduating from high school, Bryce will attend a vocational technical school in the program area of building and construction."

An important feature of a quality measurable postsecondary goal is that it focuses on the student's perspective. Measurable postsecondary goals must reflect that they are the student's goals for the future—not anyone else's. Also, remember that postsecondary goals are not set in stone. In fact, they may change each year, especially if you are working with a younger student or someone who has not had a lot of employment or educational experiences. The IDEA is very clear that the transition plan must *facilitate the movement toward* the measurable postsecondary goals. This means that everything schools provide (e.g., planning, assessment, course of study, accommodations, services) should all focus on supporting students in taking steps toward their postsecondary goals. This is why the IEP teams need to develop postsecondary goals first, so that the rest of the IEP relates to the student's future goals.

How detailed your MPG is depends on the age of the student, his or her current experiences, and future dreams. Remember, for every student you have to target an employment and education/training goal, and an independent living goal, if needed. The closer a student is to graduating, the more specific you would expect his or her goals to be. The National Technical Assistance Center on Transition (www.transitionta.org) provides helpful examples of compliant and high-quality MPGs, as well as a formula for writing them:

> (After graduation/After high school/Upon completion of high school) the student will (behavior) (where and when) (National Secondary Transition Technical Assistance Center [2009] Indicator 13 Training Materials, Charlotte, NC).

# Independent Living Postsecondary Goal
## IEP Team Decision Assistance Form

This form is designed to help the IEP team decide if a student needs a postsecondary goal in the area of independent living. *Independent living includes the skills and knowledge an individual needs to direct his or her life at home and in the community.* Transition assessment information should be taken into account when completing this form and additional assessment may be necessary to adequately identify goal(s).

Review each statement and consider whether the student possesses the identified skills.

Yes—performs independently and consistently

No—performs inconsistently or not at all; consider an independent living goal

N/A—not an area of independence being considered at this time

| | Yes | No | N/A |
|---|---|---|---|
| **Home Living** | | | |
| Follows daily living routine (e.g., personal hygiene, dressing, selecting clothes). | ___ | ___ | ___ |
| Purchases, prepares, and stores food; maintains healthy diet. | ___ | ___ | ___ |
| Performs light household maintenance (e.g., cleaning, unclogging drains or toilets). | ___ | ___ | ___ |
| Appropriately makes and receives telephone calls. | ___ | ___ | ___ |
| Follows disaster safety routines for fire and natural disasters. | ___ | ___ | ___ |
| **Household and Money Management** | Yes | No | N/A |
| Creates and maintains checking and savings accounts. | ___ | ___ | ___ |
| Manages money (e.g., counts money, makes change, budgets, pays taxes and monthly bills). | ___ | ___ | ___ |
| Evaluates cost of services (e.g., banking, telephone, leasing, credit cards, loans). | ___ | ___ | ___ |
| Locates and acquires place to live (e.g., finds housing, understands rental agreements). | ___ | ___ | ___ |
| Sets up living setting (e.g., organizes furniture, arranges for utilities and services). | ___ | ___ | ___ |
| Understands the importance of a good credit rating, how to view and interpret a credit report, and methods to improve credit rating. | ___ | ___ | ___ |
| **Transportation** | Yes | No | N/A |
| Selects appropriate method of transportation. | ___ | ___ | ___ |
| Possesses required transportation documentation (e.g., driver's license, bus pass). | ___ | ___ | ___ |
| Organizes transportation (e.g., carpool partners, door-to-door bus or cab service). | ___ | ___ | ___ |
| Navigates throughout community using preferred mode of transportation. | ___ | ___ | ___ |
| If driving, knows of automotive maintenance schedules and routines. | ___ | ___ | ___ |
| **Government** | Yes | No | N/A |
| Knows how to participate in voting and political decision making. | ___ | ___ | ___ |
| Understands basic local, state, and national laws. | ___ | ___ | ___ |
| Understands rights as a person with a disability. | ___ | ___ | ___ |

**Figure 2.2.** Independent living postsecondary goal IEP team decision assistance form. (From Erickson, A.G. [2007]. *Independent Living Postsecondary Goal IEP Team Decision Assistance Form.* Lawrence: Transition Coalition, University of Kansas; reprinted by permission.)

# Independent Living Postsecondary Goal
# IEP Team Decision Assistance Form

| | Yes | No | N/A |
|---|---|---|---|
| **Community Involvement** | | | |
| Locates and participates in leisure, recreation, and community activities. | ___ | ___ | ___ |
| Locates and uses community services (e.g., stores, banks, medical facilities, recreation facilities, health department, police department, social services). | ___ | ___ | ___ |
| Completes paperwork for medical treatment, community services, insurance, etc. | ___ | ___ | ___ |
| Plans and acquires wardrobe (e.g., select appropriate clothes, compare prices). | ___ | ___ | ___ |
| Responds appropriately to environmental cues (e.g., signs, sirens). | ___ | ___ | ___ |
| **Personal Safety and Interpersonal Relationships** | Yes | No | N/A |
| Performs basic first aid and seeks medical assistance when appropriate. | ___ | ___ | ___ |
| Practices community safety routines (e.g., when to talk to strangers, avoiding unsafe locations, locking doors, asking for directions). | ___ | ___ | ___ |
| Understands when it is appropriate to call 911. | ___ | ___ | ___ |
| Knows CPR and when it is necessary. | ___ | ___ | ___ |
| Maintains relationships with family and friends; establishes new friendships. | ___ | ___ | ___ |
| Understands the concepts of sexuality (e.g., physical self, reproductive process, dating, relationships, marriage). | ___ | ___ | ___ |
| Makes informed choices regarding sexual behavior. | ___ | ___ | ___ |
| Understands basic parenting skills. | ___ | ___ | ___ |
| **Self-Advocacy** | Yes | No | N/A |
| Expresses strengths and needs; asks for accommodations when needed. | ___ | ___ | ___ |
| Expresses preferences appropriately, identifies long- and short-range goals, and takes steps to reach goals. | ___ | ___ | ___ |
| Assertively advocates for self in situations outside of school. | ___ | ___ | ___ |
| Responds appropriately to typical exchanges with others (e.g., saying hello, being bumped or brushed against, making small talk, sarcastic remarks). | ___ | ___ | ___ |
| Resolves conflicts through discussion, reasoning, and compromise. | ___ | ___ | ___ |
| **Additional Independent Living Skills** | Yes | No | N/A |
| _____ | ___ | ___ | ___ |
| _____ | ___ | ___ | ___ |
| _____ | ___ | ___ | ___ |
| _____ | ___ | ___ | ___ |
| _____ | ___ | ___ | ___ |

*(continued)*

*Your Complete Guide to Transition Planning and Services* by Mary E. Morningstar and Beth Clavenna-Deane.
Copyright © 2018 by Paul H. Brookes Publishing Co., Inc. All rights reserved.

Figure 2.2. *(continued)*

# Independent Living Postsecondary Goal
# IEP Team Decision Assistance Form

**If "No" was answered for any of the skills identified above, a postsecondary goal should be considered for the area of independent living.** The discussion questions below help further identify an appropriate goal.

Independent living goal(s) needed at this time?     ___Yes     ___No

Is additional assessment information needed in the area of independent living? Why?

What are the three most important independent living skills to be addressed in the IEP?

1.

2.

3.

How can we work on these particular skills throughout this coming year (i.e., instruction, related services, post-school living objectives, daily living skills, and/or functional vocational evaluation)?

What annual IEP goal(s) will enable the student to meet the postsecondary independent living goal?

The following are detailed MPGs for students almost out of high school (National Technical Assistance Center on Transition, 2009):

1. After graduating from high school, Alex will enroll at Kings College (a technical school) and take business math to improve his work-related math skills and advance his career in business (education/training MPG) (National Secondary Transition Technical Assistance Center [2009] Indicator 13 Training Materials, Charlotte, NC).

2. Upon completion of high school, Paulo will assume responsibility for a share of living expenses by saving money earned at work and following a budget set by Paulo and his parents (independent living MPG) (National Secondary Transition Technical Assistance Center [2009] Indicator 13 Training Materials, Charlotte, NC).

3. Upon graduation from high school, Jamarreo will work part-time as a shop helper in his uncle's shop to gain experience in the automotive repair industry (employment MPG) (National Secondary Transition Technical Assistance Center [2009] Indicator 13 Training Materials, Charlotte, NC).

For younger students, appropriate MPGs might be:

1. After high school, I will go to school to learn about computers. (education/training MPG)

2. After high school, I will work with animals. (employment MPG)

3. After high school, I will live in an apartment with friends. (independent living MPG)

Goals may change over time as students gain experiences and fine tune their plans for the future, but the formula for writing these goals stays the same.

***Transition Services***    Transition services are used to help the student achieve his or her desired postsecondary goals. The transition services that must be considered by the IEP team include:

- Instruction

- Community experiences

- Related services

- Employment and other post-school adult living objectives

- When appropriate, acquisition of daily living skills and functional vocational evaluation (34 CFR 300.43 (a)] [20 U.S.C. 1401(34))

There should be a clear connection between the measurable postsecondary goals and needed transition services. You should be able to answer "yes" to these three questions:

1. Are the transition services in the IEP focused on improving academic and functional achievement of the student?

2. Do the transition services facilitate the student's movement from school to post-school settings?

3. Are the transition services that you listed appropriate for helping the student meet his or her postsecondary goal(s)? (Morningstar, Gaumer-Erickson, Lattin, & Wade, 2008)

Table 2.1 shows examples of Bryce's transition services and how they directly tie to his education/training postsecondary goal.

**Table 2.1.** Transition services tied to Bryce's education/training measurable postsecondary goals (MPG)

| MPG: education/training | Transition services |
|---|---|
| Upon completion of high school, Bryce will enroll in a vocational program to study building and/or carpentry. | • Visit college campuses that have building trades programs to tour programs and meet with student disability support services on campus.<br>• Learn how to calculate fractions needed for building measurements.<br>• Enroll in the trade and carpentry classes in high school.<br>• Complete an internship with a construction company as part of a work-study program in high school.<br>• On the weekends, work for a local carpenter.<br>• Develop a resume and letter of introduction focused on career interests. |

From Morningstar, M.E., Gaumer-Erickson, A.G., Lattin, D.L., & Wade, D.K. (2008). *Best Practices in Planning for Transition* [online module] www.transitioncoalition.org. Lawrence: Transition Coalition, University of Kansas; adapted by permission.

***Course of Study*** The IDEA requirements for outlining the course of study on the IEP emphasize that these must begin "not later than the first IEP to be in effect when the child is 16" (unless your state requires transition planning at an earlier age) [34 CFR 300.320(b)]. Planning usually begins the year before the student enters high school at the end of 8th grade, which means developing a course of study starts well before students are 16 years old. The course of study should focus on how the student's educational plan facilitates a successful transition to his or her postsecondary goals (O'Leary, 2005). For example, Bryce's IEP team worked with him to plan his course of study. This included taking electives in carpentry and welding, both of which were offered at his high school. Because Bryce planned to move on to postsecondary education and training, his course of study also included required coursework for graduation, as well as some other more specific classes to support his needs (e.g., career exploration, study skills class). Figure 2.3 outlines Bryce's 4-year course of study as it appeared on his IEP.

| Four Year Course of Study | | | |
|---|---|---|---|
| **9th grade** | **10th grade** | **11th grade** | **12th grade** |
| English 9 | English 10 | English 11 | English 12 |
| Algebra I | Geometry | Consumer math | Elective (building trades 2) |
| Physical science | Biology | Earth science | Elective (foods I) |
| World history | American history | Civics | American government |
| Elective (career exploration) | Elective (carpentry) | Elective (drafting II) | Career technical education program (3 hours) |
| Study skills | Health education (.5) | Elective (building trades 1) | Study skills |
| Elective (drafting I) | Study skills | Elective (work experience, .05), (study skills, .05) | |

**Figure 2.3.** Bryce's course of study. (From Morningstar, M.E., Erickson, A.G., Lattin, D.L. & Wade, D.K. [2008]. Best Practices in Planning for Transition [online module] www.transitioncoalition.org. Lawrence: Transition Coalition, University of Kansas; adapted by permission.)

The purpose of the course of study is to ensure that all courses and school experiences help students to develop the knowledge and skills needed to move toward the identified postsecondary outcomes. In helping the student plan the course of study, IEP teams should consider all possible courses and programs that currently exist at the high school. Having the course catalog handy is the first place to start. Planning the course of study provides a good opportunity to work closely with your guidance counselor, because course enrollment is typically one of his or her responsibilities. As the student's identified postsecondary goals change, so may the courses he or she will take.

Many schools now require an individual learning plan for all students in high school (Solberg, Wills, & Osman, 2012). This 4-year plan identifies the student's "course taking and postsecondary plans aligned to career goals" (Solberg et al., 2012, p. 2). It can help students understand how their school courses are tied to postsecondary goals. The National Collaborative on Workforce and Disability has an excellent how-to guide on individualized learning plans (www.ncwd-youth.info/ilp/how-to-guide). In many states, if your high school is using a plan of study for all students, this can be used as the course of study in an IEP. Check with your state or district office to confirm how you need to develop the course of study.

**Annual IEP Goals**    The annual IEP goals must link to the measurable postsecondary goals. The reason for this is to ensure that IEP goals are developed that will lead to or help the student move toward meeting his or her measurable postsecondary goals. For example, if Bryce is interested in the building and construction industry, then an annual IEP goal that will help meet his postsecondary goal should focus on skills needed for this field and not another career field. This might include an annual goal related to his skill in adding, subtracting, dividing, and multiplying fractions to measure window units as part of his building trades classes, or an annual goal focused on organizational skills and note taking so he learns skills for his high school classes that will also help him when enrolled in a postsecondary vocational technical program.

Remember, a student's postsecondary goal is a goal that the student desires to achieve after leaving high school, but an annual IEP goal is a goal that is expected to be achieved in one year's time. Bryce's measurable postsecondary goals included

- Upon completion of high school, I will attend a carpentry and building trades program to become a certified carpenter.

- Upon completion of high school, I will work part-time in the building construction industry until I finish the carpentry and building trades program, and then I will work full-time in a related position.

A few of his annual IEP goals were:

- By his next annual IEP meeting, Bryce will follow written instructions and diagrams to construct a model birdhouse with 80% accuracy as part of his carpentry class.

- By his next annual IEP meeting, Bryce will write a five-paragraph essay about a historical figure, meeting the standard on the five traits of writing.

- By his next annual IEP meeting, Bryce will demonstrate proficiency in measurement using a tape measure by accurately cutting the pieces of his birdhouse to the nearest one-eighth inch with 95% accuracy.

## Interagency Collaboration

During transition, parents, schools, students, and community agencies work together as partners to plan for a student's adult life. The IEP team can invite outside agencies if an agency is already or likely to be providing or paying for transition services. An outside agency representative must be invited to a student's IEP meeting if there is a chance that the agency will be paying for or providing services to the student once he or she leaves secondary school. These services or costs could include postsecondary tuition, job coaching, life skills training, and mental health services.

With so many partners involved in the transition planning process, who is ultimately responsible for making sure a student's transition IEP is implemented? This is especially important to determine because of the requirements related to accountability for providing or paying for transition services. If an outside agency fails to provide an agreed upon transition service, then the IEP team must reconvene to identify an alternative strategy to meet the transition needs of the student. Oftentimes, this is as simple as extending a timeline or service. For example, if vocational rehabilitation (i.e., an agency that prepares students for the work force and helps them obtain and maintain employment) was to provide a functional vocational evaluation, but could not do so due to funding restrictions at the end of a fiscal period, it could be that the time line for completing the evaluation would change. Other times, it may mean finding another agency to provide the service, such as changing job coaching providers who are supporting a student on the job the semester before exiting high school. What you cannot do, however, is drop the service or IEP goal from the student's IEP if that is essential to helping the student meet a measurable postsecondary goal. Remember, transition services are directly related to a student's outcomes and are not simply determined by what supports community agencies are able to provide. More information about interagency collaboration and strategies to promote it is included in Chapter 12.

### TIP FOR TRANSITION: Laws Don't Make Things Happen, People Do!

While IDEA mandates that transition planning must occur, what really makes a difference is how you bring individuals to the team to support the planning process. It is important that you not only understand the different roles team members play, but that you are able to encourage them and acknowledge their unique contributions. *People Make It Happen* (Morningstar, Lattin, & Sarkesian, 2009) is a free resource available from the Transition Coalition (http://transitioncoalition.org/blog/tc-materials/people-make-it-happen). It describes specific roles of critical stakeholders, including community members, peers and friends, advocates, school support staff, educators, administrators, postsecondary personnel, community service providers, family members, and last, but not least, students. It offers suggestions for how different members of transition teams can participate.

## The Age of Majority and Transfer of Rights

One year prior to the student's 18th birthday (the age of majority for most states), the school must notify both the student and his or her parents that the rights under IDEA will transfer from the parent to the student when the student turns 18 years old. (Though the age of majority is 18 in most states, some states have stipulations if the student is still in high school, and other states have an age of majority other than 18. It is recommended that you check your state regulations regarding age of majority.) At the age of majority, the following legal rights and responsibilities transfer from the parents to the student, who becomes the person of contact for

- Notification of meetings

- Notification and consent for evaluation

- Selection of participants in IEP meetings

- Approval of the contents of the IEP

- Approval regarding change of placement

In other words, when a student who is continuing to receive special education services reaches the age of majority, he or she will be responsible for making decisions about his or her transition planning and IEP. Students must be prepared to take on these important rights and responsibilities. This means that students must be knowledgeable about the legal requirements long before they are of majority age. It requires working with students before they turn 17 to first assess their knowledge about their disability, special education, and the IEP. Second, you can find out whether their experiences with IEP meetings have been positive or negative. The student must receive instruction on how to fully understand and assume his or her rights and responsibilities.

For students with more significant intellectual disabilities, this is often a time to provide parents with necessary information about guardianship alternatives, if needed, such as power of attorney, representative payee, limited guardianship, and conservatorships. This new approach is called "supported decision making" and has at its core that adults with disabilities should be supported to make important life decisions (Jameson et al., 2015). Most states have specific information about alternatives to guardianship that can be found under your state's agency serving children with intellectual disabilities. In addition, the Jenny Hatch Justice Project (www.jennyhatchjusticeproject.org) provides a wide range of resources related to alternatives to guardianship and strategies for supported decision making. Keep in mind that most individuals with intellectual disabilities can manage their own affairs with support and guidance from others, such as family members and friends. Guardianship decisions should not be taken lightly because it strips all legal decision making from the individual and seriously limits the person's autonomy and choice. Alternatives to guardianship should always be considered first.

## The Summary of Performance

This IDEA requirement provides support to families and students as they exit high school. The summary of performance (SOP) requires that schools provide current and relevant information about the student's academic achievement and functional performance and, most importantly, recommendations for ongoing supports and accommodations in post-secondary settings (34 CFR §300.305(e)(3)). The SOP does not require additional evaluations or reevaluations before the student graduates or exits special education services.

The SOP can be viewed as an opportunity to summarize and share comprehensive information that will support students as they transition into their future educational, employment, and living experiences. The SOP does not replace eligibility requirements for adult programs or services, such as vocational rehabilitation (VR) or for receiving accommodations in postsecondary educational settings. Students and families are still required to meet the proper eligibility requirements for services post-high school.

However, the SOP often includes information needed to select the most appropriate supports and services from outside agencies. For example, when Bryce applied to VR, part of his eligibility process included a review of his educational information. His SOP included both his academic and functional performance, as well as the accommodations he received in high school. This additional information assisted in determining his eligibility for VR services and which specific vocational services he would need to find and maintain employment (U.S. Department of Education, 2011, http://idea.ed.gov). For students like Bryce, who are planning to enroll in postsecondary education, the SOP is often used by disability student services to identify relevant accommodations once eligibility is determined.

States and districts are creating innovative ways to include students in the creation of their summary of performance. *Putting it All Together: The Summary of Performance Lesson* from the Zarrow Center for Learning Enrichment is an excellent resource that provides teachers with a lesson plan, PowerPoint presentation, teacher's guide, and materials to work with students to create their own SOP (www.ou.edu/content/education/centers-and-partnerships/zarrow/transition-education-materials/student-directed-transition-planning/summary-of-performance.html). From this perspective, the SOP can be thought of as a transition portfolio that is updated throughout a student's high school career.

## MAKING IT HAPPEN:
## Creating Quality Transition Planning Approaches

Now that you know about the IDEA requirements for transition and how to comply with the federal requirements, it's time to make quality transition planning happen for your students! By now, it should be clear that transition planning is more than just completing the IEP; it involves focusing on a student's strengths, preferences, interests, and needs and making sure his or her goals for the future are what drives the transition services offered. "Making it happen" requires launching effective transition planning and offering quality school and community experiences, services, and supports. It also requires collaboration with families, students, and other community members and agencies.

### Understand That Transition Is a Process

It is essential to remember that transition planning is an ongoing process. Transition should be a continual aspect of educational planning for students and not just for the purposes of compliance during the IEP meeting. One way to think about effective transition planning is to ask yourself how you will add to the transition planning process each year. Consider how Bryce's transition plan developed over time. During Bryce's sophomore year, he enrolled in his school's transition class as an elective. While taking this class, he had the opportunity to learn about different careers that matched with his preferences and interests for carpentry. During transition planning prior to his junior year, the measurable postsecondary goal and transition services related to the building and construction industry were added to his IEP. His course of study included enrolling in high school carpentry classes, and his IEP goals were directly related to his desired outcomes. During his senior year, his IEP included transition services related to work-based learning experiences in which he enrolled in the work-study program and developed his skills with a construction company in his community. Figure 2.4 summarizes the continuous transition planning process, with the IEP team reevaluating, updating, and revising the student's IEP and transition plan each year.

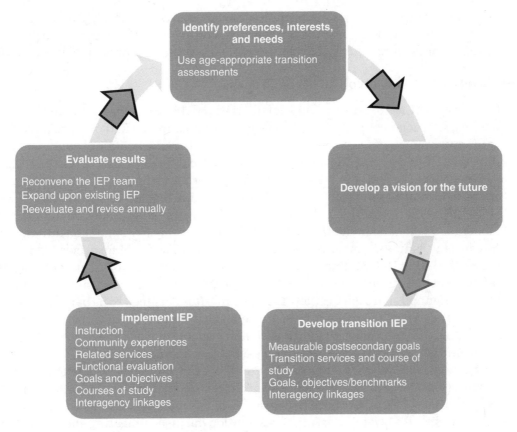

**Figure 2.4.** The transition planning process. (From Morningstar, M.E. [2008]. The transition planning process. Lawrence: Transition Coalition, University of Kansas; adapted by permission.)

The best way to identify a student's strengths, preferences, interests, and needs is to develop a PCP whereby the student, his or her family, educators, and others can gather necessary information and create a vision for the student's future. PCP is an excellent way to learn about and understand the student's strengths, contributions, interests, and dreams. Fundamentally, PCP is based on values supporting inclusive lives for individuals with disabilities so they can fully participate in and contribute to their community. There are a number of different PCP processes, such as making action plans (MAPS), personal futures planning, and group action planning, all of which include strategies for developing a vision for the future. Once the person-centered team has helped to create the vision, they then identify the steps to be taken to help the student achieve that vision.

Developing Bryce's vision for the future motivated Bryce's IEP team to think outside the box about his future dreams, especially for careers within the building and construction industry and his desire to have his own farm. His transition coordinator helped bring together the people who knew and cared about Bryce, and could motivate each other to develop a plan to support his dreams. This included the owner of the cattle farm where Bryce worked on the weekends. She was able to connect Bryce with the local contractor supply warehouse, where he was able to get a part-time job. This experience expanded Bryce's view of future employment opportunities and motivated him to work harder in school, especially on organizational and interpersonal skills most closely related to customer service. While all members of the IEP team can provide perspectives and help determine priorities, the student and his or her family ultimately decide on a desired future, because they will be working toward this future long after high school. Remember, the vision for the future is what drives the measurable postsecondary goals in the IEP.

### Keep the Student Actively Involved in the Process

If the vision for the future is the final destination and the IEP is the road map, then the measurable postsecondary goals, transition services, and annual IEP goals are the vehicles to get the student on the right road to his or her desired future. Including the student in developing the IEP and during IEP meetings is also critical for successful transition planning. Students should be active participants in their meetings, whether or not they actually run the entire meeting, as the Self-Directed IEP curriculum teaches them to do (see Chapter 3). For younger or less experienced students, some easy first steps might be to work with the teacher to identify and invite IEP team members to the meeting, and then introduce everyone who is attending the meeting. The I'm Determined One Pager form (see Figure 2.5) was created by the I'm Determined Project so that students can use it as a jumping off point for mapping out their future. The one-pager is a great strategy for younger students to prepare ahead of time and share during their IEP meeting. It is designed to be person-centered and positive, and allows the student to contribute substantially to his or her transition planning process. Bryce's teacher worked with him a couple of weeks prior to the IEP meeting to help him get ready to present the one-pager at the meeting.

Some other strategies you can use are to check in with the student throughout the meeting. Consider letting the student speak first so that his or her thoughts and feedback can be shared before others have a turn. For example, when Bryce was a freshman in high school, he shared a brief PowerPoint presentation during his meeting about his strengths, interests, preferences, and needs. As students gain experience, confidence, and skills, they can facilitate the entire meeting. Having students take an active role in their IEP meetings helps promote a more positive tone in the meeting and ensures that the meeting focuses on the student and what is needed to achieve his or her future goals (Martin & Williams-Diehm, 2013).

One curriculum aimed at increasing student involvement in transition planning is *Whose Future Is It Anyway?* This easy-to-use curriculum includes 36 lessons focused across six areas: getting to know you; making decisions; how to get what you need; goals, objectives and the future; communicating; and thank you, honorable chairperson. It also comes with a coach's guide that describes what you can do to support the student during each lesson, including materials needed, key words/concepts to be learned, and activities and suggestions for engaging students in learning. The *Whose Future Is It Anyway?* curriculum has shown positive effects on student self-determination (Wehmeyer, Palmer, Lee, Williams-Diehm, & Shogren, 2011).

### WHAT YOU CAN DO RIGHT NOW:
### Putting Ideas Into Action

Keeping track of all you need to do before, during, and after a transition IEP meeting can be intimidating. It requires you to know what is required under the IDEA to be compliant with the law and about evidence-based practices to ensure students and families are engaged in creating positive, individualized, and motivating plans for the desired future. To do this, the Transition Coalition has created a checklist to help you remember some essential steps to supporting quality transition planning (see Figure 2.6). You can begin to use this

# The I'm Determined One Pager

Name: _____          Date: _____

Address: _____

Date of birth: _____

### My strengths

### My interests

### My preferences

### My needs

**Figure 2.5.**   I'm determined one-pager. (Adapted from *I'm Determined One Pager* [n.d.] by the Commonwealth of Virginia Department of Education. All rights reserved. Reproduced by permission.)

# IEP Meeting Checklist for Transition

The following is a checklist that you might use to prepare for the transition IEP meeting. It reviews what needs to be done before, during, and after the IEP meeting. It can also be used as a tool for you to identify specific areas of the transition planning process that you would like to change or improve. Mark the checkboxes to identify the steps where you need assistance in developing knowledge, skills, methods, or materials.

## Before the IEP meeting

☐ Become familiar with community resources and services.

☐ Obtain consent from parents and student for release of information if other agencies are to be involved.

☐ Determine present level of performance in academic and postsecondary goal areas. This is determined through age-appropriate transition assessments.

☐ Identify future expectations and dreams from family, student, and community members.

☐ Identify people who should be involved in transition planning meeting(s).

☐ Determine best dates and times for family, student, school representatives, and community agencies. Always be willing to reschedule a meeting to allow for family to attend.

☐ Send written notification (invitations) of meeting to family, student, and agency representatives.

☐ Ensure that student is familiar with his or her role in the IEP meeting and possesses the skills necessary to participate fully. This should be an ongoing process, and the student may need time to practice these skills.

☐ If the student and/or family will not be attending the IEP meeting, document how their preferences, interests, needs, and strengths have been identified and how they have been involved in the transition planning process.

## During the IEP meeting

☐ Set a positive and collaborative atmosphere.

☐ Have the student introduce the people at the meeting and, if comfortable with it, facilitate the meeting. The student should be an active participant in the meeting whether or not he or she facilitates the meeting.

☐ Develop a vision for the future and/or reach agreement on vision.

☐ Identify the measurable postsecondary goals based on the vision.

☐ Review the student's present level of performance, strengths, needs, interests, and preferences.

☐ Identify the needed transition services based upon the information gathered above.

☐ Identify or review the courses of study to ensure that they will assist the student to meet his or her identified measurable postsecondary goals. Adjust as needed.

☐ Develop annual goals that address needed transition services.

☐ Identify interagency responsibilities or linkages, if appropriate.

☐ Assign any follow-up responsibilities or activities, as needed.

☐ At the IEP meeting the year before the student reaches the age of majority, inform the student and his and her family of the transfer of rights that will transfer to the student once he or she reaches age of majority.

## After the IEP meeting

☐ Implement the IEP.

☐ Share specific parts of the IEP with other teachers that are relevant to the coursework they are teaching. For example, this could include only the goal page or only the accommodations page—the information that would help them help the student.

☐ Regularly review the IEP goals and transition services for completion or to ensure that progress is being made toward them.

☐ Adapt or change curriculum, if needed, based on transition outcomes.

☐ Adapt or change instructional techniques, if needed.

☐ Provide ongoing transition assessment as needed for coursework, employment, etc.

☐ Reconvene the IEP team or part of the team, if needed.

☐ Hold any follow-up transition meetings, if necessary. Remember, if the purpose of these meetings is to discuss transition services, the student must be invited.

☐ Create an SOP for students who are graduating from or exiting high school.

**Figure 2.6.** IEP Meeting Checklist for Transition. (From Morningstar, M.E., Erickson, A., Lattin, D.L. & Wade, D.K. (2008). Best Practices in Planning for Transition [online module] www.transitioncoalition.org. Lawrence: Transition Coalition, University of Kansas; reprinted by permission.)

checklist to monitor what you need to do before, during, and after the IEP meeting; keep recommended practices in mind; and adjust your approach if necessary to best serve your students.

For transition planning to be results oriented, we must support students in preparing for an adult life that is meaningful and engaging. Transition planning requires the student, the family, and professionals to work together. The student's positive involvement in the transition planning process makes a significant difference in a student's transition outcomes. Transition planning should be ongoing throughout the student's educational career and you must be ready to support the student and family to:

- Assess student's strengths, preferences interests, and needs.

- Identify the student's vision for the future.

- Create and revise the IEP to include measurable postsecondary goals, transition services, and annual goals and services.

- Implement the IEP, including transition services.

- Provide ongoing evaluation to ensure services are being provided and progress is being made.

- Collaborate with others within and outside of the school to ensure the effort is coordinated.

Above all, in navigating the transition planning process, remember that the future belongs to the student. He or she should be as involved as possible in the journey toward a satisfying, inclusive adult life.

## ONLINE RESOURCES

National Technical Assistance Center on Transition (NTACT): www.transitionta.org

Resources for Transition Planning: Quality Transition Planning, Indicator 13, Effective Practices

Transition Coalition Online Module: Best Practices in Planning for Transition: www.transitioncoalition.org/transition/module_home.php

IMDetermined: www.imdetermined.org

Zarrow Center: www.ou.edu/content/education/centers-and-partnerships/zarrow.html

Inclusion Press: www.inclusion.com

Planning for the Future: A Workbook for Persons with Disabilities, Their Families, and Professionals (Revised, 1995). Mary E. Morningstar, University of Kansas, Transition Coalition: www.transitioncoalition.org

Person-Centered Planning: A Tool for Transition: www.ncset.org/publications/viewdesc.asp?id=1431

Person-Centered Planning Education Site Cornell University, ILR School, Employment and Disability Institute: www.ilr.cornell.edu/edi/pcp

The Beach Center at the University of Kansas: www.beachcenter.org/families/person-centered_planning.aspx

# 3

# Student-Directed Planning and Involvement

Chrissy is a junior who has attended her IEP meetings throughout high school, but she has not had many opportunities to express her interests and dreams during meetings. She also is not sure how to talk about the accommodations and modifications that help her in school and how these will translate to college and work. The IEP meetings usually run fast, with team members reviewing her current performance in classes and the accommodations and modifications needed. Ms. Atkins, Chrissy's IEP case manager, is her strongest supporter at school, but Ms. Atkins isn't yet familiar with ways to help Chrissy learn to be more self-determined. Ms. Atkins recognizes that Chrissy needs to begin advocating for herself if she is to be successful in the future. What strategies and possible first steps should she take to support Chrissy to be more involved in her transition planning process and learn the skills needed to be self-determined?

Self-determination is an essential element of transition that is necessary if we are to prepare students with disabilities for post-school environments. Student-directed IEP planning and instruction in self-determination and self-advocacy have been identified as evidence-based practices that lead to post-school success (Test, Fowler et al., 2009). Specific practices that have evidence of success include 1) teaching students to be actively involved in transition IEP meetings (Test et al., 2004), 2) supporting students to use evidence-based self-advocacy strategies and skills (Van Reusen, Bos, Schumaker, & Deshler, 1994), 3) teaching students to self-direct their IEP meeting (Martin et al., 2006), and 4) promoting self-determination skills likely to lead to improved postsecondary outcomes in employment and independent living (Shogren, Wehmeyer, Palmer, Rifenbark, & Little, 2013; Wehmeyer & Palmer, 2003).

During high school, students must be involved in transition planning and in making decisions about their educational and career experiences. This involvement provides students with the opportunities to practice self-determination skills. It may be challenging for you to consider how to balance self-determination skill instruction and decision-making opportunities for students while also supporting their academic achievement in order to graduate. The good news is that you can embed instruction on self-determination skills into the general education curriculum, which will strengthen a student's academic achievement through access to core curriculum content (Shogren, Palmer, Wehmeyer, Williams-Diehm, & Little, 2012). The strategies shared with you in this chapter will help you balance your instructional day while introducing the concepts of self-determination.

# GETTING STARTED:
## Defining Self-Determination and the Student's Role in Transition Planning

Acting self-determined is associated with skills such as advocating for your needs and interests, as well as making informed decisions about your future. But how do you know when and if your students are improving the skills needed to be self-determined? There are a variety of definitions for self-determination. Stated simply, self-determination is not about always being in control of your life, but about how you make or cause things to happen. Being self-determined means taking action based on personal preferences, choices, and interests rather than being forced to act in a certain way by others. Self-determined people intentionally and purposefully act to achieve goals in their lives (Wehmeyer & Field, 2007).

Self-determination has been described as consisting of several different components (see text box), including "the ability to make choices, solve problems, set goals, evaluate options, take initiative to reach one's goals, and accept the consequences of one's actions" (Rowe et al., 2015, p. 4).

---

### Components of Self-Determination
- Choice making
- Decision making
- Problem solving
- Goal setting and attainment
- Self-regulation/self-management
- Self-advocacy and leadership
- Self-awareness (Wehmeyer & Field, 2007)

---

Educators must be prepared to teach students the skills associated with the components of self-determination, such as self-advocacy, goal setting, choice making, and problem solving. Certain curricula and strategies for teaching and supporting self-determination have been identified as leading to improved postsecondary outcomes and are discussed later in this chapter (Test, Mazzotti et al., 2009). Unfortunately, the more extensive the support needs of students, the less likely teachers are to consider teaching self-determination skills to be important (Wehmeyer, Agran, & Hughes, 2000). It is just as important to teach self-determination skills to students with significant disabilities. Educators should equally support all students to be engaged in their own transition planning.

It is also important to consider the cultural nuances involved in teaching self-determination skills. What it means to be self-determined can look and feel different for your students and families from culturally diverse backgrounds (Trainor, 2007). In many circumstances, self-determination promotes individual rights and personal interests and goals; yet this idea of self-determination may not be acknowledged by all families, including some culturally and linguistically diverse (CLD) families for whom the cultural orientation may be collective in nature. If a family's value system promotes a collective cultural orientation, this means that familial obligations for group success take precedence over individual goals. For example, perhaps you are working with parents who believe that the first-born child should work to help support the family, but the student desires to go to college after high school. How do you balance the wants of the student with those of the family? Ideally, the transition specialist would work with the family and the student to develop mutually beneficial goals. You might have to provide information about the economic benefits of postsecondary education, share resources related to scholarships with the parents, and help the student find a part-time job in order to reach compromise with the family (Kim & Morningstar, 2005).

Educators and transition coordinators should appreciate the values and perspectives of the family and student, and have respect for their cultural orientation in terms of goals for adulthood and what it means to be self-determined. It is important for you to acknowledge and respect differences and be willing to create new strategies that can be beneficial and acceptable to both the student and the family.

## TIP FOR TRANSITION: Have Your Students Define What Makes a Good Day

The My Good Day Plan from the I'm Determined Project, a state-directed project funded by the Virginia Department of Education, is a great tool for students with disabilities to identify what makes up their "good day," and how to make the good day happen more regularly. This tool teaches self-awareness, self-advocacy, self-regulation, self-management, and problem solving. A sample My Good Day Plan and blank template is in the Chapter 3 Appendix and is adapted from the I'm Determined web site (www.imdetermined.org).

You may choose to begin teaching the components of self-determination by involving students in their own transition planning process. Even though evidence shows that if students are involved in transition planning while in high school, they will be more self-determined as young adults (Morningstar et al., 2010), students with disabilities traditionally are the least involved and engaged members of their IEP team (Martin, Marshall, & Sale, 2004). They often have little knowledge of transition planning, the goals that are being presented, the decisions that are being made, and the next steps that will be taken.

Consider Chrissy when you think about student involvement in IEP planning. Chrissy was provided few opportunities to participate during her past IEP meetings and wasn't involved in any planning prior to her recent meeting about her future. Chrissy would benefit from a process where she first learns more about herself, including her strengths and interests, to help her generate future education, employment, and adult life goals. She can learn skills to set goals and make choices. Chrissy could begin by starting the IEP meeting and introducing her present levels of performance, as well as her goals for her future, working toward facilitating the entire meeting. In this way, she would begin to learn how to advocate for her goals and the supports she needs.

## TIP FOR TRANSITION: Have Students Map Out Their Dreams Using a Dream Sheet

Using a Dream Sheet, such as the one found in the Chapter 3 Appendix, is helpful during the transition planning process. You can use it with your students and families to formulate a dream for the future, identify strengths, maximize resources available to reach their dreams, and develop action steps.

You can begin the process of having students involved in their own transition planning by supporting them to set goals for upcoming IEP meetings, invite participants, and lead the introduction to *their* meeting. Once students set their transition goals, they must then be involved in making decisions about high school courses and the accommodations needed for success. In addition, students should have the opportunity to help develop their annual IEP goals that will facilitate their progress toward meeting their measurable postsecondary goals for education, employment, and independent living. This would mean developing annual goals that will help them develop skills and experiences in the areas of academics, work-based learning, behavior, and social relationships, to name a few. Students can also learn to monitor progress on their goals. The more opportunities your students have to discuss their interests and preferences, explain their goals, and actively plan for how to achieve their desired future, the more self-determined they will become.

**TIP FOR TRANSITION: Refer to the National Secondary Transition Technical Assistance Center for More on Student-Focused Transition Planning**

The National Secondary Transition Technical Assistance Center offers a variety of lesson plan starters that help translate the research behind methods for student-focused planning and self-directed IEPs. The resources are immediately available to use in your classrooms and programs.

Like Chrissy, students who are preparing to transition to adulthood settings need to regularly practice self-determined behavior. If you instruct students on these various components of self-determination and provide opportunities to practice self-determined behavior during high school, these skills are more likely to translate to adult settings.

## MAKING IT HAPPEN:
## Supporting Student Self-Determination

How do you know if you are effectively promoting the student engagement and involvement that leads to self-determination for your students? A variety of curricula and strategies have emerged over the past two decades focused on supporting students with disabilities to become self-determined. Rowe and colleagues (2015) have worked with national experts from across the country to develop some essential methods for supporting self-determination:

- Use a student-led IEP process that allows students to demonstrate and practice self-awareness, goal setting, problem solving, and self-advocacy.

- Collaborate with general education teachers to embed student choices into daily lessons and provide opportunities to practice self-determination skills.

- Teach and provide opportunities for students to self-monitor essential skills and supports, such as accommodations.

- Ensure all students, especially those with significant disabilities, have access to methods of communication and that their choices are listened to and supported.

- Conduct age-appropriate transition assessments so students learn about their preferences, strengths, interests, and needs to set transition goals.

- Engage in honest and respectful discussions with students about their self-determination skills, progress, and needs.

- Provide direct instruction to increase skills using evidence-based curricula and instructional approaches, with guided practice in school, home, and community settings.

- Foster the development of students' leadership skills.

- Expect and support students to make routine choices through the course of their day.

- Work collaboratively with students so they achieve their goals and can be supported to take risks and learn from their mistakes.

It is important that transition programs include some essential strategies for teaching self-determination (Anctil, Ishikawa, & Scott, 2008). In particular, self-determination skills should be taught in combination rather than in isolation to best prepare students for post-secondary environments. Let's think about what this means for Chrissy, who is planning to attend a local community college and pursue a career in graphic design. Her life after high school will require that she have the skills to advocate for accommodations to support her learning needs, effectively problem solve when barriers arise, set and monitor her individual and academic goals, and make informed choices and decisions. Chrissy's teacher should use established evidence-based practices to support Chrissy to identify and act on her personal academic and transition goals, and teach her to self-monitor progress. Chrissy meets regularly with Ms. Atkins during her advisory period, where she can strengthen her problem-solving skills and adjust her goals for the future, if necessary. Chrissy can also monitor her progress toward her goals, especially during core academic courses, to ensure she receives the accommodations that she has learned are most helpful and advocate for them when needed. These opportunities to practice self-determination are embedded throughout the entire school day.

As you begin to think about enhancing your current transition program in terms of self-determination, Table 3.1 offers guiding questions to consider in terms of 1) logistics (e.g., who will provide instruction in self-determination skills and when and where it will

**Table 3.1.** Guiding questions for supporting student self-determination in your transition program

| Element of program planning | Description | Guiding questions |
|---|---|---|
| Logistics | *When and where* will instruction on self-determination skills be implemented, and who will implement it? | • When will you implement the curriculum, instruction, and opportunities for practice? Will it be taught in a pull-out or one-to-one setting? In a transition class? Or embedded within general academic classes?<br>• Which students will you focus on first? What age ranges will you consider? Who needs instruction most?<br>• Which teachers do you need to meet with to discuss planning and accommodations? How will you include the general education teachers as part of this effort?<br>• When will you meet with the teachers? Will you co-teach? |
| Curriculum and instruction | *What* curricula and instructional approaches will be used to teach self-determination skills? | • What evidence-based curricula and instructional models best fit your classroom or program? Do you need to purchase materials and curricula? What can you find online that meets your needs and adheres to best practices?<br>• Will you provide instruction as a whole group as part of a class? Or in individual student meetings?<br>• Identify natural opportunities to embed student practice of newly learned skills. Consider embedding these opportunities across multiple settings throughout the school, at home, and in the community. |
| Data | *How* will you use data to monitor self-determination in your students? | • How will you evaluate that students are learning the essential skills?<br>• What can you do to ensure that students self-monitor their progress?<br>• How will you and your students adjust instruction and experiences based on the results of the data?<br>• How will you make the data accessible to your students, parents, and other team members? |

occur), 2) selecting evidence-based curriculum and instructional approaches, and 3) how you will evaluate student progress. The curricula, models, and assessments presented next, coupled with the guiding questions presented in Table 3.1, can help you to successfully implement a transition program that supports students' self-determination.

## Selecting Self-Determination Curricula

Several published curricula are available that focus on teaching students with disabilities self-determination skills. While many may be very useful, we will focus on those that have a research base for increasing student skills and improving post-school outcomes. Because most of the published curricula must be purchased, Table 3.2 summarizes the research so you can make an informed decision when choosing a self-determination curriculum.

***The Self-Directed IEP***     The *Self-Directed IEP* curriculum developed by Martin and colleagues (1996) contains 11 sequential lessons that are typically taught over six to ten 45-minute sessions. The *Self-Directed IEP* curriculum can be taught in a variety of settings, including special education classrooms or resource rooms, study skills classes, or other similar general education classes. For students who are fully included in general education (Zarrow Center for Learning Enrichment, n.d.), the *Self-Directed IEP* curriculum teaches students to become active participants and lead their transition IEP meetings. The 11 steps to self-directing an IEP require students to learn a variety of skills, from opening the meetings and introducing participants, to reviewing past goals and performance, to identifying transition goals and working with others on the team to ensure supports are in place to achieve those goals. Research has shown that students who completed the *Self-Directed IEP* curriculum as compared to a control group were more likely to:

• Start and lead their own IEP meetings

• Talk more during the meetings

• More readily express their interests, skills, and dreams

• Have more positive perceptions of their IEP meetings

• Be more active participants (Martin et al., 2006)

***Steps to Self-Determination***     The *Steps to Self-Determination* curriculum developed by Field and Hoffman (1996) teaches goal setting and decision making, as well as improved communication and advocacy skills. This curriculum is based upon a model of self-determination that focuses on six key elements: 1) know yourself, 2) value yourself, 3) plan, 4) act, 5) experience outcomes and learn, and 6) understand the environmental context and supports for self-determination. The *Steps to Self-Determination* curriculum consists of 16 lessons that teach long- and short-term goal setting, planning, and problem-solving skills; assertive communication and negotiation skills; and how to identify dreams and challenges. The curriculum provides various lessons for multiple learning styles and can be used in multiple settings from general education classrooms to special education classrooms.

***The Self-Advocacy Strategy***     The *Self-Advocacy Strategy* (SAS) curriculum (Van Ruesen, Bos, Schumaker, & Deshler, 1994) teaches self-awareness, self-advocacy, and goal setting along with improved communication and locus of control so that students can plan and lead the transition IEP meeting. The SAS's versatility allows you to use it as an individual teacher/student meeting strategy or as a class curriculum. This curriculum consists of five steps for teaching students the skills necessary to direct their IEP meeting, represented by the IPLAN mnemonic:

I = Inventory: students complete an inventory of their strengths, areas for improvement, educational goals, and accommodations using an educational inventory form.

P = Provide your inventory information: students practice discussing their inventory using specific communication strategies.

L = Listen and respond: students learn to be active listeners and to respond appropriately when asked questions.

A = Ask questions: students focus on asking complete, appropriate questions to gather important information (who, what, when, where, why, which, how).

N = Name your goals: students summarize critical educational goals specifying what the student wants to focus on and when the goal would be completed.

The *Self-Advocacy Strategy* has been shown to help middle school students become more active participants in their IEP meetings and verbalize statements about their strengths and areas for improvement (Hammer, 2004; Test & Neale, 2004).

**Whose Future Is It Anyway?**    *Whose Future Is It Anyway?* is a curriculum developed by Wehmeyer, Lawrence, Garner, Soukup, and Palmer (2004) that addresses a variety of self-determination skills through discussion-based lessons. The curriculum is divided into six sections containing 36 lessons addressing self-awareness, decision making, identifying resources to support goals, goal setting, communicating, and participating in transition planning meetings. *Whose Future Is It Anyway?* curriculum lends itself well to a group format, with embedded opportunities for the teacher and student to meet individually to

**Table 3.2.**  Self-determination curricula with research support

| Curriculum | Skills taught | What the research shows |
|---|---|---|
| 1. The Self-Directed IEP (Martin et al., 1996) | Teaches students skills to participate in their transition IEP meetings: introduce members of IEP team, explain purpose of meeting, review performance data and past goals, discuss future goals, and close the meeting. | Has been shown to increase student engagement during IEP meetings. (Martin et al., 2006; Allen, Smith, Test, Flowers, & Wood, 2001; Snyder & Shapiro, 1997) |
| 2. Steps to Self-Determination (Field & Hoffman, 1994) | Designed to help students define and achieve goals; identify strengths, needs, and preferences; develop decision-making and goal-setting skills; improve communication skills; access resources and supports, and learn from outcomes. | Has been found to increase students' knowledge and behaviors associated with self-determination. (Field & Hoffman, 2002) |
| 3. Self-Advocacy Strategy | Self-awareness, self-advocacy, and goal setting along with improved communication and locus of control so that students can plan and lead the transition IEP meeting. | Has been shown to help middle school students become more active participants in their IEP meetings and verbalize statements about their strengths and areas for improvement. (Hammer, 2004; Test & Neale, 2004) |
| 4. *Whose Future Is It Anyway?* (Wehmeyer, Lawrence, Garner, Soukup, & Palmer, 2004) | Self-awareness; decision making; finding community resources; communicating effectively; and teaming, leading, and self-advocating. | Has been show to improve self-determination skills and transition-related skills and knowledge for middle and high school students with disabilities. (Wehmeyer, Palmer, Lee, Williams-Diehm, & Shogren, 2011) |

discuss the student's interests, preferences, strengths, and needs. The curriculum aligns with a specific research-based instructional model, the Self-Determined Learning Model of Instruction (SDLMI) (Mithaug, Wehmeyer, Agran, Martin, & Palmer, 1998), that has been shown to increase post-school outcomes, as well as increase the self-determined behaviors of students with disabilities (Lee et al., 2010; Shogren et al., 2011; Wehmeyer et al., 2012). The SDLMI includes three phases: setting a goal, taking action on the goal, and adjusting the goal or plan. Figure 3.1 provides a template for completing the SDLMI with students as they begin goal setting and problem solving.

## Assessing Self-Determination

Using assessment measures is important when implementing self-determination curricula with your students. Using an existing self-determination assessment will help you monitor student progress and determine if the curriculum is having a positive impact. The *Self-Directed IEP* and the *Steps to Self-Determination* curricula include curriculum-based assessments aligned with content. To keep track of student growth, you can administer these assessments prior to and after teaching the content. Other well-established assessments can also be useful in evaluating your students' current self-determination skills and the opportunities available to practice them. Three assessments will be described next, all of which can be found on the Zarrow Center for Learning Enrichment's web site at the University of Oklahoma (www.ou.edu/content/education/centers-and-partnerships/zarrow/self-determination-assessment-tools.html):

- The *AIR Self-Determination Scale* measures the student's capacity to exhibit self-determination skills, as well as the student's opportunities to practice self-determination. The first section, capacity, measures student ability, perceptions, and knowledge; and the second section, opportunity, focuses on how often students have been able to practice self-determined behaviors both at home and at school. The instrument is intended to be administered across key stakeholders and consists of an educator form, parent form, and student form.

- The *Arc Self-Determination Scale* (Wehmeyer & Kelcher, 1995) is a student self-report scale that examines the essential characteristics of self-determination, including autonomy, self-regulation, psychological empowerment, and self-realization. The scale is designed to 1) assess the self-determination strengths and weaknesses of adolescents with disabilities, 2) facilitate student involvement in educational planning and instruction to promote self-determination as an educational outcome, 3) develop self-determination goals and objectives, and 4) assess student self-determination skills for research purposes.

- The *Transition Assessment and Goal Generator* (TAGG) (Martin, Hennessey, McConnell, Terry, & Willis, 2015) was developed to identify students' strengths and needs, and produce annual transition goals referenced to common core standards that IEP teams may use for transition planning. It is the newest online assessment, and its items come from research on critical student behaviors associated with post-school employment and education:

  1.  Strengths and limits

  2.  Disability awareness

  3.  Persistence

| Phase 1: Set a goal | |
|---|---|
| **Guiding questions** | **My responses** |
| What do I want to learn? | |
| What do I know about what I want to learn? | |
| What must change for me to learn what I don't know? | |
| What can I do to make this happen? | |

| Phase 2: Take action | |
|---|---|
| **Guiding questions** | **My responses** |
| What can I do to learn what I don't know? | |
| What could keep me from taking action? | |
| What can I do to remove these barriers? | |
| When will I take action? | |

| Phase 3: Adjust my goal or plan | |
|---|---|
| **Guiding questions** | **My responses** |
| What actions have I taken? | |
| What barriers have been removed? | |
| What has changed about what I don't know? | |
| Do I know what I still want to learn? | |

**Figure 3.1.** Self-determined learning model of instruction (SDLMI) template. (*Source:* Wehmeyer, M.L., Agran, M., Palmer, S., and Mithaug, D., 1999.)

4. Interacting with others

5. Goal setting and attainment

6. Employment

7. Student involvement in IEP

8. Support community

## Data Collection and Evaluating Student Progress

In addition to assessment and instruction on self-determination skills, implementing an effective transition program to support and enhance self-determination involves monitoring student progress through data collection (see Table 3.1). This data is then used to adjust instruction or activities as needed to support skill development. An important step in increasing self-determination involves teaching students to self-monitor their progress on their personal goals. For example, Ms. Atkins met with Chrissy to help her identify a goal and collect data. She designed a Supporting Students in Goal Setting Checklist (Figure 3.2) to assist Chrissy to learn to set and monitor the employment goal she chose for herself. Chrissy wants to obtain a part-time job in an office setting as a work-based learning experience in her Careers class. She has decided to first complete the O*Net Interest Profiler to narrow down her preferred career interests and then review office jobs using helpful online resource sites (found on www.disability.gov/can-high-school-college-students-get-help-job-search) and the O*Net Online (www.onetonline.org), where she can watch videos and learn about educational and training requirements for careers of interest. As part of her time with Ms. Atkins, Chrissy was to narrow down her choices to five jobs in her community, develop a resume, complete applications for the jobs, and follow up with employers. Ms. Atkins and Chrissy developed a goal-setting data sheet that Chrissy could use to update her progress. Chrissy planned to work with Ms. Atkins to find solutions when there were problems. This data and information would then be used to track her progress toward annual IEP goals. For a blank version of a goal-setting sheet that you can use with your student see the Chapter 3 Appendix.

## WHAT YOU CAN DO RIGHT NOW:
### Putting Ideas Into Action

As you prepare your students for life after high school, building their self-determination is critical. Students with disabilities benefit greatly from opportunities to practice and demonstrate self-determination skills, including self-advocacy, choice making, decision making, self-awareness, and self-management. You can provide opportunities for students to practice these skills through involving your students in their IEP planning meetings and embedding opportunities to advocate for their needs and preferences throughout the school day. Educators and transition specialists should also support students to effectively communicate, problem solve, and identify supports and resources, all important skills that are needed to be self-determined.

The strategies and curricula introduced in this chapter can assist you in developing your students' self-determination so they are prepared for the decisions they will encounter in adulthood. So, how will you commit to these new strategies and practices? The I'm Determined to Support My Students: Goal Setting for Teachers form (Figure 3.3) can

Student's name: _____Chrissy_____      Goal: _To find an interesting office job in my town._

| Goal benchmark/ action step | Date attempted | Date completed | Notes |
|---|---|---|---|
| Complete the O*Net Interest Profiler. | 2/12/17 | 2/12/17 | Chrissy was able to view multiple jobs in her interest area of business management and administration. |
| Review careers of interest on Internet. | 2/13/17 | 2/27/17 | Chrissy took the information from the O*Net Interest Profiler and reviewed multiple entry-level jobs. She narrowed her choices to five. |
| Search for up to five jobs in my community. | 3/2/17 | 3/16/17 | The five jobs Chrissy researched in her community were file clerk, library assistant, receptionist, office clerk, and data entry clerk. |
| Develop a resume and fill out applications for jobs. | 3/9/17 | 3/16/17 | Chrissy completed her resume emphasizing the business classes she has completed in high school as well as her organizational skills. She then completed online applications for all of the five jobs, attaching her resume to each. |
| Follow up with employers regarding applications. | 3/20/17 | 3/20/17 | Chrissy called each of the five businesses on 3/20/17 to ask if they had received her application. As a result of the phone call, she received an interview for the library assistant position. |

Challenges or barriers to completing the goal:
One barrier Chrissy and Ms. Atkins experienced was finding time in the school day to complete the profiler, research jobs, fill out applications, and call the employers for follow-up. Additionally, Chrissy's lack of work experience made developing a robust resume a challenge.

Strategies to be successful:
Two strategies occurred to assist with this barrier: a) Ms. Atkins met briefly with Chrissy's teachers to indicate the steps Chrissy would be taking to find a job and secured their flexibility in having time to work with Chrissy during the school day, and b) a paraeducator in the high school who knew Chrissy well had a friend who worked at the library and was willing to put in a good word for Chrissy when she applied.

Ways to problem solve and overcome barriers:
Both of the strategies listed above were successful, as having time during the school day allowed Ms. Atkins to assist Chrissy in meeting her goal and having connections who could assist Chrissy with connecting to employers helped get her an interview.

Final result:
Chrissy was able to interview for the library assistant job and was offered 10 hours per week of work.

**Figure 3.2.**  Chrissy's Supporting Students in Goal Setting Checklist.

Use this form to plan for what you can do right now to support your students to become self-determined.

| Strategy or practice | Steps to your goals<br>What concrete steps can you take to implement the new strategy/practice? | Barriers<br>What obstacles are keeping you from implementing the strategy or practice in your school/classroom? | Solutions<br>How might you overcome the barriers? |
|---|---|---|---|
| Use a student-led individualized education program process. | **1.**<br><br>Date complete:_____<br><br>**2.**<br><br>Date complete:_____<br><br><br>**3.**<br><br>Date complete:_____<br><br><br>**4.**<br><br>Date complete:_____<br><br><br>**5.**<br><br>Date complete:_____ | | |
| Collaborate with general education teachers to embed self-determination skills into daily lessons. | **1.**<br><br>Date complete:_____<br><br>**2.**<br><br>Date complete:_____<br><br>**3.**<br><br>Date complete:_____<br><br>**4.**<br><br>Date complete:_____<br><br>**5.**<br><br>Date complete:_____ | | |

**Figure 3.3.** "Determined" to support my students: Goal setting for teachers. (*Source:* Rowe, Alverson, Unruh, Fowler, Kellems, & Test, 2015).

| Strategy or practice | Steps to your goals<br>What concrete steps can you take to implement the new strategy/practice? | Barriers<br>What obstacles are keeping you from implementing the strategy or practice in your school/classroom? | Solutions<br>How might you overcome the barriers? |
|---|---|---|---|
| Teach and provide opportunities for students to self-monitor essential skills. | **1.**<br><br>Date complete:_____<br>**2.**<br><br>Date complete:_____<br>**3.**<br>Date complete:_____<br><br>**4.**<br>Date complete:_____<br><br>**5.**<br>Date complete:_____ | | |
| Provide direct instruction on self-determination skills using evidence-based curricula and instructional approaches. | **1.**<br><br>Date complete:_____<br>**2.**<br><br>Date complete:_____<br>**3.**<br>Date complete:_____<br><br>**4.**<br>Date complete:_____<br><br>**5.**<br>Date complete:_____ | | |

*Your Complete Guide to Transition Planning and Services* by Mary E. Morningstar and Beth Clavenna-Deane.
Copyright © 2018 by Paul H. Brookes Publishing Co., Inc. All rights reserved.

57

**Figure 3.3.** *(continued)*

| Strategy or practice | Steps to your goals<br>What concrete steps can you take to implement the new strategy/practice? | Barriers<br>What obstacles are keeping you from implementing the strategy or practice in your school/classroom? | Solutions<br>How might you overcome the barriers? |
|---|---|---|---|
| Expect and support students to make routine choices through the course of their day. | **1.**<br><br>Date complete:_____<br>**2.**<br><br>Date complete:_____<br>**3.**<br><br>Date complete:_____<br>**4.**<br><br>Date complete:_____<br>**5.**<br><br>Date complete:_____ | | |
| Foster the development of students' leadership skills. | **1.**<br><br>Date complete:_____<br>**2.**<br><br>Date complete:_____<br>**3.**<br><br>Date complete:_____<br>**4.**<br><br>Date complete:_____<br>**5.**<br><br>Date complete:_____ | | |

| Strategy or practice | Steps to your goals<br>What concrete steps can you take to implement the new strategy/practice? | Barriers<br>What obstacles are keeping you from implementing the strategy or practice in your school/classroom? | Solutions<br>How might you overcome the barriers? |
|---|---|---|---|
| Support students to take risks and learn from their mistakes. | **1.**<br><br>Date complete:_____<br><br>**2.**<br><br>Date complete:_____<br><br>**3.**<br><br>Date complete:_____<br><br>**4.**<br><br>Date complete:_____<br><br>**5.**<br><br>Date complete:_____ | | |

be a good place to get started. Use this goal-setting form to identify and commit to using research-based strategies for promoting your students' self-determination. This form will help you develop the steps to implement each new strategy, track your progress, and problem solve when barriers arise.

Furthermore, the appendix to Chapter 3 provides additional useful forms for helping your students become more self-determined that can be filled out by students themselves with input from their families and supporters. The Dream Template helps the student envision his or her dreams for the future. The Goal-Tracking Sheet can be used by the student and his or her educational team to set measurable benchmarks or steps to the goal and track progress toward that goal over time, with space to record successes and problem solve barriers. Finally, the My Good Day Plan helps the student identify and plot events in a "good day" and determine what actions and supports are needed to make that good day happen. A student-completed example of a Good Day form, followed by a blank version, are provided.

## ONLINE RESOURCES

National Technical Assistance Center on Transition (NTACT), Lesson Plan Starters for Student-Focused Planning: www.transitionta.org

Transition Coalition Online Module: The Essentials of Self-Determination: www.transitioncoalition.org/transition/module_home.php

IMDetermined: www.imdetermined.org

Zarrow Center: www.ou.edu/content/education/centers-and-partnerships/zarrow.html

NCSET Research to Practice Brief on Self-Determination: www.ncset.org/publications/viewdesc.asp?id=962

National Gateway to Self-Determination: http://ngsd.org

# Self-Determination Forms for Students and Families

# Goal-Setting Checklist

Student's name: _____  Goal: _____

| Goal benchmark/ action step | Date attempted | Date completed | Notes |
|---|---|---|---|
|  |  |  |  |
|  |  |  |  |
|  |  |  |  |
|  |  |  |  |
|  |  |  |  |

| Challenges or barriers to completing the goal: |
|---|
|  |
| Strategies to be successful: |
|  |
| Ways to problem solve and overcome barriers: |
|  |
| Final result: |
|  |

*Source:* Rowe, Alverson, Unruh, Fowler, Kellems, & Test, 2014.

# The Dream Sheet

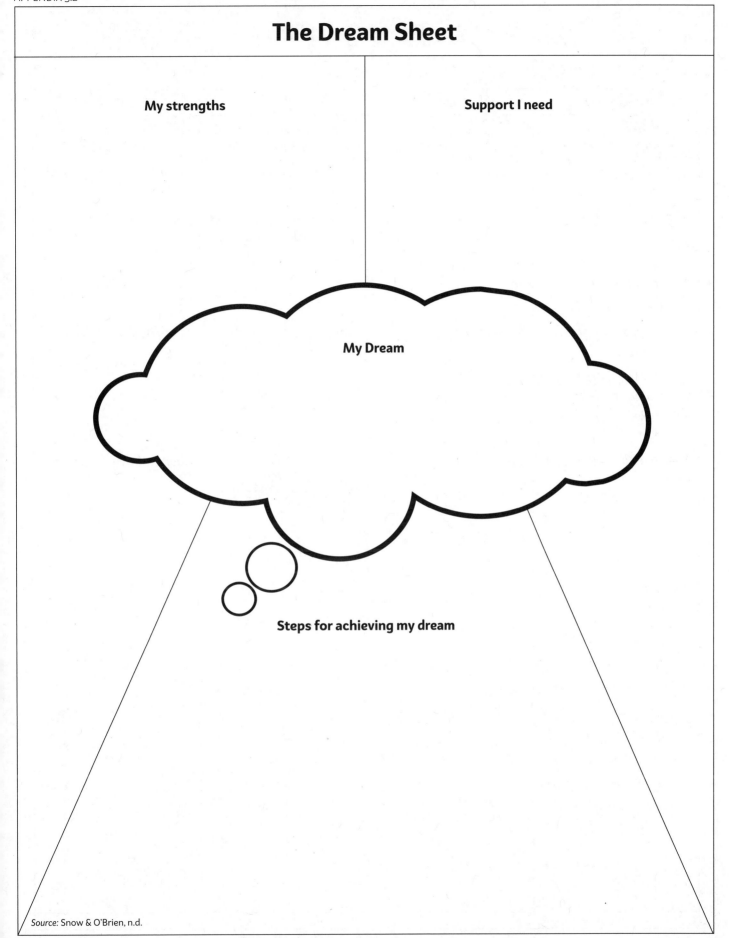

**My strengths**

**Support I need**

**My Dream**

**Steps for achieving my dream**

*Source:* Snow & O'Brien, n.d.

# My Good Day Plan

Student's name: _Chrissy_            Grade: _11th_

| GOOD DAY | NOW | ACTION | SUPPORT |
|---|---|---|---|
| **What happens on a good day?** | **Does it happen now?** | **What needs to happen to make it a good day?** | **Who or what can help me?** |
| 1. Wake up on time. | Sometimes. | Go to bed earlier so I get more sleep. | Mom/Dad or my alarm clock |
| 2. Eat a good breakfast. | Sometimes. | Have someone help me make a good breakfast. | Mom/Dad |
| 3. Get to class on time. | Yes. | | |
| 4. Do my homework. | Sometimes. | Make sure I stay focused. | Mom/Dad or my teachers |
| 5. Relax by watching TV or playing a video game with friends. | Yes. | | |
| 6. Get ready for bed on time. | Sometimes. | Make sure I turn off the TV or video game 15 minutes before it's time for bed. | Phone alarm or Mom/Dad |

# My Good Day Plan

Student's name: _____ Grade: _____

| GOOD DAY | NOW | ACTION | SUPPORT |
|---|---|---|---|
| What happens on a good day? | Does it happen now? | What needs to happen to make it a good day? | Who or what can help me? |
| 1. | | | |
| 2. | | | |
| 3. | | | |
| 4. | | | |
| 5. | | | |

# My Good Day Plan *(continued)*

Student's name: _____ Grade: _____

| GOOD DAY | NOW | ACTION | SUPPORT |
|---|---|---|---|
| **What happens on a good day?** | **Does it happen now?** | **What needs to happen to make it a good day?** | **Who or what can help me?** |
| 6. | | | |
| 7. | | | |
| 8. | | | |
| 9. | | | |
| 10. | | | |

In *Your Complete Guide to Transition Planning and Services* by Mary E. Morningstar and Beth Clavenna-Deane

# 4

# Family Involvement
## *Engaging Families During Transition*

Aja is a spirited and opinionated 16-year-old boy who loves rap music, school, and spending time with friends. Aja has cerebral palsy and an intellectual disability. He has mastered the use of an augmentative and alternative communication to express himself, although he sometimes still gets frustrated when he feels like his wants and needs are not heard. Aja is very close to his mother, Raika, who is a single mom living in a large East Indian community. She has been a strong advocate for Aja throughout his life. Aja's IEP meeting is coming up, and typically, his mom takes the lead in meetings, often speaking for Aja rather than letting him try to participate himself. Is Raika holding on too tightly to her son's future? How would you help give Aja a voice in his future planning while respecting his mother's desire to be involved?

Before a young person ever becomes a student in a classroom, he or she is first a member of a family. Families are an important part of our work. They provide vital support to students, particularly during the transition to adulthood. In fact, many families have shared that their involvement in their child's life increases during transition, especially if they desire a future for their son or daughter that is beyond the "status quo." Having families involved with schools is a clear benefit to all students. If families are involved in secondary schools, students have increased school attendance, reduced dropout rates, higher academic achievement, and more positive social skills and behaviors (Henderson & Mapp, 2002). In addition, family members often serve as role models and support systems for students once they have left high school. If families have high expectations for their son's or daughter's future and are involved in transition planning, students are more likely to graduate, have better employment outcomes, and be enrolled in postsecondary educational settings (Newman, 2004). Family expectations for their child's future help shape whether students achieve those goals, regardless of their disability label or level of functioning. All things being equal, youth with disabilities whose parents expect them to go on to postsecondary education or employment are more likely to be positively engaged in high school and achieve more post-school outcomes than youth whose parents do not share that optimism for the future (Newman, 2004).

# GETTING STARTED:
## Why Are Families So Important?

For students with disabilities, we know that planning for transition earlier leads to better post-school outcomes, and family members are crucial team players during transition planning. During high school, research has shown that families have the greatest impact on their son's or daughter's future when they:

- Hold high expectations for success

- Discuss plans for the future with their child

- Get help and assistance when needed

- Help their son or daughter to prepare for college

- Keep track of their child's academic and social progress in high school (Henderson & Mapp, 2002; Morningstar et al., 2010; Newman, 2004)

Other participants in transition planning meetings—teachers, administrators, related service personnel, and adult service providers—are likely to change from year to year, but the family members stay the same. Families help maintain continuity by providing information about students' previous transition experiences and services.

The important information that families can provide about the student include his or her strengths and abilities, likes and dislikes, and needs and idiosyncrasies. They can tell you how a student spends her spare time, what hobbies and interests he has, whether she has ever kept a checkbook, or whether the student has access to a computer at home. Parents can tell you if their son can cook a simple meal, has interviewed for a job, or reads the newspaper (Wehmeyer, Morningstar, & Husted, 1999). Families must be equal partners in decision making because they have much to gain or lose from transition. When their child exits school but is unemployed or has a job that does not provide sufficient wages to support independent living, it is the family that typically supplies a home and financial support.

## When Are Families Involved in Schools?

Families are more likely to become involved with schools and transition planning when they:

- Understand they should be involved

- Know they are capable of making a contribution

- Feel invited by the school and their children (Hoover-Dempsey & Sandler, 2005)

We also know that the strongest, most consistent predictors of parent involvement at home and school are the specific school programs and teacher practices that encourage and guide parent involvement (Epstein, 2001). Parents have reported that good relationships and communication with school professionals lead to more positive participation in transition planning (Geenen, Powers, Lopez-Vasquez, & Bersani, 2003; Kim & Morningstar, 2005). So, it is essential that if we care about successful transitions to adulthood for our students, we must identify the best ways to support and engage our families. A sage piece of advice drives this chapter: "Understanding the individual student does not mean that you will understand the family, and understanding the family is necessary to understanding the child" (Turnbull & Turnbull, 2001, p. 109). Understanding the family involves recognizing and respecting family dynamics and cultural values.

Let's take a moment and reflect on the impact of transition on Aja and his family. In Aja's last IEP meeting, his teacher discussed her ideas for beginning to plan for Aja's independence and learn the self-determination skills he would need to live on his own. Raika was caught off guard by this goal for Aja's future. She has been worrying about Aja's future since the school started discussing transition to adulthood, but it never occurred to her that Aja would live anywhere else but at home. She also doesn't understand why Aja needs to learn self-determination skills, since in her family, decisions are made that best meet the needs of all members, not just what one person wants to do. While Aja has been raised mostly in the United States, Raika still holds tightly to the traditional values of her cultural community. She wants Aja to live a happy life, with the supports he needs to make contributions within his tightknit community, but she disagrees that he should move out of the family home. If you were Aja's teacher, you might want to know more about Aja's family and the unintentional impact that transition planning may have on the family as a whole. The family systems framework (Turnbull, Turnbull, Erwin, Soodak & Shogren, 2011), which is discussed next, is one way to consider the whole family when planning for transition.

## Understanding the Family Systems Framework

*"In a mobile, all the pieces, no matter what the size or shape, can be grouped together and balanced by shortening or lengthening the strings attached, or rearranging the distance between pieces. So it is with a family. None of the family members is identical to any other; they are all different and at different levels of growth. As in a mobile, you can't arrange one without thinking of the other."*

From Satir, V. (1972). *Peoplemaking*. Palo Alto, CA: Science and Behavior Books.

As students and families move through the transition planning process, each member takes on new roles and responsibilities, thereby changing the balance of the family. As we work with families and students in transition, it is important that we have a clear understanding of how family systems affect transition and vice versa, and that we keep the mobile perspective in mind. Something that educators might think is an exciting new opportunity for a student may throw a family's equilibrium off balance. Bringing the family back into balance can be delicate work, like readjusting the strings of a mobile that has become tangled and off-kilter. It might take time and supports for the family to adjust to new circumstances.

The family systems framework (Turnbull et al., 2011) helps you see how the actions and characteristics of each family member affect the family as a whole. If you understand the family systems perspective, you will most likely answer the question, "To whom do I provide services?" differently. It can help you think about how to involve siblings, extended family members, and parents in the student's transition planning; how to gain access to the resources and networks of family and friends in order to help the student live, work, and participate in the community; and how to gauge the impact of the student's major life transition upon the entire family (Turnbull & Morningstar, 1993). There are four major elements of Turnbull and colleagues' framework: family characteristics, family interactions, family life cycle, and family functions. The sections that follow discuss specific topics related to each of these elements in detail.

***Family Characteristics*** What is your definition of a family? This seemingly straightforward question may be more difficult than you think! How you answer depends upon the lens through which you see the world. Everyone is affected by cultural and social points of view.

Today, the traditional view of the nuclear family is giving way to perspectives that better reflect family diversity. A more updated definition of family is "any unit that defines itself as a family, including individuals who are related by blood or marriage as well as those who have made a commitment to share their lives (Hanson & Lynch, 2013, p. 2).

When working with families of youth with disabilities, consider how family characteristics may influence the transition planning process. Having expectations that parents will be available to attend transition meetings during the work day or that families will actively participate in all of the school-focused transition processes may lead to frustration and disappointment if you haven't considered the reality of how the family operates. It is not necessarily the case that families do not place high values on transition planning; however, because of certain life circumstances, they may need additional supports to fully participate. As an example, one-third of youth with disabilities live in a household with a single parent, most often the mother (Turnbull et al., 2011). This can lead to difficulty in finding the right times to meet and discuss transition, particularly if the parent is working during the day to support the family.

Therefore, you may want to think outside of the typical school setting and consider alternatives for how families and students can be contributing members of the transition team. Considering the family's characteristics and life circumstances will help you when you plan for their involvement during transition.

**Cultural Characteristics**     During transition, you will likely be working with families with diverse ethnic, religious, language, and cultural characteristics. It's important to remember that not all families will share your expectations for your students' futures. Considering family characteristics such as cultural values and influences will help you collaborate with families in the best interest of the student. Aja and his family maintain cultural and religious values that are both similar and different from values held by Aja's school. For example, Aja and his family value strong familial and community relationships, but differ in the expectation that adult unmarried children should live independently. Knowing this cultural view can help the educational team to best support Aja and his family to plan for transition. For Aja and Raika, you might consider what will best meet their needs, and this might be to support Aja to learn the skills he needs to contribute to the family household and become more independent in caring for himself, including decision-making and goal-setting skills, which are critical components of self-determination (see Chapter 3). In this way, you can adapt your approach so that transition planning for Aja and Raika is more collaborative, which in turn is more likely to lead to positive outcomes for everyone.

If you consider the broadest definition of culture—the knowledge, concepts, and values shared by members of a group that is defined and characterized by the interactions between individuals in a given environment (Barrera & Corso, 2005)—then you may need to expand your views on what represents cultural diversity in your school and community. Families' cultural views about adulthood and post-school success may conflict with your views of successful transitions. For example, in some communities, leaving home to attend college is the norm; however, in some rural communities, it may be a more valued norm to forego or delay college and work on the family farm. If you are serving students and families in such a community, this must be taken into account. In other families, it may be assumed that a significant rite of passage (e.g., marriage) must occur before a young adult moves out of the family home. You may work with families who hold different values than you do, irrespective of their race or ethnicity, and this may require you to reexamine your assumptions about what really represents an ideal post-school adult outcome. Lynch and Hanson (2011) describe a continuum of values that are important to consider when providing services to families. As you work with families during transition, you might want to identify where the family falls within the continuum as a way to gauge the similarities and differences in values, viewpoints, or expectations that may emerge when working with families. The Continuum of Transition and Family Values (Figure 4.1) can help you consider how your views of transition and the family's values may or may not align in order to consider strategies for bridging the gaps.

Traditional post-school goals for students with disabilities may not meet the needs of students and families who are culturally and ethnically diverse. The cultural underpinnings of special education and transition are based upon assumptions from a dominant culture (professionalized middle class services) that may be in conflict with other cultural views (Kalyanpur & Harry, 2012). This is reflected in IDEA's emphasis on independence and individual achievement, which may conflict with values such as familialism and interdependence (Leake & Black, 2005). When the values of school professionals and parents conflict, parents may seek additional guidance from trusted community individuals. For some school professionals, this may seem as though parents are losing trust in schools' recommendations and limiting cooperation or contact. School personnel, then, often misinterpret this lack of parental involvement as disinterest, apathy, or neglect (Geenen, Powers, & Lopez-Vasquez, 2001; Greene, 2011). Considerations of family cultural and religious values will help you to avoid misinterpretation of family engagement and potentially alienating the family.

***Personal Characteristics***     As would be expected, a family member's physical health, mental health, and coping styles all affect how well the family engages with schools during transition. Part of the family's personal characteristics are influenced by the specific disability of the student; however, the specific needs of the child and the demands placed on the family, and how the family responds to these demands, are more important to consider than a disability label. Keep in mind that family priorities and needs will change over time. Also, be sure to focus on the contributions and strengths of the student with disabilities, not just the deficits. For some families, conversations with school personnel may only occur when their child has done something wrong, so you may need to consistently mention what is going well when talking with families. It is also important to consider the family's personal circumstances before making negative or hasty judgements about the family capabilities. For instance, when Aja first entered high school, Raika and Aja's dad divorced. During this period of time, Raika was having significant difficulty coping with the daily demands of Aja's care. Her communication and engagement with the school dropped off, and Aja's teacher complained that Raika wasn't returning signed forms or participating in school meetings. As soon as Raika was able to get support from her extended family and neighbors in her community, she was able to reengage with the school.

Another important characteristic of the family is how they cope with change and challenges. Families of children with disabilities do not necessarily look toward professionals and engage in long-term planning to deal with transition to adulthood, but may instead turn to their informal supports (family and friends). So, you may not be the first resource when family members are concerned about transition. You may want to have community and informal resources mapped out for the families with whom you work. When developing resources for families, also consider the family's preferences for receiving information. For example, mapping out a community resource network may help the family feel more

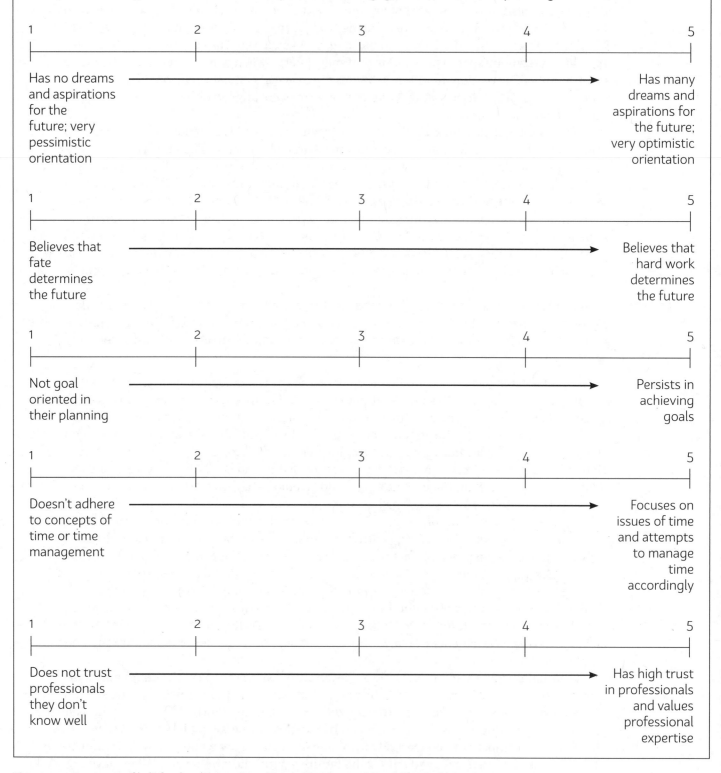

**Continuum of Beliefs Related to Transition**

For each continuum (ranging from 1–5), place an F to indicate where you believe the focus family falls in terms of their beliefs. Place a Y on a point in the continuum to indicate where you fall, from 1–5. Reflect on the extent of your agreement or disagreement with the focus family and the implications for developing a partnership with the focus family in enhancing the student's self-determination and engagement in transition planning.

| 1 | 2 | 3 | 4 | 5 |

Has no dreams and aspirations for the future; very pessimistic orientation → Has many dreams and aspirations for the future; very optimistic orientation

| 1 | 2 | 3 | 4 | 5 |

Believes that fate determines the future → Believes that hard work determines the future

| 1 | 2 | 3 | 4 | 5 |

Not goal oriented in their planning → Persists in achieving goals

| 1 | 2 | 3 | 4 | 5 |

Doesn't adhere to concepts of time or time management → Focuses on issues of time and attempts to manage time accordingly

| 1 | 2 | 3 | 4 | 5 |

Does not trust professionals they don't know well → Has high trust in professionals and values professional expertise

**Figure 4.1.** Continuum of beliefs related to transition. (*Source:* Morningstar & Turnbull, 2002.)

# Continuum of Beliefs Related to Transition

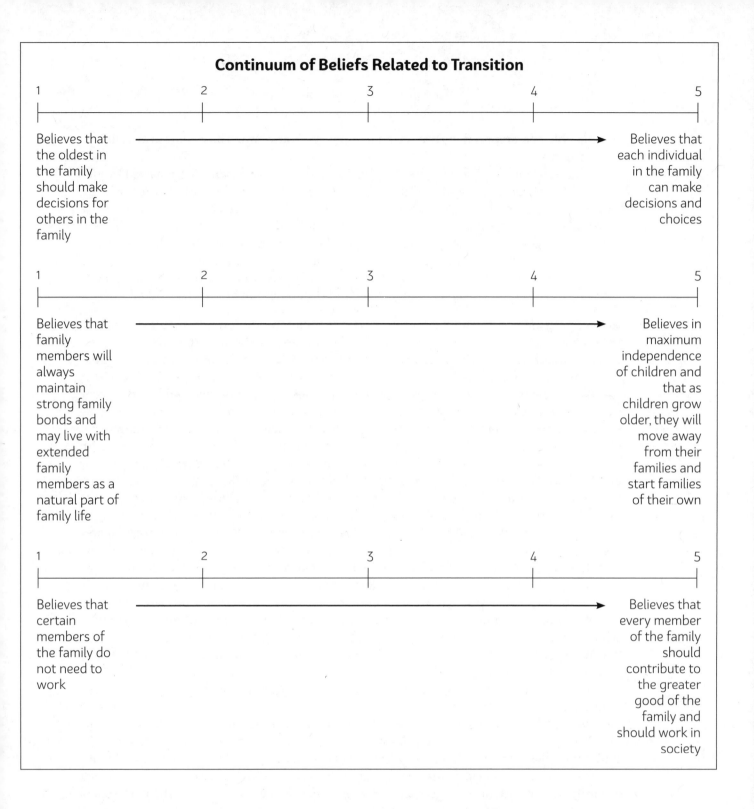

1          2          3          4          5

Believes that the oldest in the family should make decisions for others in the family     →     Believes that each individual in the family can make decisions and choices

1          2          3          4          5

Believes that family members will always maintain strong family bonds and may live with extended family members as a natural part of family life     →     Believes in maximum independence of children and that as children grow older, they will move away from their families and start families of their own

1          2          3          4          5

Believes that certain members of the family do not need to work     →     Believes that every member of the family should contribute to the greater good of the family and should work in society comfortable and prepared for transition if supports from community centers or religious groups are in place.

Finally, when developing a picture of your families, consider any challenges they may be facing, such as financial distress or constraints, physical or mental health concerns, employment changes, or exposure to violence. These issues are complex and can cause extreme stress for all family members. Families struggling with these types of burdensome challenges may find planning for their adolescent's future very difficult. In such circumstances, as previously mentioned, it is more important to go beyond just school-based services and student-focused interventions. You will need to bring together an array of community resources to support the whole family, thereby supporting the student.

**Family Interactions**      Family interactions comprise interactions between individual family members (e.g., parent, sister, grandmother) or can refer to the workings of various family subsystems (e.g., marital, parental, sibling, extended family roles and relationships). Family interactions often determine how a family is able to handle stressful challenges, as well as how the family is able to use available resources in positive and healthy ways. To collaborate successfully with families during transition planning, think about how family members interact and the differing roles they play. Recent research shows that 5.5 million children are living in households with grandparents, most often along with the child's parent or parents, and over 1.5 million children are being fully supported by grandparents as the primary caretakers (Children's Defense Fund, 2014). In many circumstances, you may be communicating and planning for transition with grandparents and other extended family members (e.g., aunts, uncles, siblings). Given this, there may be cultural and generational differences that exist between grandparents, parents, and students. For example, while Raika and the school are not at odds over how independent and self-determined Aja should be, his grandmother believes that Raika is "too hard" on Aja for making him use his communication device to ask for a drink. When Aja stays with his Nanni, she does everything for him and anticipates his every need. Aja, on the other hand, is starting to assert his own mind by insisting on listening to rap music on his computer, which is viewed by both his mother and Nanni as disrespectful of their traditions. Appreciating these kinds of family dynamics can be helpful in balancing support for Aja with respect for his family relationships and culture.

Understanding the different roles of family members is especially critical during transition, a time when society expects adolescents to assume more autonomy in making decisions and taking responsibility for their actions. Increased independence from the family may not be the case for families with young adults with significant disabilities. The major life roles typically assumed by teenagers (e.g., having an after-school job, driving a car, opening a checking account) may be significantly delayed, if they occur at all. In fact, a family may experience an increased level of direct involvement during the post-school period due to the lack of community adult services and supports (Hanley-Maxwell, Whitney-Thomas, & Pogoloff, 1995).

Perhaps what is needed is a redefinition of adulthood. Research has shown that students with disabilities overwhelmingly desire to continue their close involvement and interactions with their families, who offer both pragmatic and emotional support (Morningstar, 1997). Taking into account the preferences of the adolescent for an *interdependent relationship* with the family, a better way to plan is toward a "supported adulthood" (Ferguson & Ferguson, 2011). Adulthood might be defined by the changing roles and responsibilities *within* the family as well as the student's personal expectations for the future. In many cultures, this may be defined for all young adults, not just those with disabilities. In fact, in some cultures, moving out on one's own might be viewed as a disgrace to the family (Blue-Banning, Turnbull, & Pereira, 2000; Turnbull, et al., 2011). Therefore, as you embark on the process of transition planning, be careful to consider the preferences of both the student and family regarding his or her level of independence.

***Family Functions***     Family functions are the tasks that families perform to meet the needs of each family member and the family as a whole. Families strive to reach equilibrium through fulfillment of family functions. The following are eight primary family functions:

1. Economic: generating income and handling family finances, paying bills, earning allowances, and so forth

2. Daily care: purchasing food, preparing meals, cleaning the home, providing transportation

3. Recreation: vacations and travel, hobbies or clubs, sports

4. Socialization: developing individual and collective friendships and social skills, engaging in social activities

5. Self-esteem: self-identify and self-image, awareness of personal strengths and weaknesses, motivation, empowerment

6. Affection: developing intimate personal relationships, expressing one's sexuality, giving and receiving nurture and love, expressing emotions

7. Education: participation in school-related activities, continuing education, homework, career development, work ethic, transition

8. Spiritual: transmitting cultural and personal beliefs from one generation to the next, participating in a spiritual community (Turnbull et al., 2011)

While each family function is distinct, most families cannot perform all eight functions at the same time. For example, if a family is struggling to meet the basic necessities of daily care, then functions such as recreation, socialization, and even education may take a backseat. Also, a family may choose to devote less time to certain functions (e.g., a clean and orderly house) in order to give more time to others (e.g., time for recreation and socializing). It is important that we strike a balance between our professional expectations and the family's priorities. We often only focus on the education/vocational family function, primarily from the perspective of the student. It may be that transition is not a top priority for the family when the school is ready to start making plans, and therefore families may struggle with your efforts to bring it to the forefront. Recognizing this will help you balance what you know is important to do (e.g., long-term transition planning) with the immediate needs of the family. On the one hand, we know that families and students who begin the transition planning process early achieve better outcomes. On the other hand, some families and students report feeling pressure from schools to begin the formal transition process before they are ready (Morningstar, Kleinhammer-Tramill, & Lattin, 1999).

Understanding the goals and cultural perspectives of students and families can alleviate a lot of inadvertent miscommunication and conflict. For example, you can start planning early by asking families of middle schoolers some basic questions about where they envision their child headed in the future. This might be as simple as asking a few questions about their child's future goals. You could also share videos of older students with disabilities talking about how they achieved their dreams for the future, such as those posted in the "Parents" section of the I'm Determined web site or the resources for elementary parents available there at www.imdetermined.org/parents. These types of discussions, coupled with compelling examples of families who have high expectations for the future, can pave the way for more positive and directed transition planning. The Conversation Starters textbox provides a list of helpful questions that you might ask parents to learn about family routines and functions and jump start the transition planning process.

## Conversation Starters

Consider using these comments and questions to dialogue about the student's and family's activities, environments, and routines:

- Tell me about your son's/daughter's day. What are some common routines/activities at home and at school? What types of things happen on most: mornings? afternoons? nights? weekends? Which activities would you like to have him or her participate in?

- What activity(s) does your son or daughter not like to do? What makes this routine/activity difficult or uncomfortable?

- What are your child's daily study habits like? How does he or she feel about school?

- Who are the important people who participate in your child's life? Who provides support to your child in terms of studying and schoolwork (e.g., grandparents, big brother, neighbor, friend)?

- Does your son or daughter have regular opportunities to socialize with friends and peers?

- What are your (family's) expectations for your son or daughter? What are some of your hopes and dreams for your son's or daughter's future?

As a school professional, you are faced with the challenge of providing transition planning and services early enough to meet the complex needs of students and their families, while allowing family members to maintain a balance among their myriad roles and functions. Making it happen; that is, ensuring that students are prepared for adult life without placing undue burdens on them and their families, is the main focus of this chapter!

***Family Life Cycle***     The transition from school to adult life specifically addresses the fourth element in the family systems framework: the family life cycle. Children are born; they go to school with their friends; they learn to drive; they graduate from high school; they go to college; and they get jobs, get married, and move away from home. It is helpful to think about a family's life cycle as a picture of how families change and adapt as they move through time, but for the family with a child with a disability, the life cycle perspective may not provide enough information, particularly during transition. The life cycle is based on age-linked markers of developmental growth and reflects the child's achievement of greater levels of independence (Turnbull et al., 2011). Families of children with disabilities often do not experience the cues that lead to shifting the responsibility to the young adult. They cannot always rely on the natural process of change and must instead deliberately plan for their child's movement into adulthood.

The reality is that most families often do not go through the "normal" phases of family development at "normal" times (McGoldrick, Carter, & Garcia-Preto, 2010). Transitional periods may last much longer than life cycle theory implies. The process of making transitions, in fact, may require many different life experiences to ensure the gradual movement toward successful adult life, especially if the family and student possess a vision for their future that is different from the status quo of services and supports offered in their community. This can conflict with the IDEA, which has a fixed definition of transition as formally starting by age 16 (or younger in some states), and continuing until the student graduates or exits school at age 21.

It is important to develop an expanded definition of transition that includes more than our static view of a handoff of school services to an adult service system. To be effective, transition must be considered from the perspective of the family as a whole and the overall needs of all its members. The characteristics of families have changed in recent decades, and you must be sensitive to families whose ideas may not align with a professionalized view of transition. Expanding your understanding beyond ethnic and racial diversity to address unique family values and perspectives is essential to working well with all families. Consider how families must change as a student becomes an adult, and keep in mind that families may have different priorities than the school's or your own. Finally, remember that a smooth transition is the result of gradual changes to the family system over an extended period of time, even though the IDEA recognizes only ages 16 to 21 as the transition period.

Educators working with families that include young adults with disabilities must remember that transition is a process rather than an outcome. In this way, you can focus on how families successfully achieve their desired outcomes as part of a longer haul. Keep in mind that though you can be a reliable ally to families and students, providing supports, information, and experiences, your role is time-limited. You most likely will not be there to support the student and family upon graduation from high school. Therefore, pay careful attention to how you can meet the specific transition needs of the student and the family, as well as foster skills and attitudes that will last over time.

 **MAKING IT HAPPEN:**
## Supporting Families During Transition

Now that you understand how transition can affect the whole family, what are the strategies you can use to maintain family balance? This section includes strategies for how to develop a family-friendly transition planning process by creating welcoming places within the school. There are ideas for building meaningful family involvement, as well as ways to establish culturally responsive planning with families.

### Create Welcoming Places

*"The strongest, most consistent predictors of parent involvement at home and school are the specific school programs and teachers' practices that encourage and guide parent involvement"*

Dr. Joyce Epstein, Johns Hopkins University (From Henderson, 2009).

What does it take to increase family involvement during transition planning? We can learn from research and practices geared toward family involvement in schools in general.

Researchers consistently point out that parents are more likely to become involved in school when they:

- Understand they SHOULD be involved

- Know they are CAPABLE of making a contribution

- Feel INVITED by the school and their children (Hoover-Dempsey & Sandler, 2005)

This means that it is up to us (schools in general, and transition specialists in particular) to support families to become actively engaged during transition planning. Some strategies for creating welcoming schools include:

- Home visits

- Parent workshops

- Career/college/transition fairs

- Curriculum nights

- Parent activity nights

- Using volunteers to call, e-mail, provide door hangers, and distribute flyers about workshops, activities, fairs

- Redesigning freshman orientation so families can meet with teachers, learn about high school expectations, connect with community resources, and tour school

- Using parent liaisons to build relationships with families, train educational staff, attend parent-teacher conferences, and teach families how to use online student tracking systems (Harvard Family Research Project, 2011, *Family Engagement for High School Success Toolkit*)

## Increase Family Involvement

It is essential that the activities and strategies for reaching families are woven throughout the day to gain trust and open communication between students, parents, and staff. Oftentimes, the first step is to actively and systematically provide outreach to families instead of performing "random acts of family engagement" (Boethel, 2003). You must take time to build trust with families if you want them to be engaged during critical transition events.

***Reach Out to the Family's Support Networks***    Informal and community supports that families access can be helpful during transition, especially for families who are CLD or who are not connecting with schools. Generally, families get many of their personal, economic, spiritual, and social supports from their informal cultural networks, which often include extended family members, religious groups, and cultural centers. One approach is to connect with cultural or community liaisons, sometimes called cultural brokers (Leake & Cholymay, 2004). These are people from the family's culture who can work with schools and families to negotiate solutions. Sometimes cultural liaisons are informal members of the community, such as a friend or neighbor, but they can also be staff working for organizations supporting families, such as an interpreter or a youth minister in a church. Finding informal community members and cultural liaisons will take persistence and must be a deliberate effort.

Every community has informal and formal resource networks. You can ask families which resources they use; to whom they turn for help and guidance in their community; and which religious, social, or cultural organizations support them. You can also identify community organizations where you think your families might already be involved. This would be similar to creating a community map of religious organizations, cultural centers, and service agencies that support specific groups of families (e.g., foster care, health departments, agricultural outreach agencies). You can be proactive by visiting these agencies and finding potential allies who can then share information and resources with families.

You may find that outreach looks different than schools typically envision. For example, informal cultural networks have identified that they share information with families through means other than brochures, newsletters, and e-mails (Nix, 2010). They recommend that word of mouth is the most effective way to share information, and that who does the telling is equally important. One strategy that can work well is offering to hold a transition workshop or support group sponsored by a church, center, or other community gathering place rather than at school. It may take considerable time to build relationships with families when providing supports and training. If you offer a training and families don't attend, you may need to keep at it! The lesson here is that just offering transition training does not mean that families will be able or willing to come. You may need to be persistent and collaborate with existing community support systems to promote involvement during transition and ensure that families are best supported and understood (Geenen et al., 2001).

### Increase Family-Professional Collaboration

Building meaningful family involvement during transition requires the following elements of communication: listening, sharing information, and inviting support. As professionals who are well-versed in what we need to do for transition, we may be tempted to *act first*: identify future goals, design a plan, determine a strategy, and implement the transition plan. Yet before you start, you need to stop and listen to families about their needs, concerns, opinions, and preferences for the future. Doing so in a manner that supports active family participation may be a new twist for you when transition planning.

Keep in mind that students with disabilities most likely want and expect their families to support them. In fact, Morningstar, Turnbull, and Turnbull (1995) found that students overwhelmingly identified their families as contributing in many ways to helping them plan for their future, and that these students wanted and expected their families to be involved in:

- Making sure they stayed in high school

- Planning for and helping them pay for college

- Helping them move out on their own

- Helping them find a job (Morningstar, Turnbull, & Turnbull, p. 254)

Given that the family is the primary support for students throughout the transition period, and often well into adulthood, it is a mistake to consider student interests, preferences, and needs as completely distinct or separate from family preferences and needs. At times, it may seem hard to balance the goals of student self-direction and family involvement, but this does not mean that excluding the family is necessary in order to promote student involvement.

Remember the balancing required for the delicate family mobile when considering how to move forward. For instance, imagine what it might be like for Raika when Aja starts learning new skills to advocate for himself and participate in work experiences while in school. His transition coordinator will have to carefully consider the best approaches for supporting Aja's growth while taking into consideration Raika's concerns and values. This may mean, for example, that Aja's work-based learning may focus on experiences within a small family business in Aja's neighborhood and with employers whom Raika trusts.

*Learning to Listen*     How do you go about listening to families' concerns, wants, and needs? The transition planning process is one that must be centered on student and family preferences and interests. This is consistent with the intent in the IDEA—that transition services be individualized. Keep in mind that parents may hold unspoken and often intangible concerns and worries about a variety of topics, including safety, sex, and social contacts: Will my daughter be safe out in the community? Will my son have friends? These legitimate concerns can become barriers to successful planning if the parents are not comfortable communicating with you.

It is important to identify and be aware of families' concerns when discussing their child's future. Sometimes these concerns emerge when you ask families about plans for their son or daughter. Even a simple and desirable question such as, "What are your hopes and dreams for your child's future?" can result in expressions of concerns and fears. Families' specific concerns may be related to the services their child may need in the future. Families often express concerns about the availability of adult services (e.g., postsecondary options, living situations, supplemental security income, guardianship) that match the family's cultural values and expectations. They also want more information about the transition mandates under the IDEA and their specific role during transition planning. It is important to acknowledge and validate these concerns with families and provide information in a culturally responsive way. Culturally responsive approaches to sharing information with families are shared in this chapter.

Another aspect of learning to listen is recognizing what to listen for. Families may communicate by telling stories and anecdotes about their child or young adult. It is essential that we ask questions of families in ways that allow them to answer in their own words. This requires letting go of our jargon about transition. Families are more likely to respond if we start by asking broader questions that are nonjudgmental and focus on the family strengths rather than difficulties. By listening to families, you will lay the cornerstone for establishing mutually trusting relationships. Families have expressed that the most caring professionals were honest, clear, and knowledgeable; shared information that was responsive to family concerns and needs; and followed through on agreed-upon plans (Turnbull et al., 2011).

*Sharing Information With Families*     Building a trusting relationship with parents and family members can take time and requires that essential information about transition is offered in less structured and more person-centered ways. This can be harder than it seems, even if you are trying to respect and acknowledge the family's culture and preferences. For example, we often consider home visits as ways to show the family we are willing to come visit and get to know them where they are most comfortable. Yet for some families, this may not be the case. We must take the time to "view 'comfortable and familiar' from their lens and not ours" (Kalynpur & Harry, 2012, p. 129). This may mean meeting outside the home and in a place of the family's choosing by "entering their worlds no matter how uncomfortable that might be" (p. 130) for us. Finding places of common ground, such as their informal cultural and community networks, is one strategy for starting to develop a positive relationship with families.

## TIP FOR TRANSITION: Host Parent Information Events

Host a parent information event (PIE) Night for Families. Of course, this includes serving pie! But more importantly, parent information events can provide families with much needed information that is provided in an informal atmosphere. Think about offering one in conjunction with a community organization or center. Make sure you include activities that youth can share with families, which is often a great way to get families to attend!

Families have expressed preferences for both the content they would like shared with them as well as the way in which they want information shared. These ideas can be as diverse and individualized as each of the families you serve! First, it's very common for families to express their desires to give and receive support from other families. This may be by attending workshops or support groups. While families want to learn about specific topics (see "Transition Topics that Families Want to Know About"), they also want to be supported and engaged in positive relationships. Keep in mind that this may take time. Just because you offer a workshop, transition fair, or PIE night doesn't mean families will attend; you will need to actively engage in outreach in ways and places that make sense for families.

## Transition Topics That Families Want to Know About

- Types of adult services available
- Role models for their child
- Basic facts about transition
- Guardianship and estate planning
- Role of IEP team members
- Criteria for evaluating IEP
- Post-school options
- Social security and supplemental security income
- Student specific skills:
  - Sexuality
  - Self-care
  - Getting along with others
  - Taking responsibility

Strategies to consider when organizing transition events include:

1. Widely advertise the event with flyers, brochures, and notices in key locations in the community such as churches, grocery stores, and community centers. Don't expect that families will only pay attention if information is sent home with their child or

e-mailed to them from the school. Families will be more likely to get involved if other families recommend it or if their student is involved.

2. Plan events with the "community connectors," those families and organizations whom families listen to and trust. Often word of mouth is the best way to get families to attend. Host your events outside of school at places where families are most likely to go. Collaborate with family community organizations to host these events.

3. Maintain frequent and positive communication with your families. They are more likely to participate in events if you have already shared helpful and positive information and resources in the past.

4. Share information and resources over time and in multiple formats. Sharing information once is not enough, especially if families are not focusing on transition issues due to other competing stressors facing the family, or if they are too worried or concerned about the upcoming changes.

5. Make sure to meet the family's preferred information method (e.g., e-mail, flyers, video, online, word of mouth, radio, church bulletins).

6. Arrange linkages with other families and supports. Remember that families want to talk with other families, and while not all families want to participate in a long-term transition support groups, many families want to have time to talk with others who have had similar experiences. They also want to connect with role models—both families who have been successful and successful adults with disabilities similar to their child's.

7. Make sure to address logistics. Be sure you have child care, transportation, and food! You might consider offering a meal to families during parent-teacher conferences. Then, as families are socializing and eating, you can talk individually with a family about transition-specific activities.

*Inviting Support*    Like listening, inviting support might seem to be relatively simple on the surface. The IDEA mandates that school districts contact parents about scheduling and participating in the transition IEP meeting. In reality, however, this mandate is often an administrative process to document compliance rather than a true invitation. It may be easy to assume that parents and family members are aware of transition-related mandates and are ready to participate as partners, when in reality this may not be the case. Some parents may have become disenfranchised from their child's IEP planning or may not be confident or familiar enough with the process to feel empowered to actively participate. Often, the administrative process inadvertently creates barriers to full family participation, and it will require reaching out and inviting families into the process.

Although parents and professionals generally agree on the activities considered most important for transition planning (e.g., talking to the child about life after high school, helping the child find work, participating in school meetings), there are differing points of view on exactly how important each of these activities are. For example, it has been shown that while some parents may be less involved in school-based transition activities, they may be much more focused on family and community activities, such as talking to their child about life after high school and teaching him or her about family or cultural values and beliefs. Regardless of "race/ethnicity, culture, or income, most families have high aspirations and concerns for their children's success" (Boethel, 2003). However, external factors such as poverty are linked to both the extent and types of involvement among low-income and minority families.

Research has identified potential barriers to minority and low-income families' involvement—barriers that schools often can help to overcome. These potential barriers include logistical factors (when meetings are scheduled, child care needs, and transportation problems), language differences, cultural beliefs about the role of families in children's schooling, families' lack of knowledge and understanding of U.S. educational processes, and issues of exclusion and discrimination (Boethel, 2003). Finding solutions to any external barriers that may be keeping your families from participating can go a long way to increasing their involvement and participation if this is necessary. While transition should be a year-round activity, a focal point process is the IEP meeting. The IEP Meeting Checklist for Transition in Chapter 2 (see Figure 2.6) includes some suggestions for supporting families before, during, and after the transition IEP meeting. The next section will share ideas and resources to help you engage in culturally responsive strategies with your families.

## Understand Cultural Reciprocity to Develop Partnerships With All Families

Often thought of as a strategy to enhance professional cultural competence, using the steps associated with cultural reciprocity (Kalaynpur & Harry, 2012) is one approach to working with all families, regardless of their race, economic status, or other cultural values. The following four steps are adapted for working with families during transition planning (Kim & Morningstar, 2005):

- Step 1: Know your own world view. First, you must understand the factors that shape your personal views, beliefs, and traditions. You should be aware of your school's values and expectations related to transition planning and outcomes. Most likely, the view of adulthood that operates in your school will include living outside the family home and becoming an autonomous and independent adult. It is important that you understand these are presumed outcomes and that not all families hold them. For example, Aja's culture accepts adult children living at home into adulthood. By promoting living outside the family home after high school, the school's perspectives are conflicting with Aja's family's. This is not to say that the school's and family's ideas may not be equally valid; it is just a reminder that specific values may be associated with a particular cultural orientation.

- Step 2: Learn about your families. It will make a big difference if you learn about the general cultural characteristics and beliefs held by the communities to which your families belong, while also not making general assumptions about an individual family based on their background (Kalyanpur & Harry, 2012). Each family possesses unique aspects and values, including roles within the family, communication styles, perceptions of disabilities, and disciplinary styles (Lynch & Hanson, 2011). Knowing which post-school outcomes Aja and his family value and how family members are supporting Aja to learn certain skills for the future can help school professionals better understand areas where they and the family agree and where there are different points of view. You can use Figure 4.1, The Continuum of Beliefs About Transition, to map out how families' viewpoints align or conflict with your own values about transition.

- Step 3: Acknowledge and respect cultural differences. Be honest with families about where you and they align when thinking about transition and also acknowledge differences. You can do this and still be respectful of their points of view. Your focus on the strengths of your families and attempts to establish trust and rapport with families will provide opportunities to work together to develop mutual goals. With Aja, this might mean listening to his family's views and concerns about working in the community. Professionals can discuss the core experiences and skills they believe are essential for Aja to learn with Raika, such as communicating with co-workers, following a schedule of work-related tasks, and problem solving. *Where* Aja learns these skills may be very important to Raika, so the team can in turn brainstorm options that are agreeable to the family while also supporting Aja's goals and continued learning.

- Step 4: Compromise to reach mutual goals. Make your best efforts to develop goals that both you and the family can accept, which will most likely involve compromises. For example, Aja's family may not wish to allow him to participate in a work-based vocational experience that the educational team believes is important. In such a situation, the team will first need to explain why job experiences are an important part of their views about transition preparation. Before any decisions are made, they will need to understand Raika's views about her son participating in a work experience. It could be that she is concerned that by working, Aja won't be able to receive his supplemental security income; or perhaps she is afraid of Aja working in the particular work-based location you have identified. Reaching a compromise might mean rescheduling the work experience for fewer afternoons a week, or it could be that Raika and her family can help find a work setting where they know the owners.

## WHAT YOU CAN DO RIGHT NOW:
### Putting Ideas Into Action

Given what we know works, it is essential that we practice skills for supporting our families. This can often feel like stepping into new territory because, as teachers, we are trained to focus on the individual student's unique strengths and needs, and sometimes do not consider the role of the student's family, especially during transition. One way to begin aligning your transition activities with established parent involvement strategies is to use the Parent Transition Involvement Checklist (Knab, Pleet, & Brito, 2000). Schools that have used this checklist to increase family involvement during transition have seen increased rates of family involvement (see Figure 4.2). Check off the ways that parents and families are currently involved in your transition planning and write down other examples of how you are using these strategies and if they are working. For any family involvement strategies that are lacking, brainstorm with your transition team to generate examples of how new strategies might be incorporated in your school.

Remember that collaborative partnerships require that both families and professionals share certain characteristics and behaviors. Personal characteristics of both family members and professionals, such as being optimistic, friendly, open-minded, and caring, are important elements of collaborative interactions (Dinnebeil, Hale, & Rule, 1996). In addition, family-centered practices, such as building trust by following through on actions, being nonjudgmental, showing respect, and accepting differences, lead to stronger partnerships (Hanson & Lynch, 2011. Providing helpful, family-friendly information and resources is another important element of collaborative transition practices. Using this chapter as a guide, you can begin applying these strategies for working with families to your transition practices right now.

# Parent Involvement Checklist for Transition

| ✔ | Activity or strategy | General examples | Examples in my school | New ideas for making it happen |
|---|---|---|---|---|
| | Hold parenting workshops. | Workshops could include these topics:<br><br>Parenting your adolescent with disabilities<br><br>Sexuality and your child with disabilities | • _____<br>• _____<br>• _____<br>• _____<br>• _____<br>• _____<br>• _____<br>• _____<br>• _____ | • _____<br>• _____<br>• _____<br>• _____<br>• _____<br>• _____<br>• _____<br>• _____<br>• _____ |
| | Organize transition planning events. | Hold a community-wide transition fair where agencies and organizations share information with families and youth. | • _____<br>• _____<br>• _____<br>• _____<br>• _____<br>• _____<br>• _____<br>• _____<br>• _____ | • _____<br>• _____<br>• _____<br>• _____<br>• _____<br>• _____<br>• _____<br>• _____ |
| | Engage families in transition decision making. | Use a parent transition survey (e.g., www.transitioncoalition.org/blog/tc-materials/the-new-parent-transition-survey/) to identify critical areas families need related to transition. | • _____<br>• _____<br>• _____<br>• _____<br>• _____<br>• _____<br>• _____<br>• _____<br>• _____ | • _____<br>• _____<br>• _____<br>• _____<br>• _____<br>• _____<br>• _____<br>• _____ |
| | Support families to engage in transition learning at home. | Have parents assist with completing homework, finding a tutor, applying for colleges.<br><br>Encourage families to support their child to learn about chores, daily living skills, and community participation that will support transition.<br><br>Have families open a bank account and support their child to set budgets, use a bank card, etc. | • _____<br>• _____<br>• _____<br>• _____<br>• _____<br>• _____<br>• _____ | • _____<br>• _____<br>• _____<br>• _____<br>• _____<br>• _____<br>• _____ |

**Figure 4.2**    Parent involvement checklist for transition. (*Source:* Knab, Pleet, & Brito, 2000.)

(continued)

Figure 4.2. *(continued)*

# Parent Involvement Checklist for Transition

| ✔ | Activity or strategy | General examples | Examples in my school | New ideas for making it happen |
|---|---|---|---|---|
| | Connect families to parent advocacy and support groups. | District special education family advisory group<br><br>Disability specific family organization (e.g., Downs Syndrome Guild, The Arc, Autism support group) | • _____<br>• _____<br>• _____<br>• _____<br>• _____<br>• _____<br>• _____<br>• _____<br>• _____ | • _____<br>• _____<br>• _____<br>• _____<br>• _____<br>• _____<br>• _____<br>• _____<br>• _____ |
| | Host transition workshops. | Hold family-focused transition training and resource workshops. | • _____<br>• _____<br>• _____<br>• _____<br>• _____<br>• _____<br>• _____<br>• _____ | • _____<br>• _____<br>• _____<br>• _____<br>• _____<br>• _____<br>• _____<br>• _____ |
| | Develop a newsletter for parents. | Distribute a quarterly newsletter for families in a school or district focused specifically on transition planning and services. | • _____<br>• _____<br>• _____<br>• _____<br>• _____<br>• _____<br>• _____<br>• _____ | • _____<br>• _____<br>• _____<br>• _____<br>• _____<br>• _____<br>• _____<br>• _____ |
| | Share community linkages. | Develop a community resource directory for families.<br><br>Share information about referral procedures for VR. | • _____<br>• _____<br>• _____<br>• _____<br>• _____<br>• _____<br>• _____<br>• _____ | • _____<br>• _____<br>• _____<br>• _____<br>• _____<br>• _____<br>• _____<br>• _____ |

# Parent Involvement Checklist for Transition

| ✔ | Activity or strategy | General examples | Examples in my school | New ideas for making it happen |
|---|---|---|---|---|
| | Hold informal family events. | Hold a transition tailgate before a football game. Host a PIE night. | • _____ <br> • _____ <br> • _____ <br> • _____ <br> • _____ <br> • _____ <br> • _____ <br> • _____ <br> • _____ | • _____ <br> • _____ <br> • _____ <br> • _____ <br> • _____ <br> • _____ <br> • _____ <br> • _____ <br> • _____ |
| | Develop a transition web site (e.g., include a family section on the district web site and post helpful resources and information). | Include a family section on the district web site and post helpful resources and information. | • _____ <br> • _____ <br> • _____ <br> • _____ <br> • _____ <br> • _____ <br> • _____ <br> • _____ <br> • _____ | • _____ <br> • _____ <br> • _____ <br> • _____ <br> • _____ <br> • _____ <br> • _____ <br> • _____ <br> • _____ |
| | Take families on field trips (e.g., visit local postsecondary settings). | Visit local postsecondary settings (college, community college, vocational technical schools). Organize a trip to visit community agencies (VR, DD services, centers for independent living). | • _____ <br> • _____ <br> • _____ <br> • _____ <br> • _____ <br> • _____ <br> • _____ <br> • _____ | • _____ <br> • _____ <br> • _____ <br> • _____ <br> • _____ <br> • _____ <br> • _____ <br> • _____ |
| | Regularly communicate with families. | Develop a "note home" format or daily activity books to share activities that took place during the day. Send weekly transition e-mails with updates about upcoming events, online resources, as well as information about their child. | • _____ <br> • _____ <br> • _____ <br> • _____ <br> • _____ <br> • _____ <br> • _____ <br> • _____ | • _____ <br> • _____ <br> • _____ <br> • _____ <br> • _____ <br> • _____ <br> • _____ <br> • _____ |

*(continued)*

Figure 4.2. *(continued)*

# Parent Involvement Checklist for Transition

| ✔ | Activity or strategy | General examples | Examples in my school | New ideas for making it happen |
|---|---|---|---|---|
| | Ask families to volunteer. | Have families share careers and employment histories with students in a careers class. Invite families to join transition activities for the students such as job Olympics and job shadow events. Include families in supporting students' field trips and other school-wide events. | ● _____<br>● _____<br>● _____<br>● _____<br>● _____<br>● _____<br>● _____<br>● _____<br>● _____ | ● _____<br>● _____<br>● _____<br>● _____<br>● _____<br>● _____<br>● _____<br>● _____<br>● _____ |
| | Hold family focus groups. | Invite families to talk about school and transition practices at the beginning and end of the year for formative planning and evaluation. Invite families to talk about specific topics of concern (e.g., college admissions requirements, job-related skills). Include culturally diverse families to share information about their cultural values and how these can be incorporated into transition practices. | ● _____<br>● _____<br>● _____<br>● _____<br>● _____<br>● _____<br>● _____<br>● _____ | ● _____<br>● _____<br>● _____<br>● _____<br>● _____<br>● _____<br>● _____<br>● _____ |
| | Initiate preliminary transition planning activities. | Ensure families understand and are prepared for transition planning meetings. Well ahead of IEP meetings, share drafts of measurable postsecondary goals, transition assessment results, and IEP goals. Include families in supporting their child to self-direct the transition IEP meeting. | ● _____<br>● _____<br>● _____<br>● _____<br>● _____<br>● _____<br>● _____<br>● _____ | ● _____<br>● _____<br>● _____<br>● _____<br>● _____<br>● _____<br>● _____<br>● _____ |

## ONLINE RESOURCES

Center for Parent Information and Resources: www.parentcenterhub.org

PACER Center's National Parent Center on Transition and Employment: www.pacer.org/transition

Parents Helping Parents: www.php.com

Beach Center on Families and Disability: www.beachcenter.org

Transition Coalition (www.transitioncoalition.org) online modules:

Working with Families in Transition

Working with Cultural Diverse Families

# 5

# Transition Assessment

## *The Cornerstone of Transition Planning*

Melody is a 16-year-old student who loves art and design, excels in hands-on and group school projects, participates on the JV soccer team, and likes to spend time with a small group of friends. She was diagnosed with a learning disability in 5th grade, primarily in reading and auditory processing. She has completed her 10th grade year enrolled in the typical core academic classes, as well as electives within the art department. She enrolls each semester in a study skills class for additional support. She has enjoyed most of her classes when the instruction is highly differentiated and students are able to work on group projects; however, she often finds it hard to pay attention in class and is distracted by other students. Her reading difficulties are accommodated through access to intensive reading instruction, specialized learning strategies, digital technologies, and opportunities to obtain the notes and lectures from her teachers. In addition, she is given extra time for tests.

Melody plans to attend college and is leaning toward an interest in art and design, but has no idea about possible careers. She has had minimal work experiences thus far and is hoping to pick up a part-time job after soccer season is over. She is not willing to share information with her friends and teachers about her learning needs, and sometimes feels embarrassed in class when she is called on to read or respond to a direct question. At her last IEP meeting, her special education teacher and guidance counselor discussed the importance of planning for her college applications and preparing for her future. Melody and her family are confused about what to do next.

Transition assessment is a cornerstone of the transition planning process. Planning for adulthood is all about working with students and families to identify what a student does well, where he or she is interested in heading in the future, and what additional or ongoing supports are needed. We know that student-centered planning is recognized as an essential component of quality transition programs (Kohler, 1996). Facilitating the student's self-awareness and decision-making abilities is an important part of the assessment process, so it is crucial to help students and families understand how and where transition assessment plays a critical and ongoing role in the student's life. Figure 5.1 illustrates the continuous assessment process that is part of transition planning.

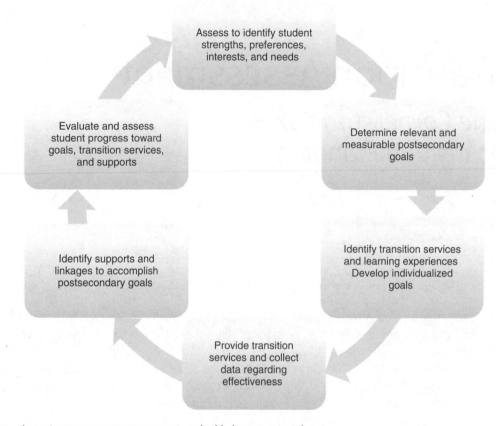

**Figure 5.1.** A continuous assessment process is embedded in transition planning.

## GETTING STARTED:
## Defining Transition Assessment

Providing the right types of planning and experiences for students requires developing and implementing a comprehensive transition assessment process. If we think about transition planning as the launching pad for a student's adulthood development, then one of the most important skills we can help students develop is decision making. This requires that they have good information about who they are, what their strengths are, and what supports they need to succeed when they face critical life choices. Melody has been embarrassed by her disability, but now she is gradually becoming less self-conscious and more self-aware. As she matures, she is developing an understanding of who she is—not just how her disability makes her different. Melody's plans for continuing her postsecondary education mean she will need a solid sense of her strengths, preferences, and interests, as well as her support needs. All of this requires the right data and information for Melody to share.

### A Comprehensive Process

For Melody and all students with disabilities, secondary special educators and transition coordinators must be able to define and operationalize a comprehensive transition assessment process. Leaders in the field of transition have defined transition assessment as incorporating a strong student-centered and ongoing approach that takes into consideration both current and future outcomes:

> Age-appropriate transition assessment is an ongoing process of collecting information on the youth's needs, strengths, preferences, and interests as they relate to measurable postsecondary goals and the annual IEP goals that will help facilitate attainment of postsecondary goals. This process includes a careful match between the characteristics of the youth and the requirements of secondary environments and postsecondary environments, along with recommendations for accommodations, services, supports, and technology to ensure they match. Youth and their families are taught how to use the results of transition assessment to drive the transition requirements in the IEP process, develop the SOP document, and advocate for needed or desired supports to succeed in meeting postsecondary goals. (Neubert & Leconte, 2013, pp. 74–75)

## Individualized Education Programs and Transition Assessment

In Chapter 1, you learned that IDEA requires that transition assessments be used to identify a student's MPGs. Assessment is one of the first components of transition planning, as you cannot plan for a student's future if you don't have the right information! Transition assessment is an ongoing process, not a single assessment completed right before a transition meeting. It is not only helpful for developing MPGs, but is essential for tracking progress toward attaining student post-school goals. Assessment helps the IEP team determine if progress is being made and if changes are needed. Therefore, assessing for transition is a dynamic process and should be incorporated throughout a school year. This includes focusing on gathering information about the student, as well as assessing the effectiveness of the transition services in supporting the student to meet his or her goals.

Keep in mind that transition assessment is as unique as each individual student. You will need to consider developing a transition assessment toolkit that includes a variety of different methods for gathering information about your students. The rest of this chapter will focus on providing you with resources to help you develop this comprehensive toolkit.

## MAKING IT HAPPEN:
## Implementing a Student-Centered Transition Process

Families and students play a critical role during transition assessment. Typically, they share unique information, particularly about the student's strengths, interests, and needs outside of the school setting. These details include sports, religious experiences, hobbies, and time with friends. Providing this information can bolster certain areas of focus, especially when it comes to preparing for postsecondary education, employment, and living in the community. We know that families and students often identify expectations for the future that are different from those of the school. Family and student expectations are important to know, given that they are the most powerful indicator of post-school success (Newman, 2005). Learning more about the family's and student's values and cultural expectations is also essential in developing culturally responsive plans for the future.

### TIP FOR TRANSITION: Use a Variety of Strategies to Gather Information

1. Take the time to get to know your student and build a good rapport with the student before you try to assess his or her abilities and interests.

2. Use surveys to help the student determine interests and direction.

3. Remember that often students are not able to effectively communicate their strengths and experiences. Consider using situational assessments to observe students in a variety of specific settings (e.g., across several different work settings) to gather information.

4. Explore possible career interests through both career interest inventories and job shadowing so students get to try out the job in person.

5. Visit your state/regional one-stop center, which is equipped with career assessment tools that measure interest and aptitudes.

6. Check with your local community college for career assessments that might be open for public use.

If the ultimate goal of transition assessment is to help students develop a cohesive view of who they are and their future roles, then the success of transition assessment depends mostly on their perspectives. New approaches to transition assessment encourage students to self-assess, interpret results, and create transition goals. Roles students can play include:

- Helping to plan for the specific domains in which they want to know more about themselves

- Participating in their assessment process by identifying the specific methods and measures they would like to complete

- Using the information gathered to develop their postsecondary goals and transition plans

- Keeping a portfolio of learning strategies, accommodations, experiences, and information about their strengths, preferences, and interests

- Focusing on student-directed planning that should be the underlying framework when implementing transition-referenced assessments (Kohler & Fields, 2003)

## Types and Approaches to Transition Assessment

There are so many different methods and types of assessments that can be used to gather relevant information for transition that it can be hard to know where to start. One place to begin is with a clear distinction between formal and informal assessments. Next, it is important to know about the many different approaches for collecting transition information, such as interviews, rating scales, observations, and person-centered discovery. Finally, pulling it all together into a process that makes sense for you and your students is essential. When designing a transition assessment process, keep in mind that transition assessment is an ongoing process of obtaining, organizing, and using information to support stakeholders, including professionals, families, and students, in students' positive transitions to successful and satisfying adult lives.

***Formal Transition Assessments***    Transition assessments are classified as formal when specific procedures have been used to standardize the instruments. These include measures that are norm- or criterion-referenced, contain sufficient evidence of validity and reliability, and include detailed administrative and scoring procedures. Many formal measures can be used as a part of transition planning, including instruments measuring academic achievement, intellectual functioning, adaptive behavior, employment and vocational aptitude, career interests, personality, quality of life, social skills, and self-determination (Clark, 2007).

The main characteristic of formal assessments is that they are designed for consistency across all elements of the test (e.g., test items, conditions for administering the test, scoring protocols, and interpretation of results). Norm-referenced assessments are designed to determine how a student's score compares with others. More recently, criterion-referenced transition assessments have been developed to ascertain if a student has mastered the criteria required for specific knowledge and skills identified as essential (Flexer, Baer, Luft, & Simmons, 2013).

An easy way to tell if the assessment is formal is that it will come with an administration manual that will describe the development process completed to strengthen the reliability and validity of the instrument. Information about how the measure is consistent and accurate (reliability), and the effectiveness of the instrument to measure what it is supposed to measure (validity) will be included. In the case of norm-referenced assessments, information will be provided about how the student's results align with the comparison group scores.

Using standardized measures is not new to secondary educational settings and can be an excellent starting place, especially if you don't know a student well. In addition, the results of formal assessments may be needed for referrals to adult services such as VR or for ensuring appropriate accommodations in postsecondary settings. However, there are limitations to using formal assessments:

- Consider the age, developmental level, reading ability, communication style, primary language, and cultural background of your students when selecting formal assessments. If your students do not match the characteristics of the norm group, then the results may not be valid.

- Be aware of some potential snares with formal assessments, such as 1) using results to label or stigmatize a student; 2) the possibility of errors due to test bias, poor validity, or low reliability; and 3) the likelihood of over-relying on a single test rather than individualizing assessments for each individual student (Rojewski, 2002).

- Realize that standardized tests are often not designed to collect data critical to transition planning. For example, such tests cannot identify whether an individual can understand and respond to social cues in various work settings. For this level of information, informal observations and rating scales may be needed.

While there is a wide range of formal assessments that can be used in educational planning (c.f., Clark, 2007, *Assessment for Transitions Planning*), only a few provide a comprehensive assessment of transition-specific skills and behaviors. Table 5.1 reviews some current formal transition instruments that include standardized and criterion-referenced assessments.

***Informal Transition Assessments***   Informal assessments are prevalent in schools and are often created or modified by practitioners and shared among educators. These measures can provide critical information on student learning characteristics and often help teachers develop and implement more personalized, individualized instruction. While formal assessments provide a more global "big picture" view of transition, informal assessments are useful because they can ask very specific questions for clarification and further in-depth information.

**Table 5.1.** Formal transition assessments

| Instrument | Target group | Content areas assessed | Procedures for standardization | Unique features |
|---|---|---|---|---|
| Transition Behavior Scale, 3rd Edition (TBS-2) (McCarney & Arthaud, 2012) | Students ages 14 to 21 with mild to severe disabilities. | Work-related, interpersonal relationships. Social/ community expectations. | Standardized with 2,624 randomly selected students from 30 randomly selected school systems across 20 states. 7th through 12th grade teachers completed the rating forms. Significant differences were found between different ages and genders. | • Includes a school form and student self-report form. • Each form contains 62 items to rate. • Estimated time to complete each is 15 to 20 minutes. |
| Transition Planning Inventory, 2nd Edition (TPI-2) (Clark & Patton, 2014) | Students ages 14 to postsecondary education; mild to moderate disabilities. | Eleven domains: • Career choice and planning. • Employment knowledge and skills. • Further education and training. • Functional communication. • Self-determination. • Independent living. • Personal money management. • Community involvement and usage. • Leisure activities. • Health. • Interpersonal relationships. | Standardized with 535 students receiving special education services ages 9 to 25 years old across 14 states. Of the 535 students, 64% were male and 36% were female. | • TPI forms completed by school, family member, and student. • Four rating forms that use a 0 to 5 scale; all contain 57 items. • Further assessments and recommendations form. • Administration and resource guide with easy to follow directions. • Incudes Informal Assessments for Transition Planning with suggestions for other assessments. • Resource CD with pdfs of forms includes language translations of parent form and a modified inventory for students with severe disabilities. |
| Transition Assessment and Goal Generator (TAGG) (Martin, Hennessey, McConnell, Terry, & Willis, 2015) | Secondary students with mild to moderate disabilities who intend to attend postsecondary education and/or be competitively employed. | Eight constructs: • Strengths and limits. • Disability awareness. • Persistence. • Interacting with others. • Goal setting and attainment. • Employment. • Students' involvement in IEP. • Support in community. | Transition educators, students with disabilities, and their parents in 38 states participated in the development and standardization of the TAGG. Teachers who were involved with the National Secondary Transition Technical Assistance Center were randomly selected. In total, more than 700 teachers, parents, and students participated in Phase I and II development, and an additional 4,250 will participate during Phases III, IV, and V. | • 34-item online assessment. • Available in three versions for student, professional (teacher), and family. |
| Enderle Severson Transition Rating Scale (ESTR) (Enderle & Severson, 2003) | Students ages 12 to adulthood; mild to severe disabilities. | Five domains: • Employment. • Recreation and leisure. • Home living. • Community participation. • Postsecondary education. | Eighty-two special education teachers from two midwestern states and their students completed a reliability evaluation. Test-retest reliability was determined by randomly selecting completed ESTR scales and sending a second copy of the scale 10 days later, asking teachers to re-rate the student (r = .93). For interrater reliability, the classroom teacher and another professional who knew the student equally well completed the ESTR scale. | • Various rating scales for parents and teachers to complete. • Separate forms for students with mild and severe disabilities. • Parent forms available in Spanish translations. • Useful in helping to plan future goals, learn student strengths and needs, and plan for adult services. • Online form where all information can be entered and summary report printed. |

Informal assessments are only as effective as the assessment questions and data that are collected. The right questions need to be asked to be certain that the information collected addresses an identified domain or skill area of importance. This can prove challenging to a practitioner with limited time. When deciding upon which informal assessments to use, it is important to consider the range of information needed for student-focused transition planning. Informal assessments are inexpensive, given that most are teacher made; however, those that are published are also a great addition to a transition assessment toolkit. Informal assessments are best used across multiple responders when collecting information, including students, parents, employers, teachers, support staff, and friends, to name a few. The major types of informal assessments are described in Table 5.2.

**Table 5.2.** Informal transition assessments

| Type of assessment | Defining characteristics | Benefits and drawbacks |
|---|---|---|
| Reviewing background information/ case files | Uses school and other records. Often used when you need to look up specific information regarding a specific skill or area of focus. | Benefits: Historical information can provide insight and information beneficial during transition planning, such as past career development experiences or behavioral interventions used previously. <br> Drawbacks: The information may be too dated to be of benefit and may focus primarily on deficits and needs, rather than the strengths, preferences, and interests needed when planning for transition. |
| Interviews: structured and informal | Purposeful, with questions identified ahead of time. Structured interviews are designed to elicit specific information about a particular topic. Interviews are conducted verbally and in person, but can be completed on the phone. Questions are open-ended, with opportunities for follow-up discussion and questions for clarification. | Benefits: Interviews allow opportunities to ask clarifying questions to gain better understanding. If kept positive, interviews build trust and enthusiasm for transition. They can provide flexibility to ask a few key questions of a student or family member. They are culturally responsive when completed in the language of the family/student. <br> Drawbacks: Students and family members may not feel comfortable answering interview questions. Students may respond with answers they think the teacher/professional wants to hear, rather than their true feelings or desires. |
| Survey/ questionnaire | Written or online, a survey asks a specific set of questions and requires a response from the person completing it. Typically, items require the person to select from among a set of responses (e.g., yes/no, check a list of skills, level of agreement). Short answer, open-ended questions can be included. | Benefits: Can be completed quickly and whenever the person has time (e.g., at home in the evening). They can be answered privately, which might relieve the stress associated with answering in person, as in an interview. <br> Drawbacks: Items on the survey need to be carefully worded so that the respondent understands and can answer to the best of his or her ability. |
| Observations and situational assessments | Probably the most common approach, and often very informal. Most often used to assess the quality of a student's performance and skills in certain situations. A checklist or some type of structured assessment is used to collect data in the actual setting in which the student is performing the skills (e.g., at work, in a social situation, in class). Anecdotal information written after the fact is not considered a systematic method. | Benefits: Does not require a student to read or write. Best results obtained when observations are purposeful and use a specific protocol or format for collecting data on certain behaviors or environments. Critical information about patterns of behaviors occurring in certain environments can be collected. <br> Drawbacks: Unstructured or anecdotal observations are highly subjective, leading to inaccurate data. |

**TIP FOR TRANSITION: Create a Profile of Discovery**

 Like a portfolio, a discovery profile uses person-centered observations and work experiences to identify strengths, interests, and preferences, as well as experiences and capabilities. It can be filled out for a student after work-based experiences and observations at school, in the community, at home, at work, and during recreational activities. The information can be used to create a customized career plan that includes school- and work-based learning, internships, and part-time employment. Discovery facilitates a process where students exit high school with a customized career plan toward integrated jobs, adult services, and transportation. More information about the process of discovery can be found at the University of Montana's Rural Transition Employment Project web site (http://ruralinstitute.umt.edu/transition/Discovery.asp).

## Implementing the Transition Assessment Process

Implementing a comprehensive transition assessment process encompasses two different roles for the transition specialist. The first role is to meet the individual needs of your students. For this, you want to individualize the methods and types of assessments so they are responsive to each student's needs. The second role you play is programmatic. It is important to develop a comprehensive system and process for thinking about transition assessment across all of your students. Here are some general rules to consider when assessing all students:

1. Be sure to customize the assessment process to capture specific information needed for upcoming decisions. For Melody this upcoming year, focusing on career awareness and career exploration will be essential. In addition, it may be important to conduct environmental assessments of postsecondary campuses to identify specific accommodations available.

2. Make sure assessment methods are appropriate to the learning and response characteristics of the student. Melody will need support and assistance with any assessments that require reading and written responses. Given that we know she excels in activity-based and group projects, an effective method of assessing her strengths might be systematic observations within specific learning situations targeting critical problem-solving and communication skills.

3. Assessments must incorporate assistive technology (AT) and accommodations when necessary. Access to AT and appropriate accommodations in postsecondary settings will significantly increase Melody's ability to participate in learning and achievement. Melody should be assessed to find out the specific technology appropriate for her. In addition, more information is needed about her abilities to request needed accommodations.

4. Assessments must occur in natural environments for sampling interests, behaviors, and skills. Formal assessments offer comprehensive data regarding broad areas of focus, and informal paper and pencil measures provide necessary and specific details. However, it is essential that you develop and implement systematic methods for observing students and collecting relevant information about their skills, preferences, and interests in the actual environment. For Melody, this will mean experiencing specific career exploration activities, such as job sampling several different arts-related fields and collecting specific information from her about these experiences. Figure 5.2 provides a sample form for collecting this level of data on work experiences and

# Assessing Student Work Experiences

Student name: _____    Employer: _____    Job title: _____

Employment dates: Start: _____    End: _____    Paid/unpaid: _____

Job responsibilities: _____

**Exit interview for student**

What I liked about this position:

What I didn't like about this position:

What parts of my job I do best:

Where I need more support and training:

What supports I use on the job:

**Employer evaluation/letter of recommendations (attach):**

**Comments about the experience (collect information from a variety of sources, including the student, family, employer, and school personnel):**

Student:

Family:

Employer:

Educational team:

**Figure 5.2.** Assessing student work experiences.

provides space to record an exit interview from the student, as well as recommendations and comments from the family, employer, and educational team.

5. Assessment methods must produce outcomes that influence the development, planning, and implementation of the transition process. Like most 16-year-olds, Melody is undecided about her future career, but plans to go on to postsecondary education as a part of her career path. In this circumstance, you might share several different career interest inventories with Melody, allowing her to identify the one that will provide the best information. Many career assessment systems also provide information about postsecondary educational requirements for a particular career. Having this type of information would certainly help Melody make decisions about her transition to college and careers.

6. Assessment procedures and transition strategies must be verified by multiple methods and persons. Under the best circumstances, multiple stakeholders should be involved in assessing and interpreting student skills. Given that transition assessment is ongoing and takes place over multiple years, it is more likely that several different people will be involved. For example, getting input from Melody, her teachers, and her family about strategies and methods for supporting her learning is essential. It is not sufficient to ask only her core academic teachers.

7. Assessment results must be stored in a user-friendly format. Students can keep their transition assessment results in a portfolio that they can share with others. Knowing what assessment information to share can be difficult, however, without proper preparation and guidance. The types of information you share might differ depending upon with whom you are sharing it. For example, when Melody attends college, information the disabled students services office might need is very different from what VR might need to determine her eligibility.

## TIP FOR TRANSITION: Assess Students' Career Awareness

Systematic, age-appropriate student assessment of career awareness (e.g., interest inventories, aptitude tests) has been identified as a predictor of post-school employment. School programs that provide career assessment are more likely to support students to learn about their preferences and aptitudes for various types of careers (National Technical Assistance Center on Transition, 2016).

## Building a Transition Assessment Toolkit

If you want to embed transition assessment throughout all that you do, then you can begin by developing a transition assessment toolkit. A transition assessment toolkit is a collection of resources and information about transition assessment, as well as actual assessments, that can be shared with all stakeholders involved in transition planning (educators, families, and students). The transition assessment toolkit includes several resources, the first of which contains general information about transition planning and the transition assessment process. It also includes a wide variety of assessments to meet the unique assessment needs of students. The textbox is a sample outline or "table of contents" for what might be found in a comprehensive transition assessment toolkit. Often, transition assessment toolkits are primarily paper-based, given the wide range of assessments still only available in paper. However, creative teachers and transition coordinators are beginning to develop online toolkits that can be shared within middle and high schools and across districts.

▪ ▪ ▪ ▪ ▪ ▪ ▪ ▪ ▪ ▪ ▪ ▪ ▪ ▪ ▪ ▪ ▪ ▪ ▪ ▪ ▪ ▪ ▪ ▪ ▪ ▪ ▪ ▪ ▪ ▪ ▪ ▪ ▪ ▪ ▪ ▪ ▪ ▪ ▪ ▪ ▪ ▪ ▪ ▪ ▪ ▪ ▪ ▪

## Outline of What to Include in Your Transition Assessment Toolkit

### Provide General Information and Resources About Transition Assessment

- Defining transition assessment
  - IDEA definition
  - Specific state/district policies related to assessment
  - What transition assessment is and is not
  - Purpose and importance of transition assessment
  - State/district policies
- Transition assessment procedures
  - Transition assessment timelines: When to assess, what to assess, who will assess…
  - Family and student involvement
    a. How to involve students and families in the assessment process
    b. How to share assessment results with students and families

### Describe and Include Types of Assessments

- Include assessments by domain
  - Career development and employment
  - Postsecondary education and training
  - Independent living and community involvement
- Include both formal and informal assessments

### Provide Guidance and Tools for Summarizing Assessment Data

- Assessment data for monitoring instruction, student progress, and decisions
- Coordinating assessment results with post-school environments
- Summarizing assessment data on the IEP

*Source:* Morningstar (2013)

▪ ▪ ▪ ▪ ▪ ▪ ▪ ▪ ▪ ▪ ▪ ▪ ▪ ▪ ▪ ▪ ▪ ▪ ▪ ▪ ▪ ▪ ▪ ▪ ▪ ▪ ▪ ▪ ▪ ▪ ▪ ▪ ▪ ▪ ▪ ▪ ▪ ▪ ▪ ▪ ▪ ▪ ▪ ▪ ▪ ▪ ▪ ▪

**Defining Transition Assessment**　　Transition assessment toolkits often start with a definition of transition assessment. This section of the toolkit includes the IDEA definition, clarification on what transition assessment is and is not, and the purpose for assessing during transition planning. If states or districts have specific policies or procedures related to transition assessment, this information is usually found here. Easy to understand definitions help schools, family members, and students understand why transition assessment is important and how to best implement the assessment process.

**Transition Assessment Procedures**　　The next section of the toolkit helps the transition planning team know how and when to assess. Developing a transition assessment timeline or checklist helps teams follow certain milestones that should be completed related to the types and levels of assessment occurring during transition. Most often, timelines begin in middle school and continue through each of the high school grades, and, if appropriate, as part of extended (18- to 21-year-old) transition programs (see Figure 5.3 for an example of a transition timeline).

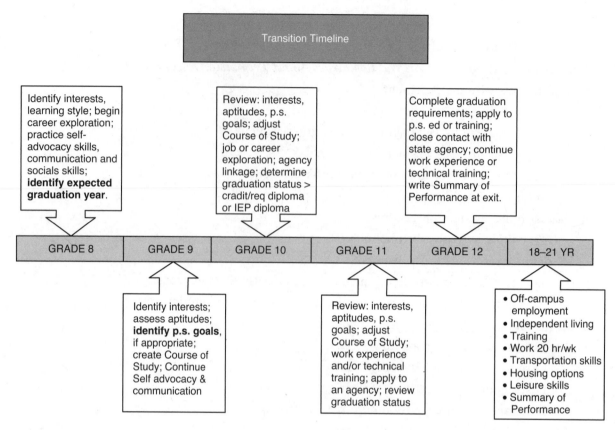

**Figure 5.3.** Transition timeline. (From Johnson, C. [2007]. Guide to transition assessment in Washington State. Seattle, Washington: Center for Change in Transition Services [CCTS], Seattle University; reprinted with permission.)

This section of the toolkit is also where you provide information about how to involve students and their families during transition assessment. Including strategies and ideas for how to provide useful information to families and students, such as brochures, letters, and videos, is important. As described earlier, families and students can play more active roles than just completing assessments when you need information. They can be actively involved in deciding the most relevant information to collect and in determining which specific assessment methods to use. For example, if you have a variety of methods and approaches in your toolkit related to career interests, you can ask students which particular career interest inventory they would like to fill out. Melody chose to complete The Leisure/Work Search Inventory (Liptak, 1994) to identify career interest areas because this particular informal inventory identifies employment opportunities related to leisure interests such as fixing things at home, going to museums, volunteering, or visiting state parks. The compiled results are categorized into 12 different career domains (artistic, scientific, mechanical, humanitarian, etc.) Because of Melody's interests in the arts, this was the assessment she was most motivated to complete.

Finally, ideas for how to share information with families and students is included in this section. All too often transition assessment results are only reported in the IEP as required by law (e.g., the present levels of academic and functional performance). However, designing and developing family- and student-friendly methods for reporting assessment results will support students to become more self-determined.

***Transition Assessments***   The heart of a transition assessment toolkit is the wide array of assessment resources! Remember, if transition assessment is individualized, then you will need a variety of approaches and methods that will best fit the needs of each student. Typically, assessments are organized by the major domains of transition: 1) current and future employment, 2) current and future education and/or training, and 3) independent living. Within each domain, you will include all of the different formal and informal assessments available in your school or district. A variety of different assessment methods, from standardized measures to person-centered approaches, should be included. Use the information and resources from this chapter to help develop your own toolkit.

***Using Transition Assessment Data***   To complete your transition assessment toolkit, provide guidance on ways to use assessment results to improve transition planning and tools for collecting ongoing assessment data to ensure that transition services facilitate progress toward the desired postsecondary goals. Remember, transition assessment results should be used for more than just developing the MPGs and annual IEP goals and monitoring individual student progress—data should also be collected on transition programs to monitor whether students are achieving their outcomes. Assessment data informs daily decisions about instructions and educational experiences, is used to monitor ongoing progress toward post-school goals, can aid in eligibility for outside services, and helps develop the IEP.

***Monitoring Instruction, Progress, and Decisions***   Educators often use assessment information to monitor progress and individualize instruction, as well as to ensure linkages to supports and services necessary for successful transitions. Daily measures are needed to ensure that students are making progress toward the goals related to academics, employment, and independent living. This can include both curriculum-based measures such as test grades and other progress monitoring procedures. In addition, measures pertaining to a student's IEP goals must be maintained (e.g., observational data regarding problem-solving behaviors and skills, employer evaluations).

Decisions regarding the programs and transition services for achieving students' postsecondary goals should be data-based. For Melody, this might mean that once the transition team has a better understanding of her interests, preferences, and strengths, the transition services she receives and her course of study will mirror these results. Right now, Melody is enrolled in an American Literature class required for graduation. She has indicated that she likes the class, but her performance is poor. Perhaps the reason behind this is that the accommodations provided to Melody do not sufficiently meet her needs, or she may not have the advocacy skills to request supports and accommodations when in class. Maybe she is not using effective learning strategies when taking notes and/or studying. Collecting the right data to be able to best support Melody toward success will include observing her in class to determine which learning strategies she is using. An environmental inventory of the class may also be needed to determine if environmental aspects are distracting her. Finally, Melody, her teacher, and the special education teacher should meet to review the results and make changes to the supports she is receiving in this class to ensure progress.

***Coordinating Assessment Results With Post-School Environments***   As students identify their post-school goals, transition assessment data can be used to identify the outside supports a student will need to be successful (Thoma & Tamura, 2013). It is important for the IEP team to be aware of the eligibility requirements of adult agencies and be able to provide relevant data and assessment results. Knowing what assessment information is needed by agencies such as VR, employment services providers, and postsecondary settings is a critical part of transition planning. To do this, a transition specialist can involve outside organizations in the assessment process, as well as structure the process to collect relevant information needed for adult agencies (Neubert & Leconte, 2013).

***Summarizing Assessment Data on the Individualized Education Program***     Because transition assessment is a key component of the annual IEP, assessment results should be included in the present levels of educational performance section in the IEP. This information must be used to assist students in making informed choices related to training, education, employment, and where appropriate, independent living. In preparation for the IEP, you can provide students with the tools needed to express their preferences, interests, and needs both prior to and during the IEP meeting. Students can summarize information obtained through the transition assessment process using a variety of unique approaches, such as picture profiles, videos, PowerPoint presentations, and student portfolios. Strategies such as the "One-Pager" from the I'm Determined web site (www.imdetermined.org) or the "representational portfolio" from the University of Montana Rural Institute (http://ruralinstitute.umt.edu/transition/portfolio.asp) are unique ways students can summarize and share assessment results.

Assessment data is also essential to crafting the SOP on the IEP. The IDEA 2004 reauthorization required that schools provide students and families with a summary of the student's academic achievement and functional performance, including recommendations for how to support the student in meeting his or her goals for postsecondary education/training, employment, and independent living. This summary can be useful in guiding postsecondary settings in providing appropriate accommodations needed so that the student can access educational environments as required under the Americans with Disabilities Act and Section 504 of the Rehabilitation Act. In addition, adult agencies, such as VR, often use the SOP to determine eligibility for employment supports and services (Clark, 2007).

To meet minimal compliance, the SOP is required to be completed and provided to the student at graduation or exit of services. However, tracking academic and functional performance tied to postsecondary goals can begin when transition planning first starts. In this way, the SOP is viewed first and foremost as a tool to be used by the student and should include his or her input about what is to be included (Flexer, Baer, Luft, & Simmons, 2013). The SOP can be considered a portfolio summarizing essential information about the student that is needed for success in the future. The four major components of the SOP described by Flexer and colleagues (2013) include:

- Student level of functioning, which describes how the disability affects performance and reports results from both academic and functional performance measures (formal and informal). Emphasis should be placed on the student's strengths and accomplishments.

- Postsecondary goals addressing the student's future education, employment, and living plans. The SOP should summarize the student's accomplishments in achieving his or her goals.

- Recommendations for the most effective accommodations and supports needed to maintain participation in specific environments associated with the student's postsecondary future goals (e.g., college, vocational technical settings, workplace settings, community living).

- Copies of assessment reports should be included in addition to the summaries to ensure that eligibility for services is not delayed or disrupted. In addition, assessment results can be used to identify the environments that are most likely to support and accommodate the student.

## WHAT YOU CAN DO RIGHT NOW:
### Putting Ideas Into Action

It may seem overwhelming to consider individualized transition assessments for every student. However, using a five-question strategy to think about planning your assessments of individual students is one way to begin putting the assessment procedures discussed in this chapter into practice. The Transition Assessment Planning Form (Gaumer-Erickson, Morningstar, Lattin, & Cantrell, 2008, Figure 5.4) is divided into the three major domains mentioned previously: employment, education and/or training, and independent living. Within each domain, specific areas of assessment are further considered (e.g., independent living includes areas such as self-awareness, money management, transportation, medical and health, communication). As you develop assessment plans for each student, you can review the domains and ask yourself each of the five questions to plan the assessment process for the upcoming year:

1. What do we already know about the student? If you already have information in a particular area (e.g., Melody's team knew her best methods of communication), then you can fill this information in and you don't need to continue to assess in that area.

2. What do we need to learn? This is where you will focus your efforts during the upcoming year. For Melody, the team knew very little about her career interests, her abilities related to self-determination, and specific AT she may need.

3. How will we gather information? Here is where you can turn to the range of formal and informal assessments and approaches available to collect information and brainstorm which assessments might be best for each student.

4. Who will gather information? You are not the only professional who should be involved in collecting transition assessment information. The student, family, and other educational and adult agency professionals should assist in a collaborative assessment process. In Melody's case, the team may have the AT specialist complete an assessment of Melody's AT needs for postsecondary settings or have Melody and her family visit colleges to identify the types of accommodations and supports offered on certain campuses.

5. When will information be gathered? Having a timeline for compiling the information is critical. If you don't set a deadline well in advance of the transition planning meeting, you will not have the information you need to develop the services and experiences related to the student's preferences, interests, and strengths. Melody has 2 more years in high school, and her team will have to carefully plan for the best ways to collect relevant assessment data for her.

The purpose of the transition assessment planning form is to help guide an individualized assessment planning process. It is not expected that you fill in every cell on the sheet, but rather view it as a long-term plan for prioritizing certain areas and domains throughout the student's secondary experiences. If you work with students with significant disabilities, you can use an adapted planning form such as the one from the Transition Coalition in Figure 5.4.

# Transition Assessment Planning Form

| Transition assessment domain | Areas of assessment to consider | What do we already know about the student? | What do we need to know about the student? | How will we gather this information? | Who will gather the information? | When will the information be gathered? |
|---|---|---|---|---|---|---|
| Current and future employment | Occupational interests and values | | | | | |
| | Work aptitude | | | | | |
| | Work readiness/ prevocational skills | | | | | |
| | Assistive technology | | | | | |
| | Temperament/ personality | | | | | |
| | Manual dexterity | | | | | |
| | Work environments | | | | | |

**Figure 5.4.** Transition Assessment Planning Form. (From Morningstar, M.E., Gaumer Erickson, A., Lattin, D.L. & Wade, D.K. [2008]. Best Practices in Planning for Transition [online module] www.transitioncoalition.org. Lawrence: University of Kansas; reprinted by permission.)

| Transition assessment domain | Areas of assessment to consider | What do we already know about the student? | What do we need to know about the student? | How will we gather this information? | Who will gather the information? | When will the information be gathered? |
|---|---|---|---|---|---|---|
| Education and/or training | Academic achievement | | | | | |
| | Learning styles | | | | | |
| | Accommodations | | | | | |
| Independent living | Self-awareness | | | | | |
| | Self-determination/ Self-advocacy | | | | | |
| | Money management | | | | | |
| | Home living | | | | | |
| | Recreation and leisure interests | | | | | |

*(continued)*

**Figure 5.4.** *(continued)*

| Transition assessment domain | Areas of assessment to consider | What do we already know about the student? | What do we need to know about the student? | How will we gather this information? | Who will gather the information? | When will the information be gathered? |
|---|---|---|---|---|---|---|
| | Transportation | | | | | |
| | Personal safety | | | | | |
| | Medical and health | | | | | |
| | Communication | | | | | |
| | Adaptive behavior | | | | | |
| | Interpersonal relationships | | | | | |
| | Community participation | | | | | |

Identifying and collecting relevant student information using an ongoing transition assessment process that includes multiple assessment methods is the foundation of quality transition planning. Each student is unique; therefore, designing individualized transition assessment plans is essential for implementing a student-centered process that takes place over time. Because a critical goal of transition assessment is to develop student self-awareness of important life choices, strategies for supporting and engaging students and families during assessment are essential. Developing a transition assessment toolkit can support all stakeholders in understanding what transition assessment means, as well as participating in a comprehensive process using both formal and informal measures. If done properly and in collaboration with all stakeholders, transition assessment can result in a clear picture of students' experiences, skills, accomplishments, and supports that over time facilitates their movement toward positive futures. But, to benefit from thorough transition assessments and transition services, and attain the best possible future, students must remain in school. Chapter 6 provides strategies for keeping students in the classroom and engaged in their education.

## ONLINE RESOURCES

Transition Assessments for Youth with Significant Disabilities: www.ou.edu/content/education/centers-and-partnerships/zarrow/transition-assessment/severe-disabilities.html

NTACT:Age Appropriate Transition Assessment Toolkit: http://transitionta.org/system/files/toolkitassessment/AgeAppropriateTransitionAssessmentToolkit2016_COMPLETE_11_21_16.pdf

Transition Assessment Reviews: http://transitioncoalition.org/tc-assessment-reviews/?cat_ID=48

Transition Assessment: The BIG Picture: http://transitioncoalition.org/online-training-modules

My Next Move: www.mynextmove.org

O*Net Interest Profiler: www.mynextmove.org/explore/ip

Transition Assessment and Goal Generator (TAGG): https://tagg.ou.edu/tagg

Life Skills Assessment: www.caseylifeskills.org

Career Planning Assessment Guide: www.ncwd-youth.info/resources_&_Publications/assessment.html

# 6

# School Engagement
## *Keeping All Students in School*
### with Megan Heidrich

Dominique is 17 years old and a junior in high school. Dominique is behind in credits to graduate and currently failing two core courses. She is frustrated with her classes and often has trouble following directions. She comes to school when she can, but it is not a priority for her. After her father moved out when Dominique was in middle school, she has been responsible for taking care of her younger brother and sister while her mother works. She is not able to participate in extracurricular activities because she has to babysit her siblings every day after school, and she often skips school to take care of them. On the weekends, she hangs out with her new boyfriend, who dropped out of school last year. Her mother worries Dominique might be drinking and doing drugs. She will be a senior next year and is not on track to graduate. Dominique's school recently collected early warning data indicating that Dominique is at risk of dropping out. What can the school do to keep Dominique in school? How do we ensure that she isn't simply considered another dropout statistic?

*Don't Call Them Dropouts,* a 2014 report from America's Promise Alliance (http://gradnation.org/report/dont-call-them-dropouts), listened to young people disclose why they left school and what supports they needed to reengage and complete their education. Thousands of young adults described how they had to overcome multiple factors, including home and neighborhood violence, absent parents, negative peer influences, and caretaking responsibilities, to complete their education. It is clear that dropping out of school isn't a snap decision among adolescents; it is usually a result of compounding pressures that lead students to gradually disengage from school and eventually drop out. Unfortunately, when students drop out, future opportunities for success in adulthood are severely limited. Though high school graduation rates have risen recently to an all-time high, as in the "2013–14 school year, the adjusted cohort graduation rate (ACGR) for public high schools rose to an all-time high of 82 percent" (The National Center for Education Statistics, NCES, 2016, para. 1), there were 33 states whose graduation rates were below 70% for students with disabilities (DePaoli, Balfanz, & Bridgeland, 2016). Thus, comprehensive supports to keep students in school are still imperative in closing the remaining gaps for students with disabilities.

Identifying and implementing effective strategies for preventing students from dropping out of school is a critical issue among all secondary schools today. It doesn't matter if you teach in an urban or rural setting, or teach students who have a range of disabilities, dropping out of school comes with very high costs to both students and society. Within the past decade, we have seen substantial increases in evidence-based strategies and community-wide approaches that increase the engagement of students at risk of dropping out. In this chapter, you will first learn about the high costs of leaving high school without a diploma and why it is so important to promote positive secondary school engagement. You will then encounter specific strategies and resources for increasing student engagement and learn about the role schools, families, and the community play to support school engagement and student reengagement.

## GETTING STARTED:
## Understanding Student Engagement

If dropping out is not a sudden decision for most at-risk students, and is most likely the result of a complex mix of pressures, then understanding how to circumvent these barriers is critical. We know that dropping out of school has consequences to not only the student and his or her family, but to the community and society at large. Therefore, it is essential that you fully understand the multidimensional aspects of student engagement in school and strategies for keeping students engaged. This section will first focus on the consequences of dropping out, and then provide examples of what school engagement entails. Finally, strategies for keeping students engaged (and reengaged) in school will be shared.

## The Consequences of Dropping Out

Since 1990, when the transition mandates first appeared in the IDEA, high school outcomes for students with disabilities have generally improved. We have seen a 17% increase in graduation rates between 1987, when post-school outcome data was first collected, and 2003 (Wagner, Newman, Cameto, Levine, & Garza, 2006). More recently, and for the first time ever, graduation rates among all students have crossed the threshold of 80% (Balfanz et al., 2014). However, youth with disabilities are not graduating at nearly the same rate as their peers without disabilities. In fact, their graduation rate is 20% lower, with dramatic variations among states (e.g., 24% of youth with disabilities graduated in Nevada, while 81% graduated in Montana in 2012) (NCES, 2013). According to the 2013 report from the NCES, 60% of all youth with disabilities received a high school diploma, with significant disparities existing among different disability groups. For example, 60% of young adults with learning disabilities (LDs) received regular high school diplomas, but among students with emotional disabilities (EDs), the rate was about 43% (NCES, 2013). Dropout rates among students with disabilities are even more troubling, with 22% leaving school without a diploma during the 2008 to 2009 school year (Snyder & Dillow, 2012). This is compared to significantly lower rates among their peers without disabilities, which during this same period of time was reported at about 8% (U.S. Department of Commerce, 2013). Within certain disability groups, dropping out of school is even more likely to occur, with the highest (40%) among youth with emotional disabilities.

Dropping out of school has serious negative outcomes for youth, including an increased likelihood of being unemployed, underemployed, and dependent on welfare (Belfield & Levin, 2007). In addition, dropping out is associated with risky behaviors, as well as increases in mental health needs (Archambault, Janosz, Morizot, & Pagani, 2009). One recent report revealed a steady decline in employment for individuals without a high school diploma: from 2002 to 2012, the percentage of young adults without a high school credential employed full-time declined from 60% to 49% (Kena et al., 2014).

Youth with disabilities who drop out are much more likely to have been arrested, stopped by police, or incarcerated (Sanford et al., 2011). Only 63% of students with disabilities who had dropped out had been employed at some point within 4 years after leaving high school, as compared to 75% of students with disabilities who graduated (Newman, Wagner, Cameto, & Knokey, 2009). The types of jobs, salaries, and opportunities for career advancements among youth with disabilities who have dropped out is reported as lower than among those who graduated (Trainor, Morningstar, Murray, & Kim, 2013). In addition, only 17% of students with disabilities who dropped out attended any type of postsecondary setting (Newman, Wagner, Cameto, & Knokey, 2009). It is clear that youth with disabilities who drop out of school are at a distinct disadvantage as they strive for independence and self-sufficiency in adulthood (Wilkins & Huckabee, 2014). As a transition specialist, you know how difficult it can be to improve outcomes for youth with disabilities. However, there is a silver lining to the crisis facing our schools: You have the power to make a difference in engaging students and leading them to graduation (Appleton, Christenson, & Furlong, 2008).

Understanding why students drop out is the first step to developing strategies to keep them engaged in school. As emphasized throughout this chapter, a student's dropping out of school is rarely the result of one quick or impulsive decision, and there are usually warning signs that a student is not engaged. As Bridgeland, Bruce, and Hariharan (2013) learned, students who drop out believed at one time that they could have succeeded in school. Most often, these students had dreams of working in careers requiring a high school diploma or higher, and many maintained passing grades while in high school. The most common reasons students dropped out were because they were bored, disengaged, and not inspired or motivated to persevere. In particular, they described inadequate support from school during complex personal and educational circumstances they were facing.

Students who disengage from school are likely to experience academic challenges, greater levels of absenteeism, and behavioral difficulties, which ultimately lead to dropping out of school (Kennelly & Monrad, 2007; Sinclair, Christenson, & Thurlow, 2005). Students with disabilities at risk of dropping out usually have high rates of absenteeism and are least likely to be involved in organized school groups (Wagner, Kutash, Duchnowski, Epstein, & Sumi, 2005). In addition, when behavioral difficulties emerge, students are more likely to be suspended both in school and out of school (Wagner, et al., 2005).

Before we move on, let's think about Dominique and why she is at risk for dropping out. Dominique has household responsibilities much greater than the typical high school student because she is taking care of her two younger siblings. This causes her to be out of school often enough to miss significant academic content, which in turn leads to failing grades. Dominique has started to hang out with older friends and others her age who have dropped out, and as a consequence, this makes school seem insignificant. Understanding why students engage in school and how we can reengage students like Dominique before they drop out will be an important focus.

## Defining Student Engagement

To get started with increasing student engagement, you must first understand what it means for students to be engaged in school. Once you know the answer to this, you can then identify students who are at risk of disengaging and, most importantly, begin to implement strategies to support them. At its most basic, engagement can be thought of as a

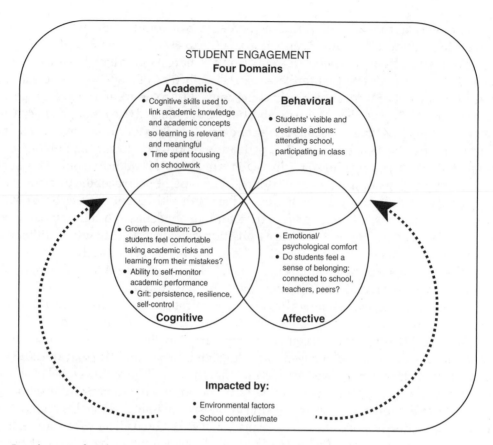

**Figure 6.1.** Four domains of student engagement. (*Source:* Christenson, et al., 2008).

combination of thoughts, feelings, and behaviors toward school (Appleton, Christenson, & Furlong, 2008). Engagement has been considered essential to promoting school completion—defined as graduation from high school with the academic and social skills to be college and career ready. Four major domains associated with student engagement have been identified, including 1) academic, 2) behavioral, 3) cognitive, and 4) affective (Christenson et al., 2008). As illustrated in Figure 6.1, these four domains are influenced by environmental factors and the context of the school.

***Academic Engagement***    Academic engagement focuses on the time spent actually engaged in schoolwork, as well as the credits accrued while in high school. Academic engagement includes the cognitive skills needed to link academic knowledge and organize academic concepts in order to make learning relevant and meaningful (Fredricks, Blumenfeld, & Paris, 2004). Academic learning is always a major focus of schools, sometimes to the detriment of the other areas of engagement. Even with our recent movement toward college and career readiness, which combines academic and nonacademic factors leading to success, most often schools tend to emphasize academic knowledge apart from the skills linking knowledge to the wider worldview.

***Behavioral Engagement***    Behavioral engagement is easiest to see because it involves student's measurable actions, such as showing up for school, participating actively in class, and joining extracurricular activities. Behavioral engagement can be thought of as the presence of active, desirable behaviors. Focusing on behavioral engagement will require you to increase positive behaviors associated with learning, while at the same time decreasing behaviors leading to dropping out of school. Positive behavior interventions and supports (PBIS) is an example of a schoolwide framework that schools implement to emphasize prosocial behaviors.

**Cognitive Engagement**     Students who believe school is relevant to their futures are cognitively engaged in school. These are students who are interested in learning and can self-monitor their academic performances. Others have referred to this type of engagement as a growth orientation (Dweck, 2008), whereby students feel comfortable taking academic risks and learning from their mistakes, which ultimately leads to making connections between school and their future lives. Associated with cognitive engagement is the concept of "grit," which has been used to refer to students who are persistent, resilient, and have self-control (Duckworth & Seligman, 2005). In essence, students who are cognitively engaged are more likely to take ownership of learning, be self-aware, set goals, and seek help from others (Farrington et al., 2012). Recall our definition of self-determination in Chapter 3 and note the similarities. The strategies you learned about in Chapter 3 can also be successfully used to support students with disabilities to stay in school.

**Affective Engagement**     A fourth area essential to keeping students engaged in school focuses on emotional and psychological processes. Students who feel a sense of belonging within school, have social connections to both adults and peers in school, and express a sense of support from their parents and others in the broader community, exhibit higher levels of engagement. An essential part of feeling connected to school includes students feeling safe and supported in the school environments (Bradshaw, O'Brennan, & McNeely, 2008). Feeling safe at school not only includes safety from violence, but means that students feel safe to disclose to a teacher or school staff member about personal issues, as well as school-related concerns (Bridgeland, DiIulio, & Morison, 2006).

**Environmental Factors**     It is interesting to note that research has not found any relationships between demographic indicators and dropping out of school. In fact, we know that the strongest predictors of students dropping out are environmental and include indicators such as absenteeism, failing academic classes, and overall grade point average. From this perspective, student engagement is the result of how well the student fits within his or her learning environment (Appleton, Christenson, & Furlong, 2008; Fredricks et al., 2011). For some time now, researchers have shown that school engagement can increase (or decrease) as the learning environment changes (Allensworth & Easton, 2007; Connell, 1990; Finn & Rock, 1997). Think about Dominique. We know she is frequently absent due to family responsibilities, failing two courses, influenced by her friends, and not on track to graduate. All of these are environmental factors are affecting her success in high school.

Students report that they go to school for a specific purpose—whether it be academic, social, or for family reasons (Yazzie-Mintz, 2010). Students who leave school without a diploma often describe their education as not relevant, state that they had few social relationships in school (with either peers or adults), or claim their family's obligations and expectations did not align with school (Keyes & Sureshkumar, 2007). In addition, many students who have left school before graduation describe toxic environmental factors, quite often at school itself, that simply outweigh school attendance (America's Promise Alliance, 2014). These factors include witnessing or enduring violence at home, in school, or in their neighborhood, and unsafe, unsupportive, or disrespectful school climates and policies.

**TIP FOR TRANSITION: Inspire Students With Other Students' Perspectives**

It's one thing to read about youth who are struggling to remain in school, but it's more inspiring for you (and your students) to actually hear from students who possess a variety of perspectives on what drove them to leave school and what resources have helped them get back on track. Watch and listen to the individual youth stories on the Boost Up YouTube Channel (www.youtube.com/channel/UCL6H_vwPVNGtzeEs6yfwExg), as well as from the documentary Don't Call Them Dropouts (www.youtube.com/watch?v=CAVvQ12AdLM).

When we consider how to improve secondary schools to support students to remain engaged, we have to consider how school organizational efforts can enhance student engagement (Sebring, Allensworth, Bryk, Easton, & Luppescu, 2006). Institutional factors that are most likely to influence student success include how schools 1) build supportive relationships, 2) maintain high academic expectations, and 3) ensure coherent and relevant instruction (Mac Iver & Mac Iver, 2009). We also know that the way secondary schools are organized plays a role. For instance, smaller learning communities (DuFour & Eaker, 1998) have been found to be more welcoming than large schools, where students can feel disconnected from peers and adults. Issues of school climate affect the academic success of students. Schools where students share the belief that they have the ability to achieve high standards have a reduced number of dropouts (McEvoy & Welker, 2000). High school administrators set the tone for providing positive and proactive supports (Dinham, Cairney, Craigie, & Wilson, 1995). How schools connect with family members and the neighborhood community is also essential to reducing the dropout rates. Finally, teachers must support student-focused learning through robust instruction and research-based teaching methods. Examples of a variety of strategies will be shared with you in the Making It Happen section of this chapter.

In summary, keeping students engaged in school is complex. It requires that you pay attention to many aspects of learning, including what and how students are learning academically, how connected students are to their school and the people in it, whether students are motivated and have the skills to persevere when times get tough, and whether students are present and participating in school. Keep in mind that there is a reciprocal relationship among the four domains of engagement. For instance, you can be a catalyst for increasing a student's positive school experiences by changing the environment (e.g., starting a mentoring program), which can change how students feel about school. Students will then likely come to school more often, which in turn motivates them to work harder and improve their academic performance. As you will learn next, supporting those students early can pay off.

## MAKING IT HAPPEN:
### Strategies to Promote Student Engagement

When resources are scarce, it is important to identify those students who truly need support. On the one hand, schools that fail to identify at-risk students will not be able to make an impact, no matter what interventions and state-of-the-art supports are available. On the other hand, when a school identifies far too many students who are not actually at great risk of dropping out, resources get spread too thin. The challenge is to develop a system whereby all students receive the supports they need to be fully engaged in learning, while students more at risk receive more intensive interventions.

Being able to accurately identify students most in need is a critical first step to intervening effectively. In this section, you will learn about three universally used predictors of students at risk of dropping out: attendance, behavior, and course completion. These three indicators will guide your efforts to identify high-risk students and can help you determine the most effective student engagement strategies. You will also learn about strategies and interventions to support students who are at high risk for disengagement and dropping out, as well as implementing more universally applied strategies that promote engagement for all students. These interventions are organized across multiple levels according to the intensity of the supports, often referred to as multi-tiered systems of supports.

## Consider "The ABCs of Disengagement"

Martha and Douglas Mac Iver (2009) summarized the research on dropout issues and found that both individual and institutional factors were associated with dropping out. For students, "high absenteeism, behavior problems, and course failure—the ABCs of disengagement—are the telltale signs" (p. 5):

A = Attendance: Middle school and high school students who attend school only 80% of the time are much more likely to drop out. This makes sense because students are missing large amounts of academic content when absent from school. Therefore, we need to pay attention to attendance rates and intervene when students are missing too much school.

B = Behavior: Getting suspended or receiving an unsatisfactory behavior grade in middle school and being suspended by 9th grade when in high school are critical predictors of dropping out. Unfortunately, even off-task, disruptive, or withdrawn behavior results in lost engagement in learning. Schools must establish positive behavioral interventions to support students who are at risk.

C = Courses: Ultimately, it's a student's transcript of credits that results in a diploma. Failing core classes like English and math in middle school is particularly risky. In 9th grade, students who fail any course (but especially core or required courses) are much less likely to graduate with their classmates. Schools should have systems and strategies in place for helping students complete their required coursework and not falling behind.

You now know what information is critical to guide educators as we support more students to graduate. Focusing on interventions that target and improve attendance, behaviors, and course completion will lead to better outcomes. Keep in mind that student-level predictors of dropping out are exacerbated in schools that do not have the infrastructure to support adequate relationships, promote high expectations, and provide instructional supports. Martha and Douglas Mac Iver's analysis of dropout prevention and recovery initiatives suggests that a combination of school reform and programs targeting individual students lead to the best results in preventing dropout and promoting student engagement (2009). A model of whole-school reform using multiple tiers of support will be described next, followed by suggested interventions for supporting the ABCs of student engagement and reengagement.

## Create Multi-Tiered Systems of Support

Multi-tiered systems of supports (MTSS) are widely accepted as a way to identify and deliver student engagement models. MTSS were originally developed to provide public health outreach. This approach is designed to provide broad information and outreach to all in a given community, and then more targeted services to some in the community, reserving highly individualized and intensive services for a few that are most in need. You may be

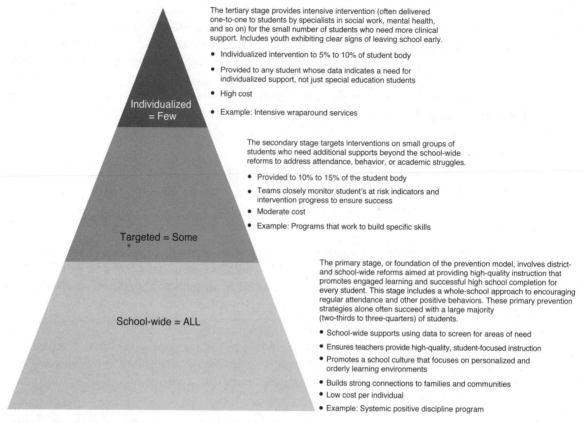

The tertiary stage provides intensive intervention (often delivered one-to-one to students by specialists in social work, mental health, and so on) for the small number of students who need more clinical support. Includes youth exhibiting clear signs of leaving school early.

- Individualized intervention to 5% to 10% of student body

- Provided to any student whose data indicates a need for individualized support, not just special education students

- High cost

- Example: Intensive wraparound services

Individualized = Few

The secondary stage targets interventions on small groups of students who need additional supports beyond the school-wide reforms to address attendance, behavior, or academic struggles.

- Provided to 10% to 15% of the student body

- Teams closely monitor student's at risk indicators and intervention progress to ensure success

- Moderate cost

- Example: Programs that work to build specific skills

Targeted = Some

The primary stage, or foundation of the prevention model, involves district- and school-wide reforms aimed at providing high-quality instruction that promotes engaged learning and successful high school completion for every student. This stage includes a whole-school approach to encouraging regular attendance and other positive behaviors. These primary prevention strategies alone often succeed with a large majority (two-thirds to three-quarters) of students.

- School-wide supports using data to screen for areas of need

- Ensures teachers provide high-quality, student-focused instruction

- Promotes a school culture that focuses on personalized and orderly learning environments

- Builds strong connections to families and communities

- Low cost per individual

- Example: Systemic positive discipline program

School-wide = ALL

**Figure 6.2.** Three-tiered dropout prevention model.

familiar with three-tiered systems commonly used within education, such as response to intervention (RTI), PBIS, and MTSS. Visit www.rtinetwork.org or www.pbis.org for an in-depth look at MTSS. Figure 6.2 illustrates an example of a three-tiered dropout prevention model that directly addresses the ABCs of attendance, behavior, and course failure.

While a multitiered system can have more than three tiers, most models use three levels of increasingly intensive supports, as is the case in Figure 6.2. When using a three-tiered model, the tiers focus on:

- Tier 1: Schoolwide/All: Tier 1 can be thought of as "Plan A" for a school. Tier 1 is provided to *all* students—it is the foundation of the model. Schools must use student and systems data to identify areas of need among students and put in place strategies that will support all students. Three essential elements that form a strong school base include 1) ensuring teachers provide high-quality student-focused instruction, 2) developing a school culture promoting personalized and orderly learning environments, and 3) building strong connections to families and communities. For example, districts often hold assemblies at the beginning of the school year in which they articulate expectations for graduation and then hold graduation-focused events throughout the school year.

- Tier 2: Targeted/ Some: Tier 2 supports take more time and money per student, with interventions only delivered to *some* students based on need. Tier 2 is provided to students who require extra support to succeed based upon the data that the school and district reviews. Typically, only about 10% to 15% of the student body will receive Tier 2 interventions, and most often in small-group settings. Tier 2 dropout prevention interventions require closely monitoring student ABC progress while providing intensive interventions, such as online or summer classes for credit recovery, additional literacy instruction, or enrollment in lab courses along with core classes (Mac Iver & Mac Iver, 2009).

- Tier 3, Individualized/ Few: Tier 3 is the most intensive level of support a school can offer. This level of individualized intervention is only provided when data indicate that for a small number of students (5% to 10%), Tier 1 and 2 supports were insufficient. While it may be assumed that because Tier 3 is so highly individualized it is reserved for students in special education, this is not the case. Any student who needs intensive and individualized supports should receive them.

In secondary schools, blending transition-focused strategies within a multitiered supports model can support student motivation, encouraging the idea that school is relevant for college and career readiness (Morningstar, Gaumer, & Noonan, 2009). Because the goal of transition-focused education is preparing students with disabilities for post-school success and the goal of dropout prevention efforts is preparing students for successful graduation, the timing is right for aligning these approaches. As noted by Fuchs, Fuchs, and Compton (2010), secondary MTSS models must be focused on adolescent interests and preferences for learning. Adolescent learners are very different from elementary students, especially in terms of their motivation to engage in learning. For many adolescents, and particularly those at risk for dropping out, they are more engaged when personal experiences and activities outside of school are linked with what they are learning in school (Brozo, 2009). Youth must see themselves as members of the learning community if they are to succeed (Rebora, 2010; Reed & Vaughn, 2010). Therefore, structuring interventions to ensure motivation and active engagement of youth is essential.

A transition-focused frame of reference has been described as a way to enhance secondary tiered intervention models (Morningstar, Bassett, Kochhar-Bryant, Cashman, & Wehmeyer, 2012; Test, Fowler, & Scroggins, 2011). This type of secondary MTSS model accounts for factors unique to secondary schools and adolescent learners (Morningstar, Knollman, Semon, & Kleinhammer-Tramill, 2012). The National Center on Response to Intervention identified several school factors as necessary for secondary MTSS models to succeed, including 1) refocusing the approaches of high school staff from an overreliance on lectures to project-based learning, 2) shifting the organizational structures of the school (i.e., creating smaller learning communities, block scheduling), and 3) aligning MTSS approaches within other district reform initiatives (Danielson, Roberts, & Scala, 2010). The textbox summarizes the features of a transition-focused MTSS model.

## Features of a Transition-Focused Multi-Tiered System of Supports Model

- Integrated school resources
- In- and post-school progress monitoring
- Greater levels of intensity
- Interventions ensure student engagement

From Morningstar, M.E. (2015). *MTSS and CCR: Are We Ready?* [PowerPoint Slides]. Retrieved from http://transitioncoalition.org/wp-content/uploads/2016/07/MTSSandCCR-UMTSS-2015.pdf; adapted by permission.

When MTSS have a transition-focused frame of reference, not only is there collaboration across educational services (general and special education), but also community agencies such as postsecondary schools, employers, and community mental health providers. Progress monitoring of students to determine their support needs would go beyond the collection of academic and behavioral data, with a focus on analyzing factors influencing graduation, dropout, and suspension/expulsion rates, as well as measuring the post-school outcomes of all students. Other MTSS models (e.g., RTI, PBIS) are designed to help students get to graduation, but they may not consider the broader goals of college and career readiness that must be brought to the table for students who are disengaging from school. In MTSS with a transition-focused frame of reference, secondary school-tiered interventions should focus on academic skills but "also promote school engagement and relevant educational experiences to ensure dropout prevention, as well as preparation for college and careers" (Morningstar, Bassett, Kochhar-Bryant, Cashman, & Wehmeyer, 2012, p.136).

An integrated approach to dropout prevention requires that schools use multitiered strategies and interventions focusing on the ABCs of student engagement, supporting students as young as middle school to attend school, improve behavior, and receive passing grades. To know the best interventions to implement, it is important for schools to collect data on how their students are performing in terms of these three important areas.

## Use Data to Keep Students on Track

Data gathered on the ABCs of disengagement—attendance, student behavior, and course completion—can be used to identify individual students in need, as well as the overall needs of a classroom, school, or even a district. You can also use school climate surveys and assessments to help understand school-level needs. Climate data can be gathered from staff, parents, and students alike. These techniques will equip you to identify which students are at high risk and to implement the best types of interventions where they are most needed.

***Early Warning Systems***     We know that data can be used to guide educators as we support more students to graduate. Early identification of warning signals associated with veering off the graduation path has been used to keep students in school (Balfanz, Herzog, & Mac Iver, 2007). All schools collect student-level data most likely to predict disengagement, monitoring attendance, behaviors, and grades; however, what is required is a system where schools can keep track of this data in a way that helps to flag students at risk and track the types of interventions used to keep them on the path to graduation. These systems are often called early warning systems. These early warning systems monitor the ABC indicators (i.e., attendance, behavior, and course completion) beginning in middle school and throughout high school to track students at risk of dropping out.

The National High School Center created the *Early Warning System (EWS) Toolkit* for use by middle and high schools. The EWS high school and middle school tools are available at no cost to schools. They rely on the ABC indicators of risk. Data can be imported or entered into the EWS tool after the first 20 or 30 days of school and after each grading period. Students at risk for dropout are automatically identified in this Excel-based program. The tool not only allows schools to make data-based decisions for students who are at risk, but gives a comprehensive view of dropout trends for that school (Therriault, Heppen, O'Cummings, Fryer, & Johnson, 2010). Visit www.betterhighschools.org/ews.asp to learn more, obtain the tools, and watch training webinars. In addition, the Everyone Graduates Center provides technical assistance and customized data analyses to schools and districts interested in creating early warning systems. To start implementing an early warning system in your school, visit http://new.every1graduates.org/ for more information.

If your school is considering investing in an early warning system, keep in mind you will want to use a system that provides both student-level and systems-wide reports. Student-level reports help individual educators support the needs of a particular student. For example, when Dominique was flagged for attendance, her educational team decided she needed additional supports. They scheduled time with Dominique and her mother to talk about how important it is to get a diploma and worked with Dominique and her mother to come up with some strategies for making sure Dominique didn't stay at home to take care of her siblings. Dominique also worked with her guidance counselor and the career and technical education (CTE) teacher during a "career exploration class" to develop a better understanding of the best career pathway for her future. These strategies helped Dominique become more engaged in her classes, which improved her attendance.

It is important to help individual students like Dominique one-on-one, but schools must also identify trends. Such summary reports are necessary to help a teacher or the school data team make overall improvements to school programs for whole school changes. If there are many students in Dominique's school who are being flagged for office referrals and in-school suspensions, the data team will want to identify any programmatic issues that are creating these problems. The solution may be to implement schoolwide positive behavior supports where all adults in the building have a consistent set of behavioral expectations they all use. This would proactively head off many individual student behaviors, but would also ensure that the adults making referrals are using consistent criteria for student infractions.

***Student Engagement Surveys***    Schools can also gather essential information about students' engagement just by asking the students themselves. Schoolwide surveys give teachers the opportunity to understand patterns and trends in their school, such as if students lack a connection with supportive adults. Here is what one student said about her experiences when someone at her school connected with her in a meaningful way: "High school is a hard time for students because there are so many self-esteem issues that come into play. When I was a sophomore, I had been suspended for the first four days of school. I was mortified. Mrs. R. acknowledged my absence without scorn or judgment. She conferenced with me at various times and only displayed faith in my abilities. She often challenged me, and rewarded my efforts with praise and my failures with support and advice." Kim, Teacher Memories (as cited in Balli, 2011, p. 250).

It is also important to screen for problems like bullying that may cause students to feel unsafe at school and pull away from their education. For example, while bullying is a national problem, it may be much more serious at your local middle school than your high school, and engagement surveys might reveal this problem. Fredricks and colleagues (2011) reviewed and summarized 21 different measures focusing on student engagement that your school might find useful. The report explains how each instrument gathers data, what information it can provide to school teams, and the statistics supporting each measure. You can find the full report at http://ies.ed.gov/ncee/edlabs/projects/project .asp?projectID=268.

### TIP FOR TRANSITION: Consider Using the Gallup Student Poll

Students and teachers can take this free and confidential survey, available at www .gallupstudentpoll.com/home.aspx, that asks students 20 questions that provide data about what they do in school and how they feel about their home, school, and community life. Your school or district can use this data for program improvements in student engagement.

Even if an early warning system or a school-wide engagement survey is unavailable to you, there are simple ways you can know that a student is veering off course. Poor attendance for any reason (even excused medical absences) is a risk. Behavior problems are a risk. Failing classes is a risk. Students need a reason to come to school and succeed. If a student is not engaged, something about their school environment must change.

One tool that you can use to support student engagement is the My Good Day Plan, which you can use to find out what it takes to ensure your students come to school. It might be their academic goals, but it might also be social life or family expectations. Sometimes there are just too many hurdles between even a motivated student and the school door. The My Good Day Plan helps plan for and overcome these barriers. Figure 6.3 depicts a sample My Good Day Plan that is focused on helping a student define what makes a good school day, with practical suggestions and plans of action to keep this student engaged and in the classroom. See the Chapter 3 Appendix for a blank template of the My Good Day Plan to use with your students.

***School Climate Surveys***     A supportive school climate is responsive to the needs of students, families, and the community. Efforts to improve school climate target five domains: safety, relationships, teaching and learning, institutional environment, and the school improvement process (Thapa, Cohen, Guffey, & Higgins-D'Alessandro, 2013). As part of a transition planning team, you may have the closest influence on a student's experiences related to positive school relationships and teaching and learning. Resources like high-quality peer mentoring, interest groups, and extracurricular involvement can help some students engage more fully in a healthier school climate.

## TIP FOR TRANSITION: Ask Your Students

Seek your students' input on school climate. Regularly measuring your students' experience of school climate is important for any school wishing to engage more students. Visit the Safe Supportive Learning web site (http://safesupportivelearning.ed.gov/topic-research/school-climate-measurement) for a wide variety of resources to get started.

Include students in the process of school climate change, with the students at the center of all decisions. View students as co-leaders and value their input in the process of changing school climate. For example, ask students for feedback on how to handle issues around bullying. It is important to not assume adults always know more than the students. Valuing youth input and encouraging their participation in changing and shaping their schools bridges the disconnect between school and the "real world," which increases student engagement (Cardillo, Freiberg, & Pickeral, 2013).

The variety and depth of data you can use to drive your dropout prevention efforts might be exciting or might seem overwhelming. Keep in mind that identifying students at risk is just the beginning. The next step is matching students to the supports they need. Collect data on student progress to ensure that the interventions and supports are working or if they need to be modified.

# My Good Day Plan

Student name: _Tim_  Grade: _9_

| Good day<br><br>What happens on a good day? | Now<br><br>Does it happen now? | Action<br><br>What needs to happen? | Support<br><br>Who or what can help me? |
|---|---|---|---|
| 1. I wake up on time. | Sometimes | I set my alarm and get up on time. | I can ask my mom to remind me to set my alarm so I get to school on time. |
| 2. I have something to eat for breakfast. | Sometimes—we don't always have food in the house. | If there isn't food in the house, I visit the counselor's office because I know she keeps food for the students. | Mrs. Smith, the counselor, will help me if I don't have breakfast. |
| 3. I get to talk to my friends. | Sometimes | I go and look for my friends if I can't find them, instead of waiting for them to find me. | My favorite teacher, Mr. Gonzales, is always friendly if I need someone to talk to. |
| 4. I have all my books for class. | Yeah, I usually have my books for class because I leave them in my locker. | _____ | _____ |
| 5. I have friends to sit with at lunch. | I don't always have friends to sit with at lunch, and I don't like to sit by myself. It's embarrassing. | I could try to sit with other people at lunch that I don't know. | I can ask other people from my classes that I recognize to eat lunch with me. |

**Figure 6.3.** Use the My Good Day Plan. (Adapted from *My Good Day Plan* © 2005 by the Commonwealth of Virginia Department of Education. All rights reserved. Reproduced by permission.)

## Use Proven Interventions

A variety of research-based interventions can be used to respond to at-risk students and address the ABCs of student disengagement. Consider how you might use these interventions, which are discussed next, to meet the needs of your students who are at risk of dropping out of school. Don't forget to think about how to keep students engaged in learning throughout their day.

### TIP FOR TRANSITION: Consult the Institute of Education Sciences for Dropout Prevention

The Institute of Education Sciences (IES) offers *IES Dropout Prevention: A Practice Guide*, an educator-friendly resource that provides clear, practical guidance on intervention practices that have a proven track record in preventing dropout. The practice guide organized dropout prevention programs around six practical recommendations for keeping students in school:

1. Utilize data systems to track the number of students dropping out and identify at-risk students.
2. Provide adult mentors/advocates for at-risk students.
3. Provide academic supports to improve academic performance.
4. Implement programs to improve student behavior and social skills.
5. Personalize the learning environment and instruction.
6. Provide students the instruction and skills needed for graduation and future success after graduation, making learning relevant and engaging (Dynarski et al., 2008).

If you are considering adopting an intervention strategy, you can use this guide to be sure it aligns with proven research. If you're not sure where to begin, use this guide to get an idea of what strengths your school may already have, as well as areas that can be improved. Find the practice guide at the IES What Works Clearinghouse web site (http://ies.ed.gov/ncee/wwc).

***Interventions to Increase Attendance***     Attendance in middle and high school is a powerful predictor of a student's risk for dropping out (Balfanz, Byrnes, & Fox, 2012; Allensworth & Easton, 2007). When students are missing school, it is important to intervene with positive approaches rather than the punitive ones that are often used, such as in-school suspension for unexcused absences. Instead, greet every student when he or she has missed school and let the student know you noticed. For students who miss school often, a daily check-in (sometimes called attendance monitoring) might support their connection to the school. School-level attendance teams can be formed to organize daily check-ins for groups of students or to facilitate problem solving with students and families. Think back to Dominique and her frequent absences. If an adult in the school was assigned to her to do a daily check-in and develop a positive relationship, the importance of attending school would be reinforced. Implementing a check-in process with an adult mentor would build rapport with Dominique and help the school get to know the barriers that often keep her from attending school. Supportive adults can then develop a plan to keep her engaged.

## TIP FOR TRANSITION: Promote Student Engagement in a Commitment to Graduate

The Get Schooled web site (https://getschooled.com/) promotes student engagement by leveraging influences in teens' lives—a blend of "sizzle and substance" to directly motivate them to stay committed to graduating from high school and going on to college. Their web site uses social media and messages students respond to (involving celebrities, powerful peers, and pop culture events) to deliver information about school engagement. The attendance calculator lets students see the toll each day of absence takes on their chances of earning a diploma. There are a variety of resources for both students and educators, including games, discussion of schoolwide challenges, and even wake-up calls from celebrities. In addition to the attendance resources, the site offers strategies for planning students' transition to postsecondary education.

Tiered interventions for increasing attendance are very focused on building relationships. There are countless reasons why chronically absent students don't show up at school each morning, which is why every absence must bring a personal response. Typically, schools notify parents when students are absent through phone calls or e-mails home; however, more comprehensive approaches may be needed, such as the strategies put in place in one rural school that recently tackled a widespread attendance problem among their 7th to 12th graders.

First, the school dropout prevention team started with data. They used an early warning system and found out that attendance was their most common predictor of dropping out. The team then talked to students, faculty, and families to develop possible solutions. Their strategy was simple but effective. They started contacting parents as soon as the absence was recorded, right at the beginning of the day, instead of their old approach of contacting parents whenever office staff had a free moment. Almost immediately, the rate of chronically absent students dropped by 30%. These unexcused absences dropped because the school immediately made it explicit to parents and students that they had noticed when students were absent and cared about students attending school. This solution increased two-way communication and improved relationships with parents and students. Not only did unexcused absences drop, but excused absences dropped as well (Wilkins & Huckabee, 2014).

This school used a Tier 1 strategy to meet the needs of about two-thirds of students who previously were thought to require more intensive supports due to high rates of unexcused absenteeism. With a stronger Tier 1 strategy in place, it turned out that a much smaller group of students were the ones who needed more targeted or possibly individualized supports related to attendance. Building parent partnerships was one essential Tier 1 strategy, as was the commitment of the school administration to make attendance monitoring a priority first thing in the day. Of course, this simple solution may not work for larger, more urban schools. It is important that you work with your school team and community to ensure the solutions fit your school context.

At the Tier 1 level, interventions to increase the attendance of all students is tied to building a culture that emphasizes that coming to school matters (Mac Iver & Mac Iver, 2009). Schools can also offer positive social incentives for good attendance to all students.

As would be expected, some students may need targeted or intensive supports to ensure their attendance is improved. Supports at the Tier 2 level might include daily check-in with an adult mentor for students who have a number of absences, while students in need of Tier 3 support might require individual counseling or community services and supports (e.g., wraparound team) (Mac Iver & Mac Iver, 2009). It can be helpful to have an attendance team monitor frequent student absences and then investigate and problem solve with individual students who are regularly missing school (e.g., a teacher, counselor, or administrator checks in with students who have two or more unexcused absences in a month) (MacIver & MacIver, 2009). Some students may require support in meeting basic needs (e.g., basic health care, permanent place to sleep). Some may need a specific intervention to address feeling socially isolated or escalating conflicts, such as bullying. Other students who are home alone in the early mornings may simply need a wake-up call.

## TIP FOR TRANSITION: Use Attendance Resources

Attendanceworks.org is a web site full of resources you can use one-on-one with students, at a school-wide level, or with community partners to increase and improve attendance. As a building-level team, you can review the resources on this web site and match the best ones to your school context.

***Interventions to Increase Positive Behavior***    Students who exhibit behavior problems in school often do so as a result of a poor fit with their environment. Very often we blame students for behavior difficulties, when changes in the environment can help reduce off-task, disruptive, or withdrawn behaviors. We do know that behavior problems result in lost instructional time due to students being removed from the classroom. Supporting positive behavior not only helps students succeed in school, but leads to more positive transitions to postsecondary education and employment. For example, Dominique has difficulty taking instruction from authoritative figures, and this has caused her to be verbally aggressive and refuse to follow directions in the classroom. As a result, she has received several in-school suspensions, whereby she is missing critical instruction and falling further behind academically. If Dominique is going to be successful in school and in her future jobs, she will need to learn strategies to control her frustration and anger when faced with feedback and criticism. Dominique may need additional behavioral supports, coaching, and counseling so that she can remain in the classroom and learn how to advocate for herself, regulate her emotions, and handle stress. It is important for schools to have behavioral interventions in place for students like Dominique, and that school is a safe, supportive, and welcoming place to learn new skills and competencies (Lehr & McComas, 2005).

Schools can support positive behavior by implementing PBIS to teach, model, and make expected behaviors explicit for all students (Mac Iver & Mac Iver, 2009). Schoolwide positive behavior interventions and supports (SWPBIS) is an example of a multitiered model of PBIS for targeting and increasing positive behavior and establishing a supportive school environment. The purpose of SWPBIS is to identify behavioral expectations for all students in the school; promote a positive and respectful school climate; and provide more intensive, individualized behavioral interventions for small groups or individual students who need additional supports. SWPBIS is operated as a schoolwide and systematic way of improving student behavior and school climate, thereby leading to higher rates of student engagement.

*Tier 1 Supports*    At the Tier 1 level, desired behaviors are explicitly taught to all students, who are reinforced for following school expectations and for prosocial behavior, while receiving clear and consistent consequences for violating school rules. School personnel keep schoolwide data on student behavior to identify students in need of more intensive behavioral support (e.g., by tracking the numbers of disciplinary referrals).

*Tier 2 Supports*     Some students may require more behavioral support at the Tier 2 level. For example, students who receive two or more office referrals might be assigned a mentor for regular check-ins and problem solving, or have a behavioral checklist reviewed each day by an adult at the school (Mac Iver & Mac Iver, 2009). Some specific examples of targeted Tier 2 interventions for improving behavior include the Behavior Education Program and Check and Connect.

The Behavior Education Program (BEP) (also called a Check-In/Check-Out; CICO), is a Tier 2 or targeted strategy for students who thrive on inappropriate attention-seeking behaviors (Crone, Hawken, & Horner, 2010). CICO is not designed for students who display dangerous behaviors or those who are uncomfortable receiving adult attention. This strategy works best when basic Tier 1 PBIS are in place throughout the school.

In brief, when a student shows off-task, disruptive, or challenging behaviors across several classes, or several days per week, the BEP team invites a student and his or her parent to participate in the program. Once a student agrees, the specific schoolwide behavioral expectations (e.g., "Be Safe, Be Responsible, Be Respectful") are explained, and the student receives one-on-one feedback addressing his or her behavior from every teacher, in every class. It is important that students receive positive feedback immediately when they succeed—not just when they have a problem. The parents also participate, receiving a brief summary each day, while providing positive feedback at home. This meets the student's need for attention, and teachers and parents reinforce school-appropriate behaviors. The school environment thereby becomes more reinforcing and more engaging for the student. For more information and resources about Check-In/Check-Out see www.pbisworld.com/tier-2/check-in-check-out-cico.

Check & Connect is a research-based intervention that has high rates of positive impact with students who need more intensive supports. It is considered a Tier 2 intervention because it requires a school counselor or other dedicated staff member to work directly with students over an extended period of time. Students "check in" with their mentor every day, which is designed to build students' social connections to the school. The mentor and student work on problem-solving skills related to academic, behavioral, or social problems and goals. The mentor also checks in with the student's family to ensure there are strong home-school supports. Visit www.checkandconnect.unm.edu to learn about Check & Connect, find training, or review the research showing how effective this intervention can be.

*Tier 3 Supports*     A very small number of students may require intensive behavioral support at the Tier 3 level. For students with significant behavior problems, an in-depth functional behavioral assessment (FBA) may be warranted, in which the school team collects data to uncover triggers or antecedents to the behavior, the function (reason for) the behavior, and the consequences that may be maintaining the behavior. This assessment data is then used to develop an individualized behavioral intervention plan (BIP) for the student. A meaningful FBA/BIP process is frequently essential to an effective transition program for students with challenging behaviors (Johnson & Walker, n.d.). A student in need of Tier 3 support may also require counseling, a referral for mental health services, and other community supports (Mac Iver & Mac Iver, 2009).

Learning positive behaviors and receiving necessary social and emotional support is strongly linked to transition outcomes for students with disabilities, particularly for students with emotional and behavioral disorders. The National Longitudinal Transition Study (NLTS) collected data in the early 1990s on the lives of youth with disabilities during high school and when transitioning to adulthood and reported troubling outcomes for students with emotional and behavioral disorders who showed a pattern of disconnecting from school, leading to academic difficulties (Wagner et al., 1991, as cited in Lehr & McComas, 2005). Over the years, research has continued to indicate that youth with emotional and behavioral disorders tend to have higher dropout rates, higher rates of arrest and unemployment, and lower rates of independent living than their peers without disabilities (Armstrong, Dedrick, & Greenbaum, 2003, as cited in Karpur, A., Clark, H.B., Caproni, P., & Sterner, H., 2005). It is important to shift from a deficits perspective to a focus on strengths so as to increase resilience among at-risk youth and to facilitate successful school experiences (Lehr & McComas, 2005). Transition-planning approaches include engaging students in coursework that is relevant to their backgrounds and interests, creating structured and supportive learning environments, and managing challenging behavior with evidenced-based strategies (e.g., providing immediate feedback using the principles of reinforcement) (Lehr & McComas, 2005).

***Interventions to Support Course Completion***      In order to get a diploma, students must earn the credits required to graduate. We know that failing grades are a sure sign of student disengagement from school; however, poor grades are also a cause for disengagement. For example, Dominique is a student who truly struggles with reading skills because of her disability, and she earns low grades in classes that require a lot of reading for information in spite of her study efforts. As her failing grades pile up, she becomes more and more dissatisfied with school, and the hurdle to graduate becomes higher and higher. The benefit of utilizing a transition-focused approach to curriculum and instruction is that it incorporates interventions emphasizing student choice, links academics to real-world experiences, and supports college and career readiness. Table 6.1 includes examples of how transition-focused approaches to curriculum and instruction can be implemented across multiple tiers of support.

At Tier 1, your school can focus on developing a schoolwide community of learners and reinforcing self-determined and self-regulating behaviors for all students. Examples of instructional methods used with all students include universal design for learning strategies instruction embedded within core academic content, differentiated instruction, mentoring (both peer and adult), and cooperative learning (including peer groups and peer tutoring) (See Table 6.2). For an expanded discussion of instructional strategies and embedding transition-related content in academics, see Chapter 7. A high school instructional lab that serves all students by providing assistance with homework and tutoring is another example of a Tier 1 support. In addition, at Tier 1, secondary curricula must make explicit connections to career and post-school goals and interests. Electives should provide a range of career readiness opportunities, including service learning, career and technical education programs, and academic units that embed preparation for the real world within lessons.

At Tier 2, supplemental transition, academic, and behavior curricula offer small-group opportunities to expand knowledge and skills and support struggling learners. Examples for how to support students with academic challenges might include using an evidence-based adolescent literacy curriculum with individual or small groups of students enrolled

**Table 6.1.**  Multitiered transition-focused approaches to curriculum and instruction

|  | Tier 1 | Tier 2 | Tier 3 |
|---|---|---|---|
| Curriculum focusing on college and career readiness. | Curriculum connected to career and educational interests for all students. Electives and available coursework provide a range of career readiness opportunities. Examples include:<br>• Service learning.<br>• Career report in language arts.<br>• Budgeting practice in personal finance course.<br>• Civic responsibility discussion in U.S. government class.<br>• A *Success 101/Freshman Focus course* for all freshmen.<br>• Chances to learn and practice critical thinking skills embedded across coursework.<br>• A variety of extracurricular activities linked to student interests and passions to promote a sense of belonging.<br>• Schoolwide models for transition and college and career readiness (e.g., *High Schools That Work; Career Academies*). | Supplemental transition, academic, or behavior curricula, coursework, and interventions. Examples include:<br>• Wilson reading.<br>• Algebra ½.<br>• Online courses.<br>• Study skills course.<br>• Adult roles and responsibilities course.<br>• Summer youth programs.<br>• Career internships.<br>• Dropout prevention models/Tier 2 behavioral interventions (e.g., *Check & Connect, CICO*). | Individualized transition curricula, programs, and coursework. Examples include:<br>• Life skills curricula.<br>• Supported employment.<br>• Community-based transition programs.<br>• Curricular modifications.<br>• Work-based learning.<br>• Vocational/careers class.<br>• *W.A.G.E.S: Working at gaining employment skills:* A job-related social skills curriculum for adolescents (Johnson et al., 2004). |
| Instruction promoting independence and engagement. | Instruction emphasizing choice and application of critical thinking that is aimed at developing a community of learners, teaching self-regulating behaviors, and engaging students and preparing them for postsecondary outcomes. Examples include:<br>• Universal design for learning.<br>• Learning strategy instruction.<br>• Differentiated instruction.<br>• Peer tutoring and mentoring.<br>• Active and cooperative learning.<br>• Career and tutoring centers. | Supplemental small group instruction or instructional supports:<br>• Co-teaching.<br>• Instructional accommodations.<br>• Transition or job club.<br>• Tutoring.<br>• Self-determined learning model of instruction.<br>• Assistive technology integrated within instruction. | Intensive and individualized instruction and supports:<br>• Instructional modifications.<br>• Small group or 1:1 instruction.<br>• Dedicated support from trained personnel.<br>• Customized interventions.<br>• Assistive technology to support communication. |

From Morningstar, M.E. (2015). *MTSS and CCR: Are We ready?* [PowerPoint Slides]. Lawrence: Transition Coalition, University of Kansas; retrieved from http://transitioncoalition.org/wp-content/uploads/2016/07/MTSSandCCR-UMTSS-2015.pdf; adapted by permission.

in a guided studies or reading lab, or extending a semester-long math class into a full-year class to slow the pace of instruction and learning. Integrating technology and particularly AT within academic instruction is another critical support for targeted groups of students.

To help students prepare for college and careers, schools might provide supplemental and small-group instructional support in the form of intensive academic tutoring tied to real-world problems and content (e.g., embedding career awareness within a reading academy for students at risk of dropping out of school). Having students enroll in an elective learning strategies course is also a way to provide more intensive Tier 2 instruction to students in need and teach critical study skills. Additionally, the school might offer supplemental support to students by providing a course in career development/transition that incorporates evidence-based interventions from both academic and transition research.

As an example, Dominique enrolled in a career class at her high school that combined instruction and opportunities to practice self-determination skills, learning strategies, and work-based learning. This comprehensive class helped Dominique gain essential skills to become a better self-advocate, helped her to approach her academic challenges,

**Table 6.2.**   Instructional methods for all transition-age learners

| | |
|---|---|
| Universal design for learning | A framework to improve teaching and ensure active learning for all students by targeting three elements of teaching and learning:<br>1) Engagement: increasing student interest in and motivation for learning.<br>2) Representation: presenting information and content in different ways to meet the needs of diverse learners.<br>3) Action and expression: providing students with different ways to express what they know. (www.cast.org) |
| Learning strategies | Used to help students access and engage with information. Students can learn to use effective learning strategies (e.g., note taking, test taking, organization, essay writing) to improve performance in school. Learning strategy instruction supports students to become active learners by teaching them how to use what they have learned to solve problems and be successful. (www.kucrl.org) |
| Differentiated learning | A process for teaching and learning that takes into account diverse students within a classroom. The intent is to maximize student growth and success by focusing on essential ideas and skills; responding to individual learning styles; using cooperative groups; integrating assessment throughout instruction; and continually reassessing, reflecting, and adjusting content, learning processes, and products to meet students' unique needs. (www.ascd.org) |
| Cooperative learning | Designed to promote shared goals through cooperation. It involves small groups of students working together to solve a problem, complete a task, or create a product. Students are individually accountable for their work, as well as the work of the group. (www.teachervision.com) |

and allowed her to engage in real-world work experiences. This class was highly engaging and interesting for Dominique, motivating her to come to school more often. The most intensive and customized interventions for students with extensive support needs occurs at Tier 3 and could include instructional adaptations and modifications, as well as intensive one-to-one supports to learn specific skills (e.g., a reading specialist working with a student on intensive literacy instruction). Tier 3 could target individual skill-based interventions, with a more specific emphasis on transition-focused curricula (e.g., life skills, employment, community-based programs).

Some students have more intensive needs that require a "wraparound support" approach. This is a model of intensive supports that addresses home, community, and school life. As noted by the OSEP Technical Assistance Center on Positive Behavioral Interventions and Supports, it is a person-centered approach that considers all critical needs of the student, including basic needs and safety, along with social, emotional, educational, spiritual, and cultural needs (see www.PBIS.org). When a student has more comprehensive needs or requires outside services and supports (e.g., social services, mental health services, health care, court involvement, safety from abuse and violence, need for food and shelter) engaging in school can be a low priority. Under these circumstances, it is necessary to provide an array of services to "wrap around" the individual, ensuring that his or her educational needs can be met. Visit www.pbis.org/school/tertiary-level/wraparound for an overview of wraparound service.

A multitiered system to supporting students in course completion and academic achievement relies on data collection and progress monitoring, which can be very helpful in revealing students at risk, as well as other schoolwide or systemic issues. As an example, in one large high school early warning data identified that a common cause of dropout from their school was 9th grade course failure in English 1. Students specifically fell off track during the second 9 weeks of the course, and it didn't take long to find out why. Each year, the school enrolls about 700 freshmen, and each one of the students must complete a term paper in the second 9-week term. This paper was the tripping point for most of this school's future dropouts (Wilkins & Huckabee, 2014).

If this was your school, what strategies might you put in place across all three tiers? Some solutions for all students might be to scaffold instruction about writing term papers that could be embedded throughout the entire semester. From the first day of English 1, teachers could provide guidance on the critical elements of a term paper in small learning units, with examples of passing work. Scaffolded instruction could include in-person lectures, examples, and activities in class blended with self-directed learning through online units of instruction. Students who need more targeted Tier 2 supports might participate in extra early morning, after school, advisement period, or "lunch buddies" sessions focusing on critical building blocks of writing the term paper. In addition, an extra elective study lab might be put in place for freshmen needing more specific and explicit instruction. For those requiring Tier 3 supports, a year-long elective class specifically focusing on the mechanics of completing a research paper may be warranted.

Besides being used as an individualized support for students, electives also play a role in helping students to be engaged and interested in school and in meeting transition requirements. Many students who leave school say that it just wasn't relevant to them (America's Promise Alliance, 2014). Most students who drop out had career aspirations, but somewhere along the way their school experiences clouded these dreams. An individualized transition planning process ensures that students have a voice in choosing their course of study while in high school. Does your school offer a variety of CTE courses or concurrent enrollment with technical schools or colleges? Not only do CTE classes offer a pathway to a career, they can also support the academic skills needed to succeed in core classes. Think of a CTE class in your school that applies math skills or requires a student to read and apply verbal information. Other electives classes—choir, painting, track, theater—can also foster a more engaging environment for a student who has difficulty seeing how high school is relevant to his or her life.

### TIP FOR TRANSITION: Think About Blending Multi-tiered Systems of Support

Recall the benefits of multi-tiered systems of support in increasing overall student engagement. The comprehensive, integrated, three-tiered model of prevention (CI3T) offers a way for schools to bring effective multitiered models together, blending both academic multitiered models (RTI) and behavior multitiered models (SWPBIS) to encompass the academic, behavior, and social needs of students in one multi-tiered system of support (Lane, Oakes, & Menzies, 2014). CI3T is a customized model to fit each school individually. Several surveys are used to identify expectations from faculty, staff, parents, and students to help guide the planning process in implementing this system (Lane, Oakes, Jenkins, Menzies, & Kalberg, 2014).

### WHAT YOU CAN DO RIGHT NOW:
### Putting Ideas Into Action

Consider Dominique, this chapter's featured student. What strategies would you have put into place to support her to stay in school? Dominique's school was using data to keep students on track. Her attendance office was aware that Dominique's absentee rates were too high, and the school did intervene at the Tier 1 level by calling her mother and talking to Dominique about the importance of staying in school. They also implemented a Tier 2 attendance intervention to support and encourage her to come to school, be engaged, and behave appropriately. In addition, the school was able to implement credit recovery with

# Checklist for Implementing Dropout Prevention Strategies

**Recommendation 1: Utilize data systems that support a realistic diagnosis of the number of students who drop out and that help identify individual students at high risk of dropping out.**

❑ Use longitudinal, student-level data to get an accurate read of graduation and dropout rates.

❑ Use data to identify incoming students with histories of academic problems, truancy, behavioral problems, and retentions.

❑ Monitor the academic and social performance of all students continually.

❑ Review student-level data to identify students at risk of dropping out before key academic transitions.

❑ Monitor students' sense of engagement and belonging in school.

❑ Collect and document accurate information on student withdrawals.

**Recommendation 2: Assign adult advocates to students at risk of dropping out.**

❑ Choose adults who are committed to investing in the student's personal and academic success, keep caseloads low, and purposefully match students with adult advocates.

❑ Establish a regular time in the school day or week for students to meet with the adult.

❑ Communicate with adult advocates about the various obstacles students may encounter—and provide adult advocates with guidance and training about how to work with students, parents, or school staff to address the problems.

**Recommendation 3: Provide academic support and enrichment to improve academic performance.**

❑ Provide individual or small-group support in test-taking skills, study skills, or targeted subject areas such as reading, writing, or math.

❑ Provide extra study time and opportunities for credit recovery and accumulation through after school, Saturday school, or summer enrichment programs.

**Recommendation 4: Implement programs to improve students' classroom behavior and social skills.**

❑ Use adult advocates or other engaged adults to help students establish attainable academic and behavioral goals with specific benchmarks.

❑ Recognize student accomplishments.

❑ Teach strategies to strengthen problem-solving and decision-making skills.

❑ Establish partnerships with community-based program providers and other agencies such as social services, welfare, mental health, and law enforcement.

**Recommendation 5: Personalize the learning environment and instructional process.**

❑ Establish small learning communities.

❑ Establish team teaching.

❑ Create smaller classes.

❑ Create extended time in classroom through changes to the school schedule.

❑ Encourage student participation in extracurricular activities.

**Recommendation 6: Provide rigorous and relevant instruction to better engage students in learning and provide the skills needed to graduate and to serve them after they leave school.**

❑ Provide teachers with ongoing ways to expand their knowledge and improve their skills.

❑ Integrate academic content with career and skill-based themes through career academies or multiple pathways models.

❑ Host career days and offer opportunities for work-related experiences and visits to postsecondary campuses.

❑ Provide students with extra assistance and information about the demands of college.

❑ Partner with local businesses to provide opportunities for work-related experience such as internships, simulated job interviews, or long-term employment.

**Figure 6.4.** Checklist for Implementing Dropout Prevention Strategies. (From Dynarski, M., Clarke, L., Cobb, B., Finn, J., Rumberger, R., and Smink, J. [2008]. Dropout Prevention: A Practice Guide [NCEE 2008–4025]. Washington, DC: National Center for Education Evaluation and Regional Assistance, Institute of Education Sciences, U.S. Department of Education. Retrieved from http://ies.ed.gov/ncee/wwc.)

Dominique by having her take a summer class, as well as enroll in an online class to make up her failed grades. Finally, the school enrolled Dominique in a careers class, an elective that helped her identify her strengths and preferences related to careers and learn more about the range of postsecondary settings where she could gain skills leading to her desired career pathway. In addition to their efforts with Dominique, the school decided to use a student engagement survey with all students to discover areas in need of improvement and ways to better support students, such as promoting involvement in extracurricular activities and service learning, and creating a more welcoming place to be.

Having a comprehensive approach to dropout prevention can support all students to stay on track for graduation and, more importantly, to be ready and prepared for future college and career plans. As a way to bring together the interventions and strategies you have learned in this chapter, consider using the Checklist for Carrying Out Drop Out Prevention Strategies, developed by the Institute of Education Sciences (see Figure 6.4) to help guide you and your school team in ensuring that you use high-quality strategies and research-based practices to keep students engaged in school. This chapter's checklist can also give you an idea of what areas need improvement in your personal practice and in your school.

Making sure that students are involved in school is only the first step, however, in ensuring a successful and fulfilling future. Students also need to access relevant and rigorous curriculum linked to their future personal and career goals. To ensure the best post-school outcomes for students with disabilities, all young adults should be fully included in the general education classroom. The following chapter emphasizes the importance of inclusion and discusses strategies for embedding transition-related content into the general education curriculum.

# 7

# Inclusion in General Education

*Strategies for Embedding
Transition Into Academic Content*

with Ryan Kellems

When Liam's IEP team met, the geometry teacher was not sure that her math class was the proper place for him and wanted to know if he could be taught math in the special education classroom. Liam is struggling with the concepts introduced in the recent unit, but is performing better than 30% of his peers and is not at risk to fail. The general education teacher expressed a general concern that other students with IEPs were also struggling in her class, and that she was not confident in how to help these students catch up. How would you explain the importance of keeping Liam and other students with learning disabilities in the geometry class? What strategies would you use to ensure that Liam and his teacher are supported?

Ensuring that all students are included in general education must be a critical focus of secondary educators. This is because we know that students with disabilities achieve better transition outcomes when they have participated in general education classes as opposed to special education settings (Test, Mazzotti et al., 2009). Students who participate in general education coursework are more likely to move on to postsecondary education and training and employment. In fact, researchers have found that students who participated in general education were five times more likely to participate in postsecondary education (Baer et al., 2003), and students with disabilities who were included with their peers were more likely to be engaged in post-school employment (Carter, Austin, & Trainor, 2012; White & Weiner, 2004).

IDEA requires that students with disabilities be included with their peers in the general education classroom to the maximum extent appropriate, supported by supplementary aids and services that are provided in the least restrictive environment. Given this perspective, the general education classroom is the preferred environment for enabling all students to engage in academic learning and participate in the range of nonacademic experiences necessary to be college and career ready (Morningstar, Lombardi, Fowler, & Test, 2015; Turnbull, Turnbull, Wehmeyer, & Shogren, 2013).

Longstanding support for access to general education exists among parents, researchers, school professionals, and advocates (Salend & Duhaney, 2011), and we now know that inclusion in general education leads to better outcomes. Inclusion succeeds when general educators and other education team members collaboratively design, implement, and evaluate the outcomes of instruction (Fuchs, Fuchs, & Stecker, 2010). Therefore, meaningful inclusion of students with disabilities in secondary general education classrooms requires transition coordinators, secondary special educators, general education teachers, and related services staff to work together. Transition coordinators can work with teachers to embed transition content within classroom academic coursework. This chapter will discuss ways to do this.

## GETTING STARTED:
## Understand That Access to the General Education Curriculum Is Critical to Transition Outcomes

Including students with disabilities in general education classes is not just best practice, federal law requires it. According to IDEA 2004, all students with disabilities must be placed in the least restrictive environment (LRE) and should be removed from the regular education environment only when this education, even with "the use of supplementary aids and services, cannot be achieved satisfactorily" (20 U.S.C. 1412 et seq). When students with disabilities are provided specially designed instruction in general education settings, they are able to engage in rigorous academic content, as well as acquire the skills necessary to be college and career ready. These skills include problem solving, communication, and relationship skills.

The level of participation in general education will vary depending on each student's unique strengths and needs. The IEP team decides the extent to which each student will participate in general education. Whether you are a secondary special educator or transition coordinator, you should always advocate for your students to be in general education classrooms with their peers to the fullest extent possible, given the academic and post-school benefits of inclusion.

### Learn the Role of the General Education Teacher in the Transition Individualized Education Program Meeting

According to IDEA, a general education teacher must be present at each student's IEP meeting. Sometimes the general educator's role during the IEP meeting is not always clear. One responsibility of special educators, including transition coordinators, is to make sure that general education teachers understand their roles, as they are integral parts of the IEP process and in helping students develop and achieve their measurable postsecondary goals. Some strategies you can use to ensure that general education teachers are fully involved in the transition IEP meeting are listed next, including examples of how each strategy was carried out with Mrs. Clarke, Liam's 11th grade geometry teacher, so that she was made to feel more comfortable in supporting Liam to succeed.

1. Ensure the general education teacher is invited to the IEP meeting and that the meeting is held at a time when he or she can participate. Liam's special education teacher worked with Mrs. Clarke to make sure the IEP meeting was scheduled at a time she could attend, such as during her planning time, after school, or during one of her classes when a substitute has been provided.

2. Make sure the general education teacher knows the student, has him or her in class, and is familiar with the student's academic work. Mrs. Clarke has had Liam in her class for 5 months. She has a good relationship with Liam and is familiar with his performance in her class. When school first started, Liam's special education teacher provided a summary of the supports and accommodations he needed. She now meets regularly with Mrs. Clarke to plan for any needed adaptations or specific evidence-based interventions Liam might need to sufficiently learn the more challenging content. The two teachers have a good relationship and are able to constructively communicate about Liam, as well as other students.

3. Meet with the general education teacher prior to the IEP meeting to discuss his or her role. The special education teacher met with Mrs. Clarke 2 weeks prior to the IEP meeting to discuss her role in the meeting. Mrs. Clarke was asked to bring performance data for Liam and be prepared to discuss how Liam was doing in relation to the course objectives and standards.

4. Have the general education teacher discuss the student's performance with the core content and standards, as well as progress on any individualized learning objectives, describing how these have been integrated into the general education content. Mrs. Clarke came to the IEP meeting prepared to discuss how Liam is performing in her class specific to the state standards for geometry. In addition, she was able to describe the specific accommodations that work best for Liam. These include allowing Liam to use a calculator on homework and assigning him a partner for in-class seatwork. She also plans to discuss some accommodations she can provide Liam for test taking other than extended test time.

5. Remember that the general education teacher is not just there to provide a signature. Mrs. Clarke was consulted multiple times during the meeting and left the process feeling like she had made a valuable contribution. Mrs. Clarke now welcomes the opportunity to participate in IEP meetings for her other students whenever she is invited.

## Understand the Common Core and Other State Standards

It is important to understand if your state adheres to the Common Core State Standards (CCSS) and, if not, what standards are being used. A majority of states have adopted the CCSS (2014) (www.corestandards.org/about-the-standards). The CCSS are learning goals that represent grade-level skills and knowledge students need in order to be college and career ready. The CCSS are different from past standards because they are common benchmarks across states for what students should know and do at each grade level. They do not dictate how things should be taught, but rather, what should be taught. Having common benchmarks for every grade pushes teachers toward a level of accountability that helps prepare students to graduate high school and enter college ready to be successful (CCSS, 2014). Common standards are also being applied to subjects other than math and English language arts. Examples include science (Next Generation Science Standards, n.d., www.nextgenscience.org) and foreign languages (American Council on the Teaching of Foreign Languages, 2015; www.actfl.org/news/press-releases/national-standards-collaborative-board-releases-iworld-readiness-standards-learning-languagesi). Specific aspects of the CCSS can easily be embedded in every class regardless of content. One example would be embedding problem-solving skills within a physical education course. In states where the CCSS have not been adopted, the state will have a set of learning standards for specific content areas and grade levels. These state standards also reflect the approach now used by the CCSS to extend student learning beyond basic facts and incorporate critical thinking and problem-solving skills. To find out if your state is a CCSS state or where your state standards are found, check your state department of education web site.

To assist teachers of students with significant disabilities who are unable to participate in general state assessments even with accommodations, states have developed or adopted alternate assessments so that these students can be included in an educational accountability system. These assessments include alternate achievement standards, often called foundational or essential elements, which are tied to grade-level standards. For example, many states are now using the Dynamic Learning Maps Essential Elements (EE, 2013; http://dynamiclearningmaps.org/content/essential-elements). The essential elements are specific grade-level expectations about what students with the most significant cognitive disabilities should know and be able to do, related to college- and career-readiness standards for students in the general population (Dynamic Learning Maps Consortium, n.d.). They are statements of knowledge and skills tied to the CCSS, but they help build a bridge so that students with the most significant disabilities can access general education content, taking into account these students' specific learning styles, content knowledge, academic needs, and expected skills (Dynamic Learning Maps Consortium, 2013). Keep in mind that essential elements are not replacements for grade-level standards, nor are they statements of functional skills or separate functional curricula. Students are expected to apply core academic skills in meaningful, personally relevant ways and are provided with supports and a learning map for reaching grade-level academic standards.

Other states have adopted a different format for supporting students with significant disabilities to address academic standards, working with the National Center and State Collaborative (www.ncscpartners.org) to ensure students with significant disabilities achieve academic outcomes and leave high school ready for postsecondary options. If you are a secondary special education teacher working with students with significant intellectual disabilities, you are most likely familiar with your state's approach. All transition coordinators should become familiar with alternate assessment approaches and how they correspond with state achievement standards. Meeting rigorous grade-level standards requires students to receive necessary accommodations and modifications to curriculum, instruction, and assessment. Typically, it is the role of the special education teacher to collaborate with general education teachers in determining and supporting what each student needs to succeed in each course. This is something that can be discussed in the IEP meeting, but is an ongoing responsibility of the special education teacher. More information about accommodations and modifications is described later in this chapter.

## MAKING IT HAPPEN:
### Embedding Transition Skills Within Core Academic Content

In many schools, transition skills have primarily been taught during pullout special education classes such as "careers," "transition skills," "life skills," or "functional skills" courses. However, these classes may not provide sufficiently robust learning experiences because students are segregated from their peers without disabilities and are not engaging in rigorous academic content. Instead, transition-related content can be embedded into your students' core content classes. This is a challenging but effective approach because it provides real-world links between core academic content and the essential transition skills *all* students will need to be successful after they graduate.

Teaching transition-related skills in an academic setting makes practical sense. If you are an educator, one of the first things you will need to do is determine what transition skills fit within each of the core academic content areas. To do this, you will want to align a student's measurable postsecondary goals and individualized IEP goals with appropriate academic content. For example, Mr. Chavez, Liam's social studies teacher, teaches the 11th grade government class required for graduation. Because it is required, this course contains a wide range of students. Typically, about 20% of the students in class have a disability. Of those students with disabilities, about 50% have measurable postsecondary goals that Mr. Chavez can embed into his government class. One of Liam's measurable post-school goals and annual IEP goals are as follows:

Measurable postsecondary goal: Upon completion of high school, Liam will enroll in the Aquarium Science Associates Degree Program at Oregon Coast Community College.

Annual IEP goal aligned with Liam's measurable postsecondary goal: Liam will write a two-page personal narrative essay with 80% accuracy for each draft over the course of the semester.

Looking at Liam's goals, Mr. Chavez considered standard 4 of the Common Core State Standards for Writing for Literacy in History/Social Studies for Grade 11–12: "Produce clear and coherent writing in which the development, organization, and style are appropriate to task, purpose and audience" (CCSS.ELA-Literacy.W.11-12.4). Mr. Chavez was able to assist Liam on his personal narrative in class. The narrative focused on Liam's volunteer work at the local library, which was a part of the school's service-learning requirement.

If you are a transition coordinator, one of your essential roles is to collaborate with all teachers to ensure that transition-focused activities and information are embedded within core academic content. In essence, transition coordinators can help all students develop skills and experiences that will ensure college and career readiness within their general education classes. For example, one transition coordinator provided summer in-service training to all of the 9th grade English Language Arts teachers in her district on how to embed self-determination skills (i.e., goal setting, problem solving, and self-advocacy) throughout the English curriculum. Academic content is a priority of the CCSS, and it is possible to embed transition skills into instruction. Table 7.1 is an example of how to embed transition-related content within 9th and 10th grade writing standards.

**Table 7.1.** Example of infusing secondary transitions skills into college and career-ready standards in English language arts

| Grade 9-10 key ideas and details | Embedded transition-focused topic |
| --- | --- |
| 9-10.1 Cite strong and thorough textual evidence to support analysis of what the text says explicitly as well as inferences drawn from the text. | Choose two postsecondary education institutions or training programs and summarize information from the web site for prospective students. Identify one that would be an appropriate personal choice for postsecondary education/training and one that is not. Provide evidence that supports your choice. |

*Source:* NSTTAC (2013). Examples of Infusing Secondary Transition Skills into College and Career Ready Standards in English Language Arts. Retrieved from http://www.transitionta.org/sites/default/files/Transition_Skills_and_CCSS_in_ELA_2013.pdf.

**TIP FOR TRANSITION: Plan for Success With CCSS!**

The first step to understanding how state standards affect your students is to learn more about what they are. Many states are using the CCSS, which were developed by The Council of Chief State School Officers and the National Governors Association. More information, including a detailed description of all of the standards, can be found at www.corestandards.org. Those states not using the CCSS have developed their own standards, which can be accessed through their web site. Once you become familiar with your state's standards you can embed transition-related content into the standards to optimize your students' success.

## Provide Access to the General Education Curriculum

Transition coordinators play an important role in a student's academic success by participating in the planning process; however, equally important is developing strategies that can be used to embed and infuse transition-focused skills and experiences within general education core academic classes and ensuring that every student has access to the general education curriculum. As a transition coordinator, you will need to make sure that you support your students and the special and general education teachers, and aid in their success. As you start the planning process for supporting students with disabilities, some important questions need to be considered by general education teachers and any others who may be involved in classroom instruction (e.g., special educator who is co-teaching, paraprofessional). Guiding questions you can use for discussion include:

- How will the student interact with the academic content?

- What academic and behavioral supports will the student need to be successful?

- What additional supports, resources, or personnel (special education teacher, paraprofessional, peer tutor) are available to assist students?

- How is general classroom management implemented, and what additional and more intensive supports are needed to support students with challenging behaviors?

- How do all students access and engage with class content? Is differentiated instruction and/or universal design for learning a focus in the class? If not, how can we ensure that learning and instruction will be enhanced so as to be accessible for all?

- How are performance and progress monitored, and what are the class grading policies? Can these policies be modified if needed? (Hughes & Carter, 2012)

Consider how the educational team planned for Liam's success in geometry class, using the above questions as a guide:

- Liam will not need to have the content modified for learning—he will learn the same content as the other students in the class.

- Liam has passed the required prerequisite classes needed to enroll in geometry. Liam did receive additional support in past math classes. The geometry teacher needs to be made aware of the accommodations Liam received in his previous math classes, such as being able to have the test read to him in a quiet environment.

- As part of the schoolwide dropout prevention program, a paraprofessional is in the class to assist all students at risk of failing, including Liam and other students with disabilities. The special education teacher will provide training and supervision of the paraprofessional.

- If needed, Liam will receive additional help with his homework from the special education teacher during homeroom. He can also attend the geometry tutoring sessions offered twice a week after school for any student.

- The geometry teacher has integrated hands-on and project-based learning and activities associated with geometry into her course. This will make the content more accessible and applicable for all students, including Liam. More hands-on learning will also assist Liam with his tendency to lose focus and attention during lectures.

- The special education teacher will work with the geometry teacher to progress monitor Liam's performance. This will require additional measures to ensure acquisition of critical skills.

## Provide Instructional Supports for Learning: Accommodations and Modifications

One fundamental way to facilitate better transition outcomes is to promote greater access to academic content for students with disabilities, and access often requires accommodations. The National Dissemination Center for Children with Disabilities (NICHY, 2010) defines an accommodation as "a change that helps a student overcome or work around a disability." An example of an accommodation would be allowing a student with a reading disability to have the history test questions read aloud to him or her. This student is still expected to learn the same content and material and show his or her knowledge on the test. Another example would be to provide this same student with an audiobook of a Shakespeare play in an English literature class.

Another strategy that ensures the general education curriculum is accessible to students with disabilities is to provide modifications to the content and/or learning goals. A modification involves altering what is being taught or expected of the student. For example, a modification for Liam is that he is only required to complete two-thirds of the homework problems most closely associated with the lesson content. There are several common areas in which accommodations and modifications are made for students with disabilities, as shown in Table 7.2.

It is important to remember that accommodations and modifications should be decided by the IEP team with student and parent input. The entire team is responsible for determining what accommodations and modifications are appropriate for a student in the classroom and on assessments. Accommodations and modifications should not be used to make a class "easier" for a student; rather, they are to be used to make learning and instruction accessible. It is often easier to simply lower the learning expectations for a student than provide appropriate supports, accommodations, and modifications. Be careful not to fall into this trap, and always maintain high expectations for all learners.

Consider some appropriate accommodations and modifications determined for Liam's 11th grade English class. This class is taught by Mrs. Guffman, a general education

**Table 7.2.**  Common areas for accommodations and modifications

|  | Example of accommodation | Example of modification |
|---|---|---|
| Environment | Give students the opportunity to work in smaller groups or one-on-one with a teacher, instructional aide, or peer tutor. You may also have the student sit in a particular location, such as in the front of the room, to avoid distractions, or by the teacher's desk if there are behavioral concerns. | Modifying the rules or equipment of a game. For example, if the students are practicing shooting free throws, the student with a disability may be allowed to use a smaller basketball or a lower basketball hoop. |
| Content delivery | Use differentiated instruction. Content is the same, but the level of the material is appropriate to the student's ability level. | Use differentiated instruction simplifying the content being presented. The overarching concepts are taught, but maybe not in as much detail. |
| Time management | Allow extra time to complete in-class work; extended testing time. | Adjusting a student's class schedule. |
| Access to instructional materials | Providing materials in an accessible format, such as audio, braille, or large print. | Only present students with the most important content. If the rest of the class is reading the entire chapter, students needing modifications only read critical parts of the chapter as decided by the instructor. |
| Communication of knowledge | Student writes an essay using text-to-speech and/or audio-to-text software. | The student writes a simplified paragraph. |

teacher, and Liam is struggling to keep up with the grade-level content. Mrs. Guffman, along with the IEP team, agreed upon the following accommodations and modifications:

- Liam will have all of the textbooks and reading materials available in an audio format (accommodation).

- Liam will have test/quiz questions read to him (accommodation).

- Liam will have access to speech-to-text software when completing written assignments (accommodation).

- Liam will complete a three-page research paper instead of the five-page paper required of his peers (modification).

As you can see, determining appropriate accommodations for a student requires consideration of a variety of different factors, such as the student's preferred mode of learning (e.g., auditory, visual), as well as learning strategies and accommodations that have previously worked well for this student.

## Access the What, How, and Why of Learning Through Universal Design for Learning

One strategy that all teachers can use to meet the needs of all students, including those with disabilities, is universal design for learning (UDL). UDL is designed to remove barriers and maximize learning for all students, so teachers who utilize the UDL principles to make content more accessible for a diverse group of learners will be helping their entire class, not just those with disabilities. UDL is based on three main principles, as illustrated in Figure 7.1.

***Principle 1: Provide Multiple Means of Representation (the "What" of Learning)***    It is important to convey content to students in several different ways. For example, students could investigate the effects of water aerobics through a web search and discuss vocabulary terms such as density, volume, and buoyancy. Another way of studying the properties of water would be to study water's role in erosion. The students could complete a project

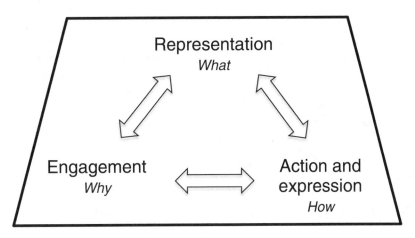

**Figure 7.1.** The three main principles of universal design for learning.

where they create a small water table with passageways made of sand in order to discuss the effects that water has on carving out river channels, such as the Grand Canyon.

***Principle 2: Provide Multiple Means of Action and Expression (the "How" of Learning)***    Students should be provided with different ways of showing they understand the content being taught. For example, in an algebra class, as an alternative to conventional worksheets, a note card activity can be used. Using this approach, algebra problems are written on one set of note cards, and the answers are on a separate set. Students are put into small groups to solve the problems. Once the problems are solved, students search the room for cards containing their answers (Kortering, McClannon, & Braziel, 2008).

***Principle 3: Provide Multiple Means of Engagement (the "Why" of Learning)***    Students should be given multiple means of engaging with the content. This is important, because what works to engage one student may intimidate another student. In English class, the teacher could encourage freedom of choice by allowing the students to choose the book they need to read for their upcoming book report. Similarly, in history class, the teacher can foster autonomy by helping the students choose any war that interests them. Students then analyze their chosen war's causes, as well as the factors that led to its resolution.

## TIP FOR TRANSITION: Use Universal Design for Learning to Support Access to General Education

In Liam's 11th grade biology class he is studying cells. At the end of the lesson, the students will be expected to label all the parts of the cell and explain what each part does. Teachers who understand that students learn in different ways can increase flexibility in how students express their knowledge about cells by allowing them several choices: to either draw the cell, create a 3-D cell using a model, or design a cell on a computer. As part of creating the model, students will label each of the cell structures.

As a transition coordinator or special educator, you can offer general education teachers information and strategies for implementing the underlying principles of UDL. General educators who implement UDL in their classes can expect to see increased learning among all of their students. Implementing UDL may feel overwhelming at first, and encouraging teachers to tackle the process in small steps over time is a great strategy. Teachers can start by implementing UDL into a few activities or lessons each semester. In subsequent semesters, they can add more UDL principles. Before they know it, educators will have developed an entire semester full of lesson plans based on the principles of UDL.

Implementing UDL principles in the classroom can be good for the teacher as well as the students. Many behavior problems in the classroom are the result of poorly planned lessons that do not fully address the what, how, and why of learning. By designing lesson plans seeking to address each of these aspects, teachers can more fully engage students in the learning process.

## Use Assistive Technology to Support Learning and Transition

Making transition content accessible within an academic setting can be easier if you utilize technology. IDEA defines AT as "any item, piece of equipment, or product system, whether acquired commercially off the shelf, modified, or customized, that is used to increase, maintain, or improve the functional capabilities of a child with a disability" (IDEA, 2004, 300.5; 20 U.S.C. 1401 [1]). The technology available to teachers will differ depending on the building, classroom, course content, and teacher skills. Some teachers will have certain technologies dedicated to their classroom (e.g., Smartboard, laptop computers), whereas others will have to check out equipment from a centralized location in the school. In addition, teachers need to determine the best technology fit for their academic subject. For example, a math teacher may choose to use a low-tech device, such as a calculator with a larger display panel. On the other hand, an English teacher may choose to use text-to-speech software to assist students with writing reports. AT can be very helpful in helping some students to access academic- and transition-related content. One example would be a screen reader for those with visual impairments.

### TIP FOR TRANSITION: Video Modeling as Technology Support for Transition.

Video modeling is an evidence-based practice that takes advantage of the latest technology and that many students enjoy using. Video prompting is a form of video modeling that uses short video clips to teach selected skills and behavior to students in steps. After watching the video clip, the learner then performs that step before the next video is shown. The student is shown the step-by-step video before completing the task. Video modeling has been used to teach a range of skills, including employment and independent living (Kellems & Morningstar, 2012). It has also been used to teach reading (Decker & Buggey, 2014). Students watched a video they created or a video of a peer reading fluently, leading to improvements in reading fluency.

Those who depend on AT and other accommodations often face challenges during the transition from high school to college. In high school, those with disabilities are given the technology and supports they need to thrive in an academic setting. Once they leave high school, the students are tasked with making the university aware of their disability and receiving the assistance they need in order to be successful. However, they may feel uncomfortable with this new responsibility. Whenever possible, transition coordinators can help with the transition process, by making sure that the university is aware of the student and providing relevant and recent test data. The same situation also occurs in the occupational field. Employers are usually willing to make accommodations for their employees, but are often unaware that accommodations are needed. Special education teachers can teach those with disabilities to be self-advocates so that they learn how to explain their disability and articulate the supports they may need in the workplace.

## WHAT YOU CAN DO RIGHT NOW:
## Putting Ideas Into Action

One way school professionals can help improve post-school outcomes for students is by ensuring they are included in general education classes. This should be a critical focus of secondary educators and transition coordinators, given the research supporting more positive transition outcomes among students with disabilities who were included in general education. This chapter presented several different considerations and strategies for both embedding transition-specific content into general education classes, as well as facilitating the inclusion of students in academic classes through strategies like UDL. Specific examples for embedding transition-focused content and activities within general education classes were also presented. Increasing your awareness of the evidence-based practices for including all students is a very important first step. In addition to using this chapter as a guide, consider perusing the resources presented in Table 7.3. All these resources expand on information discussed in this chapter and offer further information and strategies related to inclusion and embedding transition within academics.

Keep in mind that all of your efforts to increase student learning will set a positive and strong trajectory for what your students will be able to accomplish as they transition into the next stage of their life after school and beyond. The following chapters delve into how to help students achieve positive post-school outcomes, including employment, postsecondary education, independent living, and meaningful social relationships.

**Table 7.3.** Further resources on inclusion and embedding transition skills into academic content

| Web site | Description |
|---|---|
| Common Core State Standards (CCSS) Initiative www.corestandards.org | This web site provides a list of all of the Common Core State Standards. Standards can be searched by content area and grade level. The web site also provides an overview of the process used to develop the CCSS in addition to other CCSS related resources. |
| CCSS Application to Students with Disabilities www.corestandards.org/assets/application-to-students-with-disabilities.pdf | Document describing how the CCSS apply to students with disabilities. |
| Dynamic Learning Maps—Essential Elements http://dynamiclearningmaps.org/content/essential-elements | This web site lists and describes the essential elements, which are statements of knowledge and skills that are tied to grade level standards in the common core. |
| Center for Parent Information and Resources www.parentcenterhub.org/repository/accommodations/#part1 | Description and definition of supports, modifications, and accommodations for students with disabilities. Further examples of commonly used modifications and accommodations are also listed. |
| Assistive Technology and Secondary Transition Annotated Bibliography http://nsttac.org/content/assistive-technology-and-secondary-transition-annotated-bibliography | Annotated bibliography designed to provide an overview of research that has been conducted related to assistive technology and transition. |
| Assistive Technology and Transition www.transitioncoalition.org/wp-content/originalSiteAssets/files/docs/attransitionpacket1224259340.pdf | Wisconsin procedural guidelines for using assistive technology in the transition process. |

# 8

# Preparing for Employment and Career Development

Anne is a 17-year-old high school student with an emotional disability. She spent time in a residential setting at the beginning of the year, but is now back in her local high school. Anne loves animals, and after completing a comprehensive transition assessment and online career interest inventories, she has decided that she would like to pursue veterinary science as either a technician or a veterinarian. She would like to gain some experience first to determine if she likes all aspects of the job; however, Anne will most likely require support for her emotional disability as she begins to engage in work-based experiences. When she misunderstands something someone tells her, she often refuses to speak, may not complete her tasks, or leaves the setting without permission. In middle school she became physically aggressive when she felt she was being pushed too far. It will therefore be necessary for Anne and her team to find a job placement related to her interests while supporting her emotional and behavioral needs.

Secondary special educators and transition specialists are often involved in career development efforts for students with disabilities like Anne who may be facing unique personal challenges. Career planning and experiences have always been a component of transition programs for students with disabilities, with participation in work-based learning as one of the most significant predictors for employment success (Luecking, 2009; Wagner, Newman, Cameto, Levine, & Garza, 2006; NSTTAC, 2011). Studies have indicated that work experience can be beneficial (Wagner, Newman, Cameto, Levine, & Garza, 2006; Wehmeyer & Palmer, 2003) and that having a paid position prior to exiting high school is a powerful indicator of employment after high school (Carter et al., 2012). However, while opportunities to work in the community can open the door for students to be prepared for employment after high school, more is needed to truly be career-ready. As a result, districts should offer comprehensive career development programs that provide both school- and work-based learning experiences for students with disabilities.

This chapter will offer several important reasons for why effective career and employment programs can support a wide range of students with disabilities and will emphasize the positive employment outcomes associated with high-quality work-based learning.

Examples of effective career development programs, resources, and materials will be provided, and evidence-based models of inclusive school- and work-based learning will be presented. Finally, you will learn about coordinating student progress through the phases of career development. The Chapter 8 Appendix also includes a helpful collection of forms that may be used in your career development program.

## GETTING STARTED: Planning for Careers

Anne's experience is typical for many juniors in high school: choosing a career goal, wanting some experience in the career area to see if it is the right choice, and so on. Anne, like many students with disabilities, may need more support than her typically developing peers to be successful in an employment setting. Throughout this chapter, many terms associated with employment will be used—career, work, job—yet these varied terms all share common defining characteristics. For most adults, employment is a critical aspect of daily life, taking up more than one-half of their day. Whether it is a full-time job, part-time job, career opportunity, or seasonal experience, employment offers individuals opportunities to socialize; enhance their current skills; increase their financial and emotional stability; and gain a sense of inclusion, camaraderie, and pride (Wehman, Brooke, & Revell, 2007). Employment in any form is a natural component of being an adult in our society and allows people the opportunity for advancement and financial growth, as well as increased self-confidence and self-esteem. Being valued in a job and recognizing that one's skills are important and useful can have a significant influence on an individual's well-being. When researchers surveyed over 1,200 adults with disabilities about what they would change in their adult life, more than 40% reported a strong desire to obtain a better, more satisfying job (Repetto et al., 2011). Working toward a meaningful career should therefore remain a consistent post-school goal for high school students with disabilities.

Career development focuses instruction on long-term careers through the development of career awareness and exploration, career preparation, integrated coursework, and meaningful community-based work experiences related to the student's targeted career interests (National Alliance for Secondary Education and Transition, 2010). This model begins with assessing the student's career interest areas, preferences regarding working conditions, capabilities, and current experiences. Then, it aligns these assessment domains with related career exploration opportunities. Career development also provides skill-based instruction in areas such as completing a job application, preparing for an interview, and learning the social aspects of different career choices. Career development programs should ultimately lead to quality work-based opportunities for students that arise from their developing career awareness, exposure, and experiences.

### Effective Career Development: An Evidence-Based Practice for All Students

So, what makes a career development program effective and comprehensive? The most effective programs focus on providing both school-based learning experiences, such as classes, advising periods, and career-related extracurricular activities; and work-based learning experiences that are formally tied to school programs, such as industry-based internships, school-business partnerships, and summer work programs. The importance of providing youth with disabilities with effective career development and quality work experiences prior to exiting special education is well-established. Research has shown that work experiences have been described as a critical factor leading to successful post-school outcomes for students with disabilities (McConnell et al., 2013; Test, Fowler et al., 2009).

The types of career development and transition services that students with disabilities receive while in school particularly influence their long-term employment outcomes. We know that students with disabilities who have experienced employment and work-based learning during high school have a greater chance of obtaining paid integrated employment as an adult (Carter, Austin, & Trainor, 2012; Flexer, Daviso, Baer, Queen, & Meindl, 2011; Lindstrom, Dorien, & Meisch, 2011). Yet in spite of all this promising evidence, the overall employment rate for young adults with disabilities remains below the rate of their peers without disabilities (Repetto et al., 2011; Wagner & Newman, 2012; Wehman, Brooke, & Revell, 2007). Why? Given the employment disparities among adults with disabilities and same-aged peers without disabilities, we need to ask, "What is missing for students with disabilities?" Most often this comes down to comprehensive career development and experiences if students are to be successfully employed (Luecking, 2009).

Unfortunately, not all students with disabilities participate in school- or work-based learning during high school. In fact, one study found that among all of the high schools surveyed in one state, less than half (49%) offered work-based courses such as internships and work experiences (Guy, Sitlington, Larsen, & Frank, 2009). In addition, almost 75% of the career courses that were offered were classroom-based only, with less than 20% of classes including a combination of school- and work-based learning opportunities.

It is also possible that the type of employment coursework provided does not adequately prepare students for the varying demands of an adult career setting. This was noted by Guy and colleagues (2009) when they found that for the most part, classroom-based courses focused mostly on teaching technical skills with very few designed to offer "employability" or career readiness skills, such as those identified by the U.S. Department of Labor as "21st century" skills (e.g., work ethic, communication, problem solving). Even when students do learn some soft and job-specific skills through part-time or summer employment, these entry-level jobs are often inadequate in preparing students for full-time adult employment. Explicit engagement in career development experiences is often more essential for future success.

## TIP FOR TRANSITION: Skills to Pay the Bills

The U.S. Department of Labor, Office of Disability Employment Policy, created a free curriculum that was designed in collaboration with over 100 youth with disabilities. *Skills to Pay the Bills* teaches the basics of the "soft skills" needed to succeed in the workplace, including communication, professionalism, attitude, teamwork, networking, problem solving, and critical thinking. The curriculum is designed for use with students who are 14 to 21 years old and focuses on introducing essential work-related skills to youth. Remember, teaching students soft skills in a classroom will not be enough; this curriculum was designed to introduce, develop, refine, practice, and reinforce these critical soft skills throughout a student's high school years. The curriculum, video, and other helpful materials can be downloaded at www.dol.gov/odep/topics/youth/softskills.

Because employment clearly affects a person's future well-being and happiness, there is a clear imperative to help your students prepare for careers and make informed, meaningful career choices. What does this mean for you as a transition specialist? In your work supporting students to transition to adulthood, you should first examine current vocational and career programs and then enhance them to incorporate a comprehensive career development focus. A well-established, comprehensive career development program can provide you with the necessary structure to put evidence-based programs and practices into place that increase your students' chances for career success. In this chapter, you will learn how secondary educators and transition coordinators can make this kind of program a reality in the schools where they work. First, let's learn about the various stages of career development that you should consider when planning for your students.

## The Stages of Career Development

The stages of career development provide guidance on how students can identify and explore careers in which they may be interested. These include:

1. Career awareness: often begins in preschool, continuing through middle school, and focuses on discovering the existence of work, jobs, and careers.

2. Career exploration: usually begins in elementary school and continues throughout high school, where students learn about various aspects of work-related skills and the range of career pathways and postsecondary requirements.

3. Career preparation: becomes the focus during high school, when students begin to learn career-specific and work-related skills through on-the-job experiences and through planning for postsecondary education and training.

4. Career assimilation: most often occurs post-high school when young adults begin to work and understand career advancement or changing jobs within a career.

Students with and without disabilities begin learning about and exploring various jobs in their schools, neighborhoods, and most importantly, with their families, much earlier than high school. Often, elementary school lays the foundation for the first stage of career development: career awareness. In elementary school, jobs and careers are often learned incidentally through family and neighborhood experiences. In middle school, the focus shifts from awareness to career exploration, such as volunteering in school and in the community, touring businesses, and completing initial career interest inventories. In addition, during 8th grade some schools require that all students develop an individualized career plan where they start to map out a program of study for high school.

By high school, students should be planning and preparing for careers that match their strengths, preferences, and interests through a variety of experiences, including working part-time and enrolling in courses that align with a career pathway (e.g., health services, government and public administration, agriculture, food and natural resources). For more information about career pathways and clusters, be sure to visit the National Association of Career and Technical Education (www.careertech.org/career-clusters), as well as your state's CTE division, usually an office within the state Department of Education. Students can also enroll in elective courses focused more specifically on career development, work-based learning, and community work experiences.

### TIP FOR TRANSITION: Individualize Career Development

You can include career development activities in existing courses to be more individualized. For example, rather than having students fill out a sample job application, you can have students complete an actual online application for a job aligned with their career interests.

It will be much more relevant and motivating to them to apply the skills they are learning to real-life situations. You can reinforce interview skills as part of a career class by having employers role play with students with real interview questions. In a recent project, a career counselor worked with students with autism to film and evaluate a mock job interview. Once they evaluated their own interview, they then learned about and created a video illustrating their best interview skills. Then, they participated in a second mock interview, and their ratings nearly doubled across most of the interview skills areas (Munandar, 2016). This was a unique way to use video modeling for job interviews. A great way to generalize these skills would be to interview with an employer for a work-based internship or community work experience.

Students with disabilities may or may not have the same experiences as is typical for students without disabilities, and may not sequentially move through the stages of career development. Where students are in the career development process often depends upon their early experiences. If families are highly engaged with career development, youth may enter high school more prepared. This may include simple and informal experiences learning about family members' jobs, as families are often early role models for students with disabilities (Morningstar, 1997). Others with more significant disabilities may not be as prepared because of barriers associated with their disability. They may need more rigorous and intensive career development experiences. For Anne, much of her elementary experiences were focused on stabilizing her behaviors. The school prioritized behavioral goals and, as a result, she did not experience some of the career awareness activities that were occurring (e.g., trips to local businesses, volunteering, business mentors tutoring students). If she had had such exposure earlier, perhaps more information about her interest in animal care would have been available when she entered middle and high school. However, it certainly isn't too late for Anne to catch up. As a junior, she has been researching and exploring her interest areas, and this will help her launch her career preparation.

It may be overwhelming for you to think about how early a quality career development program begins, but it is never too late to start! The research is pretty clear: As long as students with disabilities experience high-quality career development opportunities, they are more likely to be successful in a post-high school setting, whether it be attending a postsecondary training or educational setting or going right to work. In the Making it Happen section next, you will learn about several strategies to assist you in building and/or improving a comprehensive career development system.

##  MAKING IT HAPPEN:
## Buiilding a Quality Career-Development Program

As a transition specialist or secondary educator, your role should be to support and enhance career development for your students. First, it is important to understand the big picture and all of the necessary elements that lead to career development before you can start enhancing your program. Figure 8.1 provides an overview of the components of a school-sponsored career development program for students with disabilities. In this model, the curricular and instructional elements are organized under school- and work-based learning. Recall that career development programs begin with an assessment process to discover student interests and preferences so as to develop an individualized career plan for each student. School-based learning immerses students in coursework, extracurricular activities, career education programs, school-based enterprises, and service learning to enhance career awareness and exploration, and help students acquire important skills.

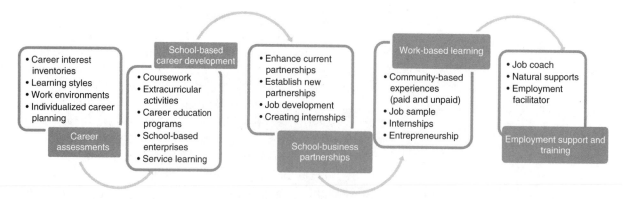

**Figure 8.1.** Essential components of career development programs.

Through developing school-business partnerships, effective career development programs also offer a variety of work-based learning opportunities for students within the community, including paid and unpaid jobs, internships, and entrepreneurship. Finally, career development programs should provide students with the necessary training and supports for success. Several steps and strategies can help in achieving this kind of career development model, beginning with establishing a collaborative career development team.

## Coordinate a District-Wide Career Development Team

Given what we know about how early career development actually starts, transition specialists should consider working with the administration to coordinate a district-wide career development planning team. The members of this team can include general education and career/technical education program coordinators, guidance and career counselors, and special education transition and work experience coordinators. The district team should focus on career development in elementary, middle, and high school in order to design a comprehensive program (Evers, Beckman, & Owens, 2012).

Meeting regularly will allow the team to first communicate and evaluate the current status of career development activities throughout the district. Once the team has a solid understanding of the range of career activities, experiences, and programs, you can then identify critical areas for improvement. This may include discussions about school-based learning and coursework, community work experiences and internships, and extracurricular activities that focus on career-related experiences. It is important to recognize that at any level of implementing a career development program, whether classroom-based or districtwide, you will be shifting from merely assisting your students in finding a part-time job to guiding them through a student-centered career interest program providing more beneficial and lifelong experiences.

## Build Programs Aligned With the Components of Career Development

You can help ensure school-sponsored career readiness by aligning your program with the five essential components of career development as depicted in Figure 8.1: 1) career assessment, 2) school-based career development, 3) school-business partnerships, 4) work-based learning, and 5) employment support and training. Let's think about Anne's career experiences through the lens of these five components. She has been able to begin her career planning by completing several career assessments that helped her identify her interests, her preferences for types of working conditions, how she learns best, what her work styles might include, and some of her volunteer experiences. As far as school courses, she plans to enroll in a more general transition and career elective, and perhaps then could enroll in a career and technical education pathway associated with animal care. The school has reached out to some new school-business partnerships and has some worksites with mentors who might be a good match for Anne. These partnerships will help to establish a possible work-based learning opportunity for Anne in the area of animal care. Anne will need support in this new work setting, especially at first, so establishing a strong partnership with the business where Anne will be trying out jobs will be critical. Anne's experiences help illustrate the benefits of the career development process, which can be individualized to meet each student's personal desires, goals, and hopes for the future.

***Career Assessment***    Assessment occurs at the start of the career planning process, but is ongoing because students will alter their preferences based on their experiences and expanding knowledge of careers. Career assessments should be systematic and ongoing to help educators, adult service providers, students, and parents understand career preferences. Assessments take many forms, and not all are paper and pencil tests. They may include observations, anecdotal information, on-the-job tryouts, classroom performance, tests, and work samples. Through the assessment process, parents and professionals learn about the student, and the student learns about himself or herself. Students generally emerge from the career assessment process with increased self-awareness and a better understanding of their skills.

One type of assessment frequently used is the career interest inventory. Most career interest inventories are based on Holland's theory of matching a person's work personality types to certain work environments (Holland, 1997). Most often, career inventories assess the student's interests and propensity toward six common types of work personalities (realistic, investigative, artistic, social, enterprising, and conventional), which are then matched to corresponding occupational environments. Once a student gets a score, he or she can then choose from among a wide range of careers that most closely align with their interests. Then students can begin to research educational and job requirements, as well as working conditions.

## TIP FOR TRANSITION: Use the O*NET Resource Center

The O*NET Resource Center at www.onetcenter.org is a web site sponsored by the U.S. Department of Labor that provides a wide range of free career information, assessments, and videos. Students discover occupations by taking the online *Interest Profiler, Ability Profiler*, and *Work Importance Profiler*. If they already have an occupation in mind, they can learn more about it from the My Next Move web site. My Next Move is an interactive tool where students can explore over 900 careers and learn about the skills, tasks, salaries, and employment projections. A partner web site is the Career One Stop (www.careeronestop.org), which has a video library of over 500 careers organized by the 16 career clusters. The up-to-date videos can help your students "see" jobs and careers they may not know about. These videos are also narrated in Spanish.

There is a wide range of career interest inventories available and you will want to consider how you might need to make necessary accommodations to these assessments for students with different learning needs. Some career assessments have been developed specifically for students with disabilities, especially for students with more significant disabilities.

**Table 8.1.**　Informal career assessments

| Name | Purpose/administration | What it measures |
|---|---|---|
| Picture Interest Career Survey (PICS) | Uses pictures to help students select career interests; appropriate for nonreaders or low-level readers. Test taker is presented with three pictures and chooses the one in which they are most interested. Thirty-six sets of pictures are included. Can be self-administered and self-scored. | A career profile of interests is created based on Holland's six career personalities: realistic, investigative, artistic, social, enterprising, conventional. |
| Job Knowledge Scale | Uses responses to 60 true/false statements to discover job search skills needed to find a job. Includes guidance on job search methods and includes room for developing job search goals. | Assesses knowledge in these areas: how to identify job leads, how to apply for jobs, how to write resumes and cover letters, interview skills, and following up after an interview. |
| Your Employment Selection | Includes full-motion online video clips of jobs, allowing students with limited reading to watch videos, listen to descriptions, and select preferred jobs from among 120 different jobs. Students first select preferred work environments; based on this process, they then view 20 jobs matching these preferences and make additional selections. | Shows 2- to 4-minute video clips of the critical tasks involved in particular jobs. Students can review jobs either by work conditions (e.g., inside vs. outside jobs, jobs that involve working alone or working with others), or by job tasks (e.g., use of computers or heavy equipment; animal care). For each job, students can click for more information. |
| Career Interests, Preferences, and Strengths Inventory (CIPSI) | This is an informal assessment for middle school to high school students. Students identify personal interests for careers. | Careers are aligned to the U.S. Department of Education 16 career clusters. |
| Informal Assessments for Transition: Employment and Career Planning | Includes over 60 easy-to-use informal assessments that provide focused data related to careers and employment. Most are paper-and-pencil or interview-style. Assessment can be completed on paper or on the computer. Reports are generated linking student interests and strengths to career information for further exploration. | Four assessment areas critical to transition planning and decision making are included: 1) interests and preferences, 2) abilities and skills, 3) career exploration, and 4) job search. |

A great place to find a variety of formal and informal career assessments for students with disabilities is on the Transition Coalition web site, under Assessment Reviews (www.transitioncoalition.org). These assessments have been reviewed and rated by other practitioners. The list of assessments includes those to purchase, as well as free and online options. Table 8.1 provides examples of several available informal career assessments, with a brief description of how they are administered and what they measure.

As a result of a continual assessment process, by a student's senior year in high school, a comprehensive career portfolio should be completed that showcases the student's interests and preferences, experiences, educational plans, and choices for future careers. If started in 9th grade, a career portfolio can prompt the students, teachers, and family to consider important career development action steps. The format and content will vary, with some portfolios set up in binders and others being digital. Examples of different types of portfolios can be found on the web site Life After IEPs (http://lifeafterieps.com/transition-portfolios). Anne could benefit from a career portfolio as she begins looking for work experiences in the field of veterinary science, especially because she has had little opportunity to research and explore her career area of interest. The portfolio would guide her in collecting information about herself, as well as provide insight into the working conditions of different types of veterinary jobs. It can also provide her with information about her preferred working conditions and support needs. Having this information will help her stay current with her career pathway of interest and help her make decisions about the career she truly wants.

**School-Based Career Development**    School-based career exploration takes into account specific skills needed for certain career pathways and also helps establish workplace "soft skills." Developing soft skills is important because they facilitate social inclusion of students with disabilities. We know that this is an essential reason most people keep jobs—the strong workplace relationships that develop with co-workers and supervisors. In addition, employers have indicated that certain skills are essential when working in today's industries: communication, enthusiasm and attitude, teamwork, networking, problem solving and critical thinking, and professionalism (Office of Disability Policy, n.d.). The good news is that focusing on soft skills can take place throughout a student's day in school, whether that is during academic classes or more specific career or transition elective classes. An important element of teaching soft skills is making sure you help students connect the dots back to employment. For example, Anne has been learning effective social problem solving so that she is able to control her frustration levels, which is not only beneficial in her classes, but also essential for her future. It is important to help Anne see the connection between these skills and the successful navigation of daily responsibilities and pressures, especially those that occur on the job.

**Career-Focused Classes**    Career or transition classes are often created just for students with disabilities as electives so they can focus more specifically on career development. However, before you create a new class, carefully examine what is currently offered in your high school. It could be that a much more inclusive approach would be to enhance an existing class, such as an advisory period, that includes students with and without disabilities. What high school student doesn't need to develop and enhance his or her soft skills? Check with your high school or district guidance and counseling department to find out if they offer any electives or special classes that you can co-teach.

Once you identify the best and most inclusive approach to supporting school-based career development, you can begin to plan the most critical content to teach. Typically, courses include career assessments so students identify their strengths, preferences, and needs. In addition, the class time emphasizes the soft skills we talked about earlier. There are some excellent resources available to support and enhance a focus on soft skills, including the curriculum associated with *Skills to Pay the Bills* on the U.S. Department of Labor web site (www.dol.gov/odep/topics/youth/softskills). For each of the six soft skills (communication, enthusiasm and attitude, teamwork, networking, problem solving and critical thinking, and professionalism), specific lessons and activities are offered. The lesson plan ideas found in Table 8.2 offer examples of strategies you can embed across school programs and grade levels.

Another excellent resource is found on the Utah Education Network, in the Utah K-12 Core Lesson Plans for Career and Technical Education/Work-based Learning (www.uen.org/Lessonplan/LPview.cgi?core=1211). This web site provides a variety of activities and lessons that align with many of the critical soft skills we have talked about. Finally, the Perkins Collaborative Resource Network describes an *Employability Skills Framework* that offers a variety of lesson plans for developing employability skills in the classroom (http://cte.ed.gov/employabilityskills).

**Community Experiences While Still in School**    Be sure to think about how students can apply the work-related skills they are learning during their school-based experiences. Before students fully engage in community-based work experiences, there are ways you can incorporate real-life experiences and practice into their lives. Being able to tie lessons to

**Table 8.2.**   Career development lesson plan ideas

| Lesson | Skill | Questions or activities |
|---|---|---|
| Choosing careers | Teaching students to identify their interests, experiences, and abilities. | **Questions**<br>• What am I interested in?<br>• Do my abilities match my interests?<br>• What volunteer experiences do I have?<br>• What job experiences do I have?<br>• Do I have the necessary skills for the career I am interested in?<br><br>**Activities**<br>• Complete a career interest inventory.<br>• Organize high-interest areas by careers you like.<br>• Tour and job shadow in businesses related to your career interests.<br>• Research technical schools and colleges to determine training requirements. |
| Gaining work experience | Providing opportunities for students to participate in work experiences during high school. | **Questions**<br>• How many work experiences can I participate in?<br>• What businesses in my community offer the career I am interested in?<br>• What employability skills do I need experience with (social skills, communication, taking initiative, self-management, etc.)?<br>• What type of help will I need at my job to be successful?<br>• Do I have a resume? If not, who can help me create one?<br><br>**Activities**<br>• Participate in a work experience course.<br>• Meet weekly with your employer and teacher to evaluate skills.<br>• Set goals to continue to improve employability skills.<br>• Ask employer if you can shadow various jobs at job site. |
| Developing a career portfolio | Compiling a comprehensive career portfolio with your students. | **Questions**<br>• Have I organized my experiences, both volunteer and paid, by the career areas I have chosen?<br>• What training options match the careers I have chosen and the experiences I have gained?<br>• What job skills have I mastered, and what skills do I still need to develop?<br>• How do I use all of this information to make my resume up to date and ready to be given to an employer?<br><br>**Activities**<br>• Inventory skills attempted and mastered, as well as goals set and completed.<br>• List skills that still need assistance.<br>• Organize researched training options by match to careers and preferences for postsecondary environments.<br>• Organize work experiences by match to careers and postsecondary training options.<br>• Compile list of future employers to consider for career experiences. |

*Source:* Evers et al. (2012).

authentic, realistic situations and problems helps students learn what skills work best so they are more likely to apply successful solutions in the future. Offering opportunities to visit and try out jobs at least one day a week as part of a careers course is ideal, especially for younger students who may not be as likely to be working. Many schools support job shadow programs that allow students to first identify careers of interest to them and then to go visit a job site to learn about particular occupations and jobs within that career pathway. Even if you cannot get out into community settings, a virtual job shadow may encourage and promote student learning (see www.virtualjobshadow.com). Other programs bring employers into school to share information about potential careers or invite business volunteers to hold mock interviews and other job-related skill development activities.

Career development doesn't happen exclusively in courses. For many students, extracurricular activities, clubs, and service associations all promote and support school-based career development. This may include career-related student organizations such as DECA,

Future Business Leaders of America, and National FFA (see www2.ed.gov/about/offices/list/ovae/pi/cte/vso.html).

*School-Based Enterprises*        Many innovative schools have started school-based enterprises to reinforce work-related skill development in a real-world context. A school-based enterprise is a student-run business, most often conducted within a school. It is designed to replicate a specific business or segment of an industry. School-based enterprises are effective educational tools in helping prepare students for the transition from school to work or college (Gugerty, Foley, & Frank, 2008). For many students, they may provide a first work experience; for others, they provide opportunities to learn applied academic skills and build management, supervision, and leadership skills. When operating a school-based enterprise, make sure students have high levels of involvement in all aspects of the business—from budgeting, to ordering supplies, to customer service and sales. Often the business provides a service or sells a product just within the school, such as a coffee shop in the cafeteria or a student store selling snacks and school materials (to see a school-based enterprise in action, check out this video of a real-life, student-run coffee shop, The Crow's Nest, at https://youtu.be/g6rTMA7jLZc). Some school-based enterprises have expanded to the broader community, such as a catering business for community events. Start by building a team and bringing students, parents, and community leaders to the table. Explore viable business ideas and search for seed money.

*School-Business Partnerships*        As you develop and improve your school-based career development program, you will want to consider school-business partnerships. Often, work experience or vocational programs have established partnerships with businesses in the community where students can gain work-based experiences. Because your school likely already has partnerships with businesses in your community, finding job sites may not be a formidable challenge in and of itself. However, as you shift to a career development approach, the student's interests should be driving the work experience options, which may require you to expand your business partnerships and create new partnerships. Other educators may teach in smaller communities or may not have started a school-business partnership program yet. In all cases, you will need to make a concerted effort to develop partnerships with your students' unique career goals foremost in mind. New partnerships should be regularly developed that increase the opportunities available to your students.

## TIP FOR TRANSITION: **The Fine Art of Networking**

Networking involves having your current, successful business partnerships assist in expanding your list of community work settings. It will require you to ASK, ASK, ASK the right questions. Ask, and it is likely you shall receive, especially if you choose the right people. First, meet with three to five currently supportive businesses with successful partnerships with your school or district. Remember, these can be partnerships of any type, not just those involving work-based learning opportunities. Find out from your district where there are existing partnerships, such as businesses whose employees volunteer time or materials to the school. Starting with those businesses that are already committed to a school is a great way to begin. Then, ask some important questions:

- Ask if they are concerned about the workforce in your community and whether they are willing to assist the school to build essential workplace soft skills.

**Table 8.3.** Guide for expanding and improving your school-business partnerships

| Partnership steps | Questions to ask | Special considerations |
|---|---|---|
| 1. Know about your community. | • Is your community primarily a professional career economy, a technically skilled career economy, an industrial economy, or a combination of these?<br>• What concerns do employers have about workplace skills for teenagers and young adults?<br>• Does the business community want to participate in improving entry-level skills? | • Consider expanding relationships employers already may have with your school district through STEM (Science, Technology, Engineering, and Math) alliances, vocational/technical programs (e.g., building trades, culinary), or current work experience sites.<br>• Check whether your district already supports a school-business partnership program, even if it is not employment-focused. That is a good first step.<br>• Form a school-business advisory group of business organizations (e.g., Chamber of Commerce) and private employers to help you develop your program. |
| 2. Narrow choices and set up meetings with employers. | At the meeting, ask:<br>• What are the various jobs available?<br>• What are the physical and task-specific demands of each job?<br>• What are the duties and expectations? | • Make sure to sell your program while also accurately describing its purpose and the benefits to the student, employer, and community workforce.<br>• Emphasize the supports your program can provide to make a job placement successful (e.g., job coaching, weekly evaluations). |
| 3. Encourage the employer. Once placement occurs, encourage employer to become more than just a job site. | • Ask the employer to be a presenter in a careers class.<br>• Invite the employer to participate in the local community transition council or team that supports transition efforts for all young adults with disabilities. | • Establish a mentoring/community service program between their employees and your student for tutoring assistance or goal-setting experience. Many businesses have mentoring or community service programs as part of their long-range goals. |

*Source:* Morningstar, Gaumer-Erickson, Lattin, & Wilkerson (2012).

- Ask if they are aware of other businesses that may be interested in partnering with the school.

- Ask if they would be willing to reach out to those businesses on the program's behalf or be a reference when you contact the business.

- Ask if they are interested in having a potential new business owner come and observe the work program in action at their place of business. (Morningstar, Gaumer-Erickson, Lattin, & Wilkerson, 2012)

A step-by-step guide outlined in Table 8.3 provides you with details for how to establish new school-business partnerships that expand your current career program's connections. All of these recommendations lead to valuable school-business partnerships for you, but even more importantly, a better career development experience for your students. Having work-based opportunities and developing a career portfolio, including a resume of unpaid internships and paid work, results from career assessments, and recommendations from business mentors, can be the keys to a successful transition to employment for your students.

***Career Exploration in Work-Based Experiences***    Work-based learning is a supervised program sponsored by an education or training organization that links knowledge gained at the worksite with a planned program of study. The experiences range in intensity, structure, and scope and include activities such as field trips, job shadowing, paid and unpaid internships, on-the-job training, and apprenticeships. Work-based learning helps students to gain basic workplace skills (including teamwork, communication, problem solving, customer service, and social etiquette skills), learn about specific occupational skills, and develop an understanding of different industries in order to make informed career choices (National Collaborative on Workforce and Disability for Youth, n.d.; www.ncwd-youth.info/work-based-learning).

These programs make a difference for students with and without disabilities! We know that when students have an opportunity to engage in community work-based learning they are more likely to:

- Be motivated to stay in school and graduate.

- See the relevance of learning to postsecondary and career goals.

- Gain access to adult role models and mentors who may be important, especially for youth at risk of dropping out.

- Improve their overall career awareness, leading to more specific and realistic postsecondary goals.

- Earn income that may be critical to supporting them to remain in school.

There are a wide variety of ways schools can support work-based learning, starting with less intensive opportunities in elementary school, such as career days or having employers as guest speakers. These typically do not cost you or your school much or require a substantial amount of your time to set up. More intensive experiences should be occurring by the time students are in high school. See Table 8.4 for a list of possible work-based experiences organized by stage of career development.

As you consider expanding or developing new work experiences, think about what we know leads to quality work experiences. First, positive partnerships between the school and participating businesses are essential. The business community sees this partnership as a way to help develop an educated and well-qualified workforce rather than as a way to find student workers. Be sure to connect with your students to help them translate their community work experiences into career self-knowledge (e.g., employability skills, attitudes, knowledge) so that work-based opportunities are about more than just acquiring job-specific skills.

As you now know, success is less about specific job skills and more about the soft skills. Cultivate on-the-job adult role models and mentors for students, and make sure that students are involved in meaningful work roles and learning about the industry. Facilitate social inclusion so students may form appropriate workplace relationships with co-workers and supervisors. Such an effort goes beyond social activities on the job (e.g., taking breaks, participating in parties at work) and includes making sure that students are working well with their co-workers by providing opportunities for collaboration. As

**Table 8.4.** Career development and work-based experiences

| Career awareness | Career exploration | Career preparation |
|---|---|---|
| · Field trips | · Mentorships | · Career and tech ed classes |
| · Guest speakers | · Job shadowing | · Job training |
| · Career fairs | · Transition/Career class | · Work-study program |
| · Career days | · Career research | · Internships |
| · Career assessment | · Course projects | · Apprenticeships |
| | · Individual career plans | · Paid employment |
| | · School-based enterprise | · Cooperative vocational education |

*Source:* Morningstar, Gaumer-Erickson, Lattin, & Wilkerson (2012).

always, be sure to link school-based learning across disciplines. This is especially important when connecting what students learn in school with their work-based experiences. Access to AT and appropriate adaptations on the job will also increase the likelihood of success. Following are some general guidelines for ensuring that students are engaged in work-based learning, throughout their school experiences, organized by grade level:

- 8th or 9th grade: Set up job shadows for students to observe and interview workers in careers of their choice.

- 10th grade: Coordinate volunteer explorations and encourage enrollment in career courses in your students' career interest areas.

- 11th grade: Establish community-based work experiences that can be tied to careers classes in school or more time-intensive internships or apprenticeships while students are still taking classes.

- 12th grade: Students should pursue a part-time job to earn spending money and learn basic job skills that they will use for life. This part-time job is not likely the career that your students will have for their adult lives, but it will provide them with the foundation to be an acceptable and employable individual as they begin their career pathway.

***Employment Support and Training***      When students are ready to engage in work-based learning, a well-designed model of support for each student's success is needed. An employment support model must reinforce the lessons students learned in their career coursework, as well as support the students to become independent employees on the job. A quality employment support model aligns the student's interests and desire to be independent with school-business partnership goals (Wehman, Brooks-Lane, Brooke, & Turner, 2007). Two important areas are required for successful job placement training and supports: natural supports and systematic instruction.

*Identifying Natural Supports on the Job*      At the start of a job placement, work experience programs may assign a job coach or employment specialist to provide support on the job site. A job coach can be a resource for a student and facilitate his or her success on the job. The intended goal should be to enhance the student's independence and performance by providing instruction and accommodations, collecting data, and monitoring progress. At the same time, the job coach or employment specialist must ensure that the employer's perspectives and needs are considered. Job coaches must balance their time between consulting with and supporting the business and other co-workers while also providing systematic instruction for the student.

A job coach can provide both direct and indirect support to the student and employer on the job site (Wehman, Inge, Revell, & Brooke, 2007). Direct support enhances the student's work speed and work quality and assists in generalizing skills across various job tasks. Providing direct support is often the dominant role job coaches assume. However, providing indirect support is more critical, as it leads to the emergence of natural supports that the students can utilize on the job, such as assistance and encouragement from co-workers. The importance of natural supports is essential; in fact, if the culture of the work setting is one that discourages supportive co-workers, it most likely will not be a positive work environment for your students. In fact, many strong programs encourage natural supports and frequently will train and support co-workers who will assist the student. Some areas you should consider when supporting students in work experiences include the following:

1. Natural supports within the workplace: Identify and engage co-workers in training and other types of assistance.

2. Student communication and advocacy: Watch for the student's authentic experiences with the employer or co-workers and encourage student's effective communication and self-advocacy skills.

3. Expanding the student's job duties: Consider tasks that can be added to the student's responsibilities to expand his or her independence and experiences.

4. Supporting co-workers: Model positive and natural interactions with the student to co-workers, teaching them how to motivate and reinforce the student on the job (Morningstar, Gaumer-Erickson, Lattin, & Wilkerson, 2012).

*Systematic Instruction*     Even before a student is placed in a work experience, you should visit the job site and complete an ecological inventory of the job site, often called a job analysis (see the job analysis form in the Chapter 8 Appendix). The job analysis will identify the sequence of tasks to be completed and help you get an overall feel for the workplace. The purpose of the job analysis is to provide consistent, organized skill training and facilitate natural supports. Once the job analysis form is completed, you may need to collect baseline data comparing the student's ability to complete required tasks and job responsibilities with on-the-job task requirements. This will help you decide how best to train the student and also what job responsibilities may need to be modified. If you do need to modify a job sequence, try to keep it as natural as possible, deviating as little from the natural sequence of steps as you can. For example, if the student cannot remember the sequence of job duties, you may need to develop a way to support him or her. This might include a written list, photos, assignment board, or flowchart. Choose the method that will be least intrusive for your student in the work setting.

Before the student starts the job, you should also have worked out whether the student will need a co-worker mentor or any other needed supports and have these designated and ready for when the student begins working. You might hold an orientation for your student, similar to orientations other employees receive, and perhaps provide some additional support. Acquaint the student with the new worksite, including all areas he or she will need to access (e.g., break room, bathroom). Review the work schedule, safety concerns, and make sure the student is introduced to key personnel. Regardless of support needs, the student should be treated the same as any other new employee.

## Meet the Requirements of a Work-Based Learning Program

Not only should a work-based learning program include all the components of a career development model (i.e., based upon student's interests and preferences, includes school-based learning and classes, supports positive school-business partnerships, and offers a range of work-based learning experiences), some additional considerations are also essential for a well-run program.

All community work-based learning programs should adhere to the guidelines required by the Fair Labor Standards Act (FLSA) Agreement for unpaid training sites. There are specific guidelines and procedures required in order to ensure that an unpaid training site is educational in nature and not a true employment relationship. Several excellent resources are available to ensure that you are in compliance with the FLSA Agreement. The main requirements that must be documented include:

- An IEP reflecting instruction and training goals and objectives relevant to the work-related training experience

- A written individual training agreement outlining the FLSA requirements and signed by all participants, along with attached individual training plan

- Records of student experience (i.e., log of hours spent in work-based learning activities, progress reports, observation reports, safety training, and performance evaluations)

The Chapter 8 Appendix provides some helpful forms and agreements that you might use as part of a compliant and effective work-based learning program. Further resources, including a handbook that describes all of the FLSA requirements and a webinar outlining the procedures, are also listed at the end of this chapter.

## WHAT YOU CAN DO RIGHT NOW:
### Putting Ideas Into Action

Work experience programs and vocational coursework have existed in most high schools for decades, yet within the last 5 to 10 years a shift has occurred from simply finding a job for students with disabilities to increasing awareness and exploration of careers that match students' interests and preferences. As you build a quality transition program for your students with disabilities, it is important to determine whether you need to transfer to a progressive career development model, which establishes a career development plan based on students' interests and preferences, and then creates school-business partnerships that match those interests.

Embracing career development means you may need to shift your thinking from helping your students get "a job, any job" to ensuring they are college and career ready. It also starts with evaluating your current career development program. Figure 8.2 provides a checklist of essential career development activities, organized by grade level and aligned with the career development strategies discussed in this chapter. When you view and complete this student-centered checklist, keep in mind that these are suggested activities and that you may want to add in new experiences. You can personalize the checklist to meet the needs and experiences of your students and help you enhance and expand your current program's offerings. Another high quality resource to evaluate your current career development program is the *Guideposts for Success (2nd edition)*, developed by the National Collaborative on Workforce and Students with Disabilities (www.ncwd-youth.info/guideposts).

By starting to provide work-based learning activities and embed career awareness and career exploration coursework and experiences into each student's course of study, you will lay the foundation for a successful career development model. Such a model provides valuable career preparation for students with disabilities as they transition to adulthood and work toward their goal of achieving satisfying employment.

# A Checklist of Career Development Activities: What Your Students Should Be Doing Year By Year

| Grade | Career development activities |
|---|---|
| 9th | ❑ Student takes a career preparation course.<br>  ❑ Focuses on learning different career areas and the training and job requirements.<br>  ❑ Develops a career plan.<br>❑ Student completes career interest and working conditions inventories.<br>  ❑ Analyzes the inventories to determine if career interests match the working conditions associated with the career.<br>❑ Student attends field trips to local businesses to see first-hand the jobs onsite.<br>❑ Student participates in a mentorship program with a local business, if available.<br>❑ Student meets with case manager to create a measurable postsecondary goal for employment that aligns with career interests, preferences, experiences, and capabilities. |
| 10th | ❑ Student completes further career assessments and updates previous ones.<br>❑ Student participates in career explorations related *to his or her career interests.*<br>  ❑ Takes part in a job shadow for 1 day, 2 weeks during an academic seminar time, or a quarter if student's course load allows it.<br>  ❑ Completes the job shadow business' job application.<br>❑ Student takes a social skills class to learn the social aspects of job sites.<br>❑ Student attends college and career fairs at school.<br>  ❑ Representatives from apprenticeship programs and vocational/technical schools attend these, in addition to representatives from colleges.<br>❑ Student observes a vocational course in high school related to career interests.<br>  ❑ Determines if he or she can enroll in it for junior year.<br>❑ Student meets with case manager to update measurable postsecondary goal for employment. |
| 11th | ❑ Student updates career assessments and career plan.<br>❑ Student attends a work experience class that provides volunteer hours in businesses related to *student's career interests.*<br>  ❑ Attempts to rotate through two or three different businesses and different jobs at each business.<br>  ❑ Participates in mock interviews related to each of these jobs.<br>❑ Student participates in a vocational/technical course in high school related to career interests.<br>❑ Student seeks a part-time, after-school, or summer job in addition to volunteer experiences.<br>❑ Student meets with case manager to narrow career goals based on work experiences. |
| 12th | ❑ Student updates career assessments to narrow interests.<br>❑ Student considers dual enrollment at the community college or local technical school to participate in coursework aligned *with his or her career choices.*<br>❑ Student attends college and career fairs at school.<br>  ❑ Views college departments that align with chosen careers; determines the type of training provided.<br>❑ Students apply to a community college, 4-year college program, or vocational/technical school based on which one provides the program best suited to career interests, preferences, needs, and strengths.<br>  ❑ Education and training after high school is often necessary to obtain a career position.<br>❑ Student continues working a part-time job after school and in the summer.<br>❑ Student meets with case manager to prepare for what accommodations will be needed in a job setting.<br>  ❑ Assists with developing his or her Summary of Performance so that he or she is aware of the accommodations that will be helpful on the job. |

**Figure 8.2.**  A checklist of career development activities: What your students should be doing year by year.

## ONLINE RESOURCES

Transition Coalition Enhancing Employment Outcomes Online Module and the Assessment Reviews: www.transitioncoalition.org

Project Search: www.projectsearch.us/Home.aspx

Virginia Commonwealth University, Rehabilitation Research and Training Center: www.worksupport.com

National Collaborative on Workforce and Disability for Youth: www.ncwd-youth.info

National Technical Assistance Center for Transition: www.transitionta.org

Office of Disability Employment Policy, U.S. Department of Labor: www.dol.gov/odep

Virtual Job Shadow: www.virtualjobshadow.com

Dream it! Do it! Career Quiz: www.dreamit-doit.com/content/toolkit/quiz.php

Handbook for Implementing a Comprehensive Work-Based Learning Program According to the Fair Labor Standards Act (2005): www.ncset.org/publications/essentialtools/flsa/NCSET_EssentialTools_FLSA.pdf

Ensuring that Work-Based Learning for Students with Disabilities Aligns with the Fair Labor Standards Act Training Agreement (Webinar): www.transitioncoalition.org/transition/section.php?pageId=192

# Helpful Forms for Your Career-Development Program

# JOB INFORMATION FORM

## Employment Information

Business: _____

Employer: _____

Address: _____ Phone: _____

Supervisor: _____ Phone: _____

## Job Information

Job title: _____ Rate of pay: _____

Work schedule: _____

Company benefits: _____

| Co-workers:    Name | Job |
| --- | --- |
|  |  |
|  |  |
|  |  |
|  |  |

Uniform: _____

Breaks: _____

Lunch: _____

## Employee Information

Name: _____

Address: _____ Phone: _____

Home contact person: _____ Phone: _____

# JOB ANALYSIS FORM

Employee: _____

Job title: _____ Hours: _____

Supervisor: _____ Phone: _____

Availability: _____

## Work Environment

Time clock/sign in: _____

Locker room/personal storage: _____

Bathrooms: _____

Emergency exit: _____

Telephones (use agreement?): _____

Other information: _____

## Materials and Equipment

| Materials | Location | Use |
|---|---|---|
|  |  |  |
|  |  |  |
|  |  |  |
|  |  |  |
|  |  |  |
|  |  |  |
|  |  |  |
| Refill supplies |  |  |

From Morningstar, M.E. (2008). Lawrence: University of Kansas.

In *Your Complete Guide to Transition Planning and Services* by Mary E. Morningstar and Beth Clavenna-Deane.

## SEQUENCE OF JOB DUTIES

___ Daily jobs                                ___ Jobs vary each day

<u>Approximate time</u>                <u>Task/job duty</u>                <u>Day of week</u>

_____          _____          _____

_____          _____          _____

_____          _____          _____

_____          _____          _____

_____          _____          _____

_____          _____          _____

_____          _____          _____

_____          _____          _____

_____          _____          _____

Quality control issues (production rates, accuracy, etc.): _____

_____

Possible adaptations: _____

_____

Potential natural supports: _____

_____

_____

_____

# 9

# Preparing for Postsecondary Education

Dennis is a 16-year-old sophomore in high school and plans to attend community college after graduation. He is interested in community activism and helping others, and he enjoys spending time with his friends, playing video games, going to movies, and walking his dog. Dennis is diagnosed with autism spectrum disorder (ASD). He struggles with conversing with others, not spending too much time on topics of interest, staying organized, being on time, and making effective decisions. He is enrolled in primarily academic courses and receives co-teaching support. He also receives special education support, enrolling in a study skills class, as well as receiving specific accommodations in the classroom.

Carol Martin, Dennis' case manager, met with him to plan for an upcoming transition IEP and determined that Dennis is regularly using only some of the accommodations listed in the IEP and not asking for needed accommodations. She learned that the paraprofessional was really making accommodation requests. The community college Dennis is planning to attend will require that he disclose his disability and take an active role in requesting and managing his accommodations. With only 2 years left to learn these skills, it is time for Dennis to begin to have more opportunities to self-direct his supports; however, it may be difficult to persuade the staff to encourage Dennis to ask for accommodations. How should the team help Dennis develop his self-advocacy skills and opportunities to practice?

College is a goal for many high school students like Dennis, whether it means attending a 2-year community college or a 4-year university. Students may also consider attending a vocational technical school or enlisting in the military. Students with disabilities and their families often expect that college will be a part of the student's future, but may not have considered all of the academic and nonacademic skills needed to achieve postsecondary educational outcomes. In the past, transition primarily focused on employment (Will, 1983), perhaps because we may not have believed college was a reality for many students with disabilities. Now, this outcome has become a viable possibility for many, with students with learning disabilities being among the largest group attending postsecondary education programs (Morningstar, Trainor, & Murray, 2015). From 2004 to 2011, the overall percentage rate of students with disabilities attending postsecondary programs increased from 31% to 60%, with 2-year community colleges and vocational and technical colleges having the highest enrollment (Newman et al., 2011). Even more exciting are the new college programs developed especially for students with intellectual disabilities. In 2005, roughly 15% of students with intellectual disabilities had attended some postsecondary educational setting. By 2011, that number had almost doubled to 29% as a result of the Higher Education Opportunity Act (HEOA; 2008; Hart, Mele-McCarthy, Pasternack, Zimbrich, & Parker, 2004; Newman et al., 2011). Through the HEOA, federal incentives are in place for comprehensive transition to postsecondary programs to partner with districts and adult agencies to increase access for students with intellectual disabilities.

## TIP FOR TRANSITION: Think College

Think College (www.thinkcollege.net) is the top resource for learning about postsecondary programs for youth with intellectual disabilities. They have an extensive database of programs you can search to find those in your state. It is important to determine which models of support your students and families are interested in, given that there are variations among programs. The range includes fully inclusive programs, as well as those where students with intellectual disabilities are predominantly engaging only with others with disabilities (Grigal & Hart, 2010). Most models can be supported through collaboration between a school district and postsecondary campus to provide transition services for youth aged 18 to 21 years old, who typically continue to receive special education services (Gaumer, Morningstar, & Clark, 2004).

As the need for academically and technically skilled workers continues, all students will need to participate in post-high school education and training to be competitively employed. Therefore, an essential aspect of the work you do during transition is to support students while in high school to make this dream a reality. There are many postsecondary educational options for students with disabilities including:

1. Four-year colleges and universities: offering bachelor's degrees as well as advanced graduate programs

2. Community colleges: public, 2-year programs that can lead to an associate's degree, primarily serving students from surrounding communities and offering academic, technical, and continuing education courses

3. Career-technical schools: offering a variety of options, including associate's degrees for certain careers (e.g., accounting, dental hygienist, computer programs), certificates (e.g., automotive, information technology, pharmacy technicians), and work apprenticeships for specific service trades (e.g., carpentry, plumbing) (Kochhar-Bryant & Greene, 2009)

For Dennis, preparing for the transition to postsecondary education includes learning the skills he will need for facing both academic and social challenges. Because Dennis does well academically, his teachers and perhaps even his family might assume that he does not need to carefully prepare for the new roles and challenges of a postsecondary education setting.

Dennis' situation is far too common in high school special education departments and, thankfully, there are tools, resources, and organizational strategies that can help you and your students prepare for the dynamics of postsecondary education settings. Helping students and families prepare for the changes ahead when students will be attending postsecondary settings is highly relevant to your work. A good place to begin is to provide families and students with an overview of the differences between high school and college, as well as helping students learn about self-advocacy, decision making, and self-determination (see Chapter 3). The transition to postsecondary education must begin early by emphasizing several critical areas: 1) enrolling in challenging academic coursework, 2) exploring career and academic interests while in high school, 3) developing effective study skills and learning strategies for postsecondary settings, and 4) perfecting social problem solving and relationship building (Getzel & Briel, 2013). Strategies for each of these crucial steps will be described in this chapter to help you support your students to make successful transitions to postsecondary settings.

## GETTING STARTED:
## How Does High School Compare With Postsecondary Education?

Your students and their families will need to know the specific differences between high school special education services and the supports and accommodations afforded to students with disabilities in college. During high school, your students are entitled to the services outlined in their IEP. The IDEA dictates that services, accommodations, and modifications are provided to meet the student's academic and functional needs. However, unlike the IDEA, laws that mandate specific services and supports as educational entitlements do not bind postsecondary programs. When students enroll in college, they must meet certain eligibility requirements in order to access reasonable accommodations mandated by Section 504 of the Rehabilitation Act and the Americans with Disabilities Act (ADA) (Shaw, Madaus, & Dukes, 2010).

### TIP FOR TRANSITION: Opening Doors to Postsecondary Education

The Wisconsin Department of Public Instruction created an excellent resource for students, families, and teachers, *Opening Doors to Postsecondary Education and Training* (http://transitioncoalition.org/blog/tc-materials/opening-doors-to-post-secondary-education-and-training-planning-for-life-after-high-school/), that includes a detailed chart comparing high school to postsecondary settings in terms of laws and responsibilities, classes, instructors, study skills, testing, grades, and other factors that can be used to help students and families understand postsecondary settings. Ask your students how often they have made independent decisions, inquire about what goals they have self-set academically or personally, and see if they know what type of disability documentation is required to receive services in college.

### Shifts in the Law and Access to Services

How students access needed services is very different once students are on postsecondary campuses (see Table 9.1 for a summary of what colleges do and do not provide). For example, in postsecondary settings, reasonable accommodations cannot change the content or standards expected for all students. This differs from modifications in high school, in which content can be altered. Reasonable accommodations can only increase "access to the content and reduction of barriers to learning" (Kochhar-Bryant, Bassett, & Webb, 2009, p. 27). What is "reasonable" may also depend upon the type of postsecondary setting. This is a shift from special education services, where accommodations are designed to support a student to obtain a free and appropriate education. The laws governing postsecondary settings (i.e., the ADA and Section 504 of the Rehabilitation Act) require only that

**Table 9.1.** What colleges do and do not provide

| Colleges do: | Colleges do not: |
|---|---|
| • Provide equal access to the curriculum ("level the playing field"). <br> • Provide reasonable accommodations to students with disabilities. | • Modify or fundamentally alter admission requirements, tests, courses, requirements for majors, or graduation requirements. <br> • Provide personal services to students with disabilities (e.g., specialized tutoring), but some may offer this at an additional cost or through university services. |

Reprinted with permission from *What Every Special Educator Must Know: Professional Ethics & Standards*, p. 124. Copyright 2015 Council for Exceptional Children.

individuals with disabilities obtain access to school programs through accommodations that do not place undue burden on schools (Hamblet, 2011). For example, most colleges and universities will provide sign language interpreters for students who are deaf because this allows access to the program as it currently stands. However, they are not required to provide one-on-one tutoring for students who struggle. Services such as individual tutoring are considered personal services which postsecondary settings are not required to provide under the ADA (34 C.F.R. § 104.4 [b][iii] & [iv]).

Parents and students should be made aware that there might be shifts in how students access accommodations and which accommodations will be provided. This is especially important to investigate because some types of postsecondary programs do provide more personalized services, sometimes because of the mission of the program (e.g., community colleges often provide more services because they serve a wider and more diverse student body due to open admissions policies); or at other times, certain programs are provided at a cost to the student (e.g., schools may offer intensive and disability-specific services at a cost above what the typical student would pay).

## Shifts in Responsibilities

Another notable shift comes in terms of responsibility. In high school, educational systems are responsible for identifying students with disabilities and providing needed specialized services and accommodations to ensure a free and appropriate education. In college, however, students are responsible for self-identifying their disability, communicating their disability to university support staff, and seeking out needed services and accommodations. Often, this requires that the student provide documentation about his or her disability to meet eligibility requirements for receiving services, and then coordinate his or her services with the postsecondary disability office, as well as advocate for accommodations during classes (Shaw, Madaus, & Dukes, 2010).

These student roles and responsibilities may seem very different from those of a student receiving special education services in high school, but this does not have to be the case! As students progress through high school, they can begin to learn to advocate for accommodations and practice this process so they are ready for college. This would be the step Dennis and the special education staff should begin to do, in addition to continuing to support him to learn to make effective decisions, problem solve, and self-manage his study habits. All of these skills are necessary for students to be best prepared for college (Getzel & Thoma, 2008). Students should begin practicing decision-making skills while in high school when they are engaged in enrollment decisions with their guidance counselor and teachers. They can be taught the skills needed to problem solve when they need to make up a test due to an absence, or learn how to approach their teacher if they want to re-take a test or work on extra credit in order to improve their class grade. Most importantly, they

**Table 9.2.** Strategies for learning college responsibilities

| Responsibilities in high school | Responsibilities in college | Lessons to teach |
| --- | --- | --- |
| Fewer responsibilities. | More independent living (e.g., car, insurance, gas). | Teach students to manage a monthly budget of required versus desired expenses. |
| Career decisions not yet established. | Student expected to know career goals tied to a major or occupational area. | Have students complete career interest inventories; research career interests through the Occupational Outlook Handbook (www.bls.gov/ooh). |
| Teachers provide help on a regular basis. | Student expected to seek out and ask for assistance when needed. | Have students review their accommodations and needs and practice talking with their core academic teachers about needs. |
| Limits set by parents and teachers with reminders for studying and completing work. | More self-monitoring required; independent reading and studying required; student individually accountable for completing and turning in work. | Beginning sophomore year, have students practice setting academic or personal goals for their individualized education programs. On a weekly basis, have them complete a chart or checklist to evaluate their progress. |
| Schedule set by school. | Student responsible for setting a schedule that will allow them to be successful (e.g., time of day, number and type of courses). | Have students develop a schedule for their evening activities for 2 weeks and evaluate the number of activities and levels of participation. |
| Attendance and progress actively monitored by teachers. | Attendance and progress not monitored by others or only on semester basis when it may be too late to make up work. | Support students to set up a self-monitoring schedule for grades using an online grading system and weekly check-in meetings until independently monitoring grades and work. |
| Student's time structured by home and school. | Student responsible for managing time and commitments; more free time during the day; time management and organizational skills are critical. | Teach and use time management strategies (e.g., chunking assignments, setting up phone calendar prompts), then have the students set up digital prompts and organize their study time/schedule; after 2 weeks have them evaluate their progress. |

*Source:* Boyer-Stephens et al. (2010).

should regularly practice self-advocacy, such as negotiating accommodations (e.g., receiving a copy of class notes, taking a test in an alternate setting), so they will be prepared for this responsibility when in a postsecondary setting. Table 9.2 provides examples of strategies for teaching different types of responsibility to high school students so they will be college-ready.

## Developing Self-Advocacy and Self-Management

Think about this saying: "If a student wears a life jacket for 12 years, and then you take it off, would you expect the student to be able to swim?" All too often, high school special education staff advocate, make decisions, problem solve, and organize accommodations for students. Yet for postsecondary education to become not only a reality but a success, your students must be the ones requesting and coordinating the supports they need. This means first and foremost they must be aware of their disability and the specific needs associated with it. To increase their chances of success in postsecondary settings, students need to display:

- Self-advocacy to request and receive accommodations

- Self-awareness, self-realization, and acceptance of their disability

- Persistence at improving their academic competency and overcoming obstacles

- Informed career decision making based on interests, experiences, and capabilities (Anctil, Ishikawa, & Scott, 2008)

Many students, like Dennis, are unprepared for the increased independence that colleges require and often struggle with managing both their course loads and their daily lives (Getzel & Briel, 2013), so an essential time to consider the four qualities of postsecondary success (i.e., self-advocacy, self-awareness, persistence, informed decision making) is during high school before the transition to postsecondary settings.

Consider how often you have included activities and skill-building opportunities related to these attributes in your work with students. It can be hard to think about adding one more skill to be taught, but opportunities to practice the skills for postsecondary success can easily be embedded across academic content and incorporated as part of the general education curriculum, especially because these skills are critical for all students to learn, not just those with disabilities. For instance, Dennis would benefit from a focus on persistence and self-advocacy as embedded components of his English Language Arts unit on *The Outsiders* by S.E. Hinton. This particular novel provides an array of embedded stories and plotlines that can fuel reflections, activities, and student-designed projects devoted to self-awareness, persistence, decision making, and self-advocacy. As a result of the teacher centering on content that incorporates developing one or more of these skills, Dennis would have opportunities to acquire the knowledge of skills, as well as apply their concepts in his daily life, and then evaluate and reflect on his own persistence or self-advocacy during challenging events in his life. Furthermore, Dennis' special education teacher could follow up on his reflections during his study skills class to assist him in applying these skills to situations that occur throughout his school day, such as when he avoids lunch in the cafeteria because he may encounter a student there who he had a small disagreement with once. In this situation, the components he learned in *The Outsiders* about self-awareness, self-advocacy, and decision making could be applied to finding a way to eat in the cafeteria with his friends while successfully avoiding conversations with the student who challenges him.

Similarly, as a special educator or transition coordinator, some of the problems you may be facing regarding your students' academic, social, or behavioral challenges can be transformed into opportunities to support your students to learn to self-advocate, self-manage, and make decisions for themselves. Learning these skills and having opportunities to practice in the classroom will ultimately translate into good career and education decision-making skills. For example, Dennis struggles with organizational skills and procrastinates when stressful assignments are due. Currently, the special education staff are inconsistent in how they address these issues, and Dennis is subsequently not learning strategies that will help him manage his daily life when he goes to college. Much of his high school preparation has focused on academic performance, yet his ability to manage and organize his academic progress will be critical to his successful participation in a postsecondary setting. His special education teacher can begin supporting him to use his phone or other digital technology to set prompts and reminders to be on time for classes and organize his materials. The teacher then can reduce the time managing Dennis' needs as he increases his self-management capabilities.

## TIP FOR TRANSITION: **Have Students Self-Monitor Accommodations**

Starting in 9th grade, have your students work with you to regularly update their accommodations list on their IEPs. The resulting accommodations may better represent reasonable accommodations that they will be eligible for in college and will increase their active participation in the decisions made about their support needs. Efforts to include students in this type of decision making will not only make their accommodations more appropriate, but will also increase the likelihood that students will ask for accommodations and begin to develop much-needed self-determination skills.

## MAKING IT HAPPEN:
## Preparing Students for Postsecondary Education

Knowing that the goal of enrolling in a postsecondary setting is steadily increasing for students with disabilities (Newman, Wagner, Cameto, & Knokey, 2009), what further steps can you take to assist students and families in choosing the right type of postsecondary program? How can you prepare students for success as they continue their education after high school? Two important prerequisites for a successful transition to postsecondary education include 1) completion of the core academic coursework in the general education classroom, and 2) comprehensive transition planning and services (Kochhar-Bryant, Bassett, & Webb, 2009; Thoma & Getzel, 2005).

### Overview of Prerequisites

Why is it necessary to complete coursework in the general education classroom instead of receiving access to the general education curriculum through a special education class setting? All colleges require a certain level of competency in reading, writing, and mathematics for entry-level courses. Your students will need to show competence either through their high school transcript or (and more often) as part of college entrance or placement exams (Kochhar-Bryant et al., 2009). If students are completing high school core courses in the general education classroom, they will be exposed to the educators with specialized core area content and will have a better chance of learning the most current and accurate information about the subject. If the placement exams indicate that your students are not ready for freshman-level coursework, they may be required to complete remedial coursework first. Therefore, the best supports you can provide to your students may be through establishing strong co-teaching approaches and inclusive practice (as described in Chapter 7).

### TIP FOR TRANSITION: Students Should Know Their Learning Styles

Have students complete a learning styles inventory so they will know about how they learn best. This can then be used to communicate with postsecondary services and supports and professors. Two free inventories include the *Learning Styles Inventory* (www.personal.psu.edu/bxb11/LSI/LSI.htm) or the *CITE Learning Styles Inventory* (http://transitioncoalition.org/tc-assessment-reviews/?cat_ID=48).

The second critical factor of postsecondary success involves embedding comprehensive transition services across your students' academic and nonacademic school experiences, which can be a challenge. Meeting the daily academic needs of your students can require a significant amount of time and attention, perhaps with limited time to focus on specific transition services and preparation for life after high school. Yet we know having access to evidence-based transition practices is necessary for an increased chance of success in postsecondary education (Test et al., 2009). Sometimes it can be challenging to know where to focus the most needed attention. Table 9.3 provides seven steps for success in college, outlining necessary knowledge and skills that students need to navigate postsecondary

**Table 9.3.**   Seven steps for success

| 7 steps | Pathway to success |
|---|---|
| **Step 1:** Learn about laws governing postsecondary settings. | • Understand the differences between the Individuals with Disabilities Education Act and special education (high school) versus the Americans with Disabilities Act of 1990 and Section 504 (postsecondary settings and services). |
| **Step 2:** Know your rights and responsibilities. | • Obtain accommodations and services.<br>• Disclose information about disability to receive services.<br>• Understand student grievances and code of conduct. |
| **Step 3:** Develop essential personal skills. | • Develop self-determination and self-advocacy skills.<br>• Understand disability.<br>• Communicate effectively. |
| **Step 4:** Develop college survival skills. | • Understand and meet academic expectations (classes, exams, reading assignments, studying).<br>• Talk with professors.<br>• Utilize technology.<br>• Acquire study skills, organization, and time management.<br>• Learn life skills; adapt to dorm life.<br>• Develop social skills. |
| **Step 5:** Understand accommodations. | • Understand reasonable accommodations.<br>• Request accommodations.<br>• Advocate for appropriate accommodations.<br>• Use assistive technology. |
| **Step 6:** Find the right college. | • Research colleges.<br>• Find out about disability services, types of supports offered, and other resources for academic and social supports. |
| **Step 7:** Document your strengths, interests, and needs. | • Know the types of documentation needed and where to obtain proper documentation (e.g., summary of performance, transcript, diagnostic information from a medical professional).<br>• Anticipate obstacles to documentation (e.g., gathering information from a medical professional may take some time).<br>• Complete a transition portfolio with all necessary information and documentation. |

*Source:* Hamblet (2011).

settings. When working with an individual student, consider with which of the seven steps the student might need the most assistance and be sure to make that a focus of transition planning.

Helping students choose the right program is one key to their success in postsecondary education and should be a vital part of transition planning. Students and families need to identify preferences for postsecondary programs based on many different factors, including:

1. Preferred pace of work (fast, medium, slow, hands-on)

2. Desired length of time in college (1, 2, 4, or more years)

3. Living arrangements (live at home or away; single room or shared room)

4. Distance from home (in town, in the same state, more than 5 hours away)

5. Class and campus size (small: fewer than 1,000 students, medium: up to 5,000 students, large: more than 5,000 students)

6. Urban, suburban, or rural campuses

7. Extracurricular activities (athletics, clubs, fine arts)

8. Cost and financial requirements (price per class, food, housing, transportation)

9. Support services for students with disabilities (types and intensity of accommodations)

This list of considerations helps your students to choose between a small state school, a community college, or a large university. It assists students in identifying their comfort levels and preferences and deciding which environments best suit their personality and needs.

## Postsecondary Survival Skills

As students with disabilities prepare for the transition to postsecondary education and training, academic skills and supports are often at the top of the list of areas of concern. However, equally important is ensuring that students are successful in the emerging set of adult responsibilities and "soft skills" associated with postsecondary settings. The next sections will focus on ideas for supporting your students to be equally prepared in academic and nonacademic survival skills.

***Academic Survival Skills***    It is important to support your students in learning the academic skills needed to be successful in postsecondary programs. At the top of this list are the postsecondary academic expectations for using higher order thinking skills (Hamblet, 2011). With the changes to educational state standards, the increased focus on critical thinking, problem solving, and communication skills is already more likely to prepare your students for postsecondary settings. Revisit Chapter 7 for strategies and resources to support your students to be included within general education academic core classes. The chapter also provides examples of how to embed transition-related skills within general education classes.

How postsecondary class schedules operate is often a shift for students, and it is important to help them understand that postsecondary classes will not meet every day and will most likely last longer than high school classes. If your school is on a block schedule, your students may be better prepared because their classes may already be scheduled every other day for longer periods of time. Another significant difference is that students may not have a full day of classes like they do in high school and classes may be scheduled with several hours of unstructured time in between. Students will need to develop effective time management and organizational skills, including setting and following a schedule. You can help by teaching your students to develop organizational techniques, such as maintaining a weekly planner or using their phone calendar. You might even set up some lessons where you provide examples of a variety of postsecondary schedules and have your students plan each day for a week—taking into consideration time for working, going to classes, and studying. Consider preparing for the transition by asking former students to share how different it is to manage time when at college with your high schoolers.

Necessary study skills and time spent studying also can be very different for students once they go off to college. Strategies students used in high school may not work best when attending a postsecondary program. Often, poor time management and a lack of self-discipline when faced with unstructured time can lead to underachievement (Balduf, 2009). It has been found that students with disabilities are successful when they are able to set realistic and attainable goals and actively use problem-solving strategies (Martin, Portley, & Graham, 2010). These abilities are associated with self-determination skills, which are extensively described in Chapter 3. Hamblet (2011) suggested some actions students with disabilities can take to ensure they are able to manage workloads, such as finding out about tutoring, learning, or writing centers that can help students plan assignments, set deadlines, organize notes, and edit drafts of papers. As an example of a resource for improving study skills that colleges might offer, Figure 9.1 provides an Estimating My Weekly Study Hours Worksheet, as developed by Utah State University. This helpful form includes a study hour calculator to help students accurately estimate the hours of study needed for certain classes.

## TIP FOR TRANSITION: College Study Tips

The College Atlas web site (www.collegeatlas.org) offers a wide range of homework, studying, memorizing, reading, essay writing, and test-taking tips for students enrolled in colleges and other postsecondary settings. They strongly encourage each student to find the tips that work best for them, based on their individual learning styles, strengths, and preferences.

*Nonacademic Survival Skills*      Being successful in a postsecondary program requires more than academic skills. For many students, the myriad other nonacademic responsibilities can cause undue stress and difficulties. Therefore, you will want to consider how to prepare your students for diverse adult living, including using technology and assistive technology, living away from home, finding a new social group, and maintaining finances. Suggestions for supporting students in some of these various areas follow.

*Using Technology*      Students should be aware that postsecondary programs rely heavily on technology to communicate with students. Online technologies are almost always required for registering for classes, submitting assignments, and even for learning content, particularly with the rapid expansion of online classes (Allen & Seaman, 2015). For the current generation of students, being fluent in technology is essential to college survival (Banjerjee, 2010). High school students with disabilities must be well prepared to enter educational environments where technology is regularly used in order to engage in and assess learning. Students should have basic competencies for online access, word processing, presentation software, online courses, and online databases if they are to successfully engage with the instructional technologies in use in postsecondary settings. This means you must be supporting students to acquire basic instructional technology skills and experiences while in high school.

In addition to the regular use of technology for academics and other basic college activities, some students with disabilities will require additional AT to support their success in postsecondary educational settings. AT helps to bridge the gap between a student's abilities and academic functioning and is defined as "any item, piece of equipment, or product...that is used to increase, maintain, or improve functional capabilities of individuals with disabilities" (Technology-Related Assistance for Individuals with Disabilities Act, PL100-407, §140.25). AT provides both compensatory supports for students with disabilities as well as supports to bridge learning gaps (Bryant, Bryant, & Ok, 2014). AT supports to bridge those gaps are often used in high school but are less frequently found on college campuses. This type of AT is most often used to improve basic reading, writing, or math skills using strategies such as chunking a writing assignment into smaller tasks to make the assignment more attainable to complete. As students with disabilities are preparing to transition to postsecondary settings, you might help them develop a list of credible web sites and resources they can use to improve these basic academic skills, such as Kahn

# Estimating My Weekly Study Hours Worksheet

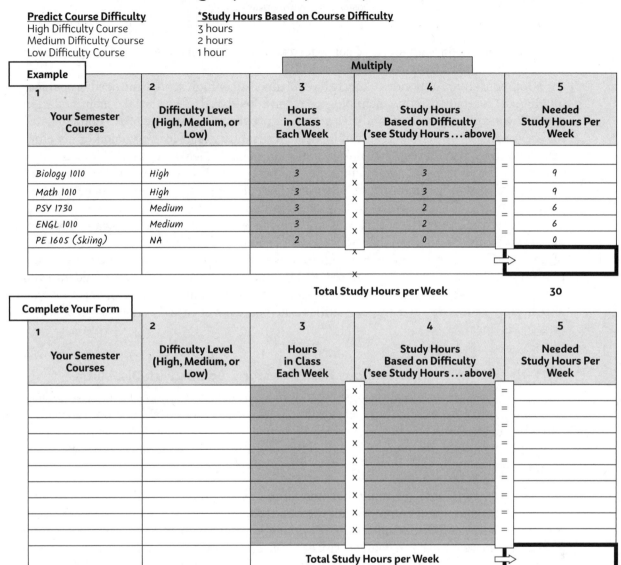

**Predict Course Difficulty**
High Difficulty Course
Medium Difficulty Course
Low Difficulty Course

***Study Hours Based on Course Difficulty**
3 hours
2 hours
1 hour

**Example**

| 1 Your Semester Courses | 2 Difficulty Level (High, Medium, or Low) | 3 Hours in Class Each Week | | 4 Study Hours Based on Difficulty (*see Study Hours . . . above) | | 5 Needed Study Hours Per Week |
|---|---|---|---|---|---|---|
| | | | Multiply | | | |
| Biology 1010 | High | 3 | x | 3 | = | 9 |
| Math 1010 | High | 3 | x | 3 | = | 9 |
| PSY 1730 | Medium | 3 | x | 2 | = | 6 |
| ENGL 1010 | Medium | 3 | x | 2 | = | 6 |
| PE 1605 (Skiing) | NA | 2 | x | 0 | = | 0 |
| | | | x | | | |
| | | **Total Study Hours per Week** | | | | 30 |

**Complete Your Form**

| 1 Your Semester Courses | 2 Difficulty Level (High, Medium, or Low) | 3 Hours in Class Each Week | | 4 Study Hours Based on Difficulty (*see Study Hours . . . above) | | 5 Needed Study Hours Per Week |
|---|---|---|---|---|---|---|
| | | | x | | = | |
| | | | x | | = | |
| | | | x | | = | |
| | | | x | | = | |
| | | | x | | = | |
| | | | x | | = | |
| | | | x | | = | |
| | | | x | | = | |
| | | | x | | = | |
| | | **Total Study Hours per Week** | | | | |

## My Study Hours Improvement Plan

| Total Number of Hours I Typically Study Each Week | Needed Study Hours Per Week (based on worksheet above) | Column A (–) Column B | |
|---|---|---|---|
| A _____ | B _____ | C _____ | Numbers of Hours I Need to Add to My Weekly Study Schedule |

**Final Thoughts:** There's no need to get discouraged or perfectionistic about a new study plan. Instead, the goal is to become aware how much time it takes to succeed in college. If it seems overwhelming or unrealistic to add this many hours to your study schedule, you have some options:

- Consider taking fewer credits — believe it or not, college is not a race. It's better to go a little slower and get better grades.
- Try to keep your work hours less than 20–25 hours per week.
- Try adding one more hour of study per day to begin with. This will increase your weekly total by 5 to 7 hours!

**Figure 9.1.** Estimating my weekly study hours worksheet. (From Estimating My Weekly Study Hours Worksheet. From: Utah State University, Academic Success Center. www.usu.edu/asc; reprinted by permission.)

Academy, which offers all levels of self-paced courses to learn content and bridge gaps in learning (Banerjee, 2010).

Compensatory AT is more likely to be continued after high school and used in postsecondary settings because this technology is often considered an essential accommodation that allows students with disabilities access to programs. This type of AT compensates for a need that is either the result of a physical disability (e.g., loss of vision or hearing) or has not been shown responsive to instruction to bridge learning gaps. For example, a note taker is a common accommodation found both in high school and in postsecondary settings. In college, the human note taker may be replaced with AT such as speech-to-text and text-to-speech software, recording lectures, and other note-taking technologies (e.g., Pulse smartpens, www.livescribe.com), all considered reasonable and allowable postsecondary accommodations. High school students should be well versed in appropriate use of needed compensatory AT and in essential elements to emphasize in their transition planning. This means you will need to first identify appropriate AT for your students and ensure they are able and willing to use needed AT while in high school. In addition, you should support them in learning the skills to advocate for necessary AT when in postsecondary settings.

## TIP FOR TRANSITION: Technology Resources for Students with Disabilities

An overview of the legal parameters surrounding AT, as well as resources for understanding access and use of AT in postsecondary settings, is provided on the Best Colleges web site (www.bestcolleges.com/resources/disabled-students). You can use this information with your students to prepare them for the changes in how AT must be requested and how it can be used.

*Postsecondary Life Skills*      Students moving into postsecondary settings face expanding environments and a wide range of adult roles and responsibilities. This is particularly true for students who will be living away from home in a college dorm or apartment. Helping students prepare for certain changes can ease the stresses often associated with the transition to postsecondary education. If they are not currently practicing essential life skills, they should:

- Learn how to do their own laundry and household cleaning.

- Manage finances (e.g., banking accounts, debit card, bills, budgets, car insurance).

- Use a planner or other organizational methods.

- Set up and check e-mail.

- Prepare simple and nutritious meals.

- Understand health care services and make their own appointments.

Independent living skills may not typically be taught in your school, but by collaborating with families and students themselves, you can support a plan to develop these types of survival skills. In addition, electives may be offered at your school to reinforce and support learning (e.g., foods/home economics, personal finance classes), and you can research community classes or partner with the business community to develop workshops related to these skills.

Financial decision making may be an overlooked area for your students. It is important for students to have a solid understanding of budgeting, bank accounts, credit and debit cards, and other finances. The sharp increase in students taking out loans to attend postsecondary programs reinforces the need for increasing your students' knowledge and awareness of student loans and credit cards (Ellis, 2013; Lee, 2013). Better knowledge may assist them in making informed decisions when they enroll in postsecondary programs and are facing the need to take out student loans. This may be especially important given that students with disabilities often attend postsecondary programs for longer periods of time than their peers without disabilities (Newman et al., 2011), which may lead to the accumulation of additional debt. Encourage your students to take consumer finance classes if available. You can also collaborate with a community bank or financial institution to develop a budgeting workshop. You could include in these lessons keeping a monthly budget, opening a checking account, and understanding interest rates for credit cards and loans.

In addition to learning about adult living, students enrolling in postsecondary programs will have to navigate many new social activities and situations. Finding a new social network and learning how to deal with the challenges of certain social situations, such as excessive drinking, can be a steep learning curve for all students, but may be especially difficult for students with certain learning and social disabilities (i.e., ASD, attention-deficit/hyperactivity disorder). The HEATH Resource Center has developed several modules for students with disabilities, including one on joining clubs and organizations, often a good way for students to build new friendships by connecting with others with similar interests (http://heath.gwu.edu/campus-life-joining-clubs-and-organizations).

## Evidence-Based Practices: The *ChoiceMaker* Series

NTACT identifies effective transition programming as a research-based practice that predicts postsecondary education success (NTACT, 2016). Effective transition programming is achieved through the development of high-quality post-school goals, ongoing transition assessment, opportunities to engage in multiple transition activities related to those post-school goals, and developing self-advocacy and self-determination skills, just to name a few. The *ChoiceMaker* series allows you to work with your students to provide effective transition programming throughout their secondary school career. The series provides opportunities for the students to 1) choose educational, employment, and personal goals; and 2) inventory their interests, work habits and learning styles, personality and characteristics, and skills and experiences. Then, you work with your students to rate their goal and how well they have attained it, as well as use the inventory results to narrow their career and college choices.

*ChoiceMaker* aligns well with the many resources provided within this chapter that assist you in preparing your students for postsecondary education environments. In addition, much like the suggestions in Chapter 3 on self-determination, your students will learn how to self-direct their IEP. Martin and colleagues (2006) found that students who participated in the self-directed IEP process talked more at their IEPs, viewed the IEP process more positively, and rated their involvement in transition issues higher than students who were involved in teacher-directed IEPs. Considering that students transitioning to college are required to direct their services and supports, an increase in student direction during the IEP process in high school would directly impact their success in college.

| High school year | Transition activities for students |
|---|---|
| 9th grade | — Develop a transition plan that facilitates postsecondary goal for postsecondary education or training.<br>— Meet with counselor/case manager to enroll in courses aligned with IEP transition course of study.<br>— Ensure courses are college preparatory.<br>— Complete transition assessments to identify career interests, strengths, and preferences.<br>— Practice self-advocacy by requesting accommodations for high school core classes.<br>— Enroll in and complete core coursework in general education classrooms.<br>— Participate in extracurricular clubs, sports, and activities.<br>— Practice organization, self-management, test-taking, and study skills.<br>— Identify independent living skills to focus on at home. |
| 10th grade | — Complete transition assessments and experiences to continue narrowing career interests, preferences, and strengths.<br>— Meet with counselor/case manager to update course of study.<br>— Update measurable postsecondary goal for education and training based on new interests or experiences.<br>— Research postsecondary education options that align with interests and preferences.<br>— Attend college and career fairs at high school.<br>— Practice self-advocacy by participating in IEP meetings and advocating for accommodations in classes.<br>— Learn about different rights and responsibilities under the IDEA, ADA, and 504.<br>— Align high school accommodations with expected postsecondary reasonable accommodations.<br>— Enroll in and complete core academic coursework.<br>— Enroll in electives related to career interests, preferences, and strengths.<br>— Take practice entrance exams if planning to attend a 4-year college (e.g., PSAT).<br>— Request accommodations for entrance exams based on IEP accommodations.<br>— Participate in extracurricular clubs, sports, and activities.<br>— Refine and expand organization, self-management, and study skills that best suit you.<br>— Explore needed technology/assistive technology to support academic skills. |
| 11th grade | — Complete transition assessments to continue narrowing interests, preferences, and strengths based on experiences.<br>— Meet with counselor/case manager to update course of study as needed.<br>— Narrow postsecondary education options based on career interests and preferences.<br>— Update measurable postsecondary goals based on any new interests or experiences.<br>— Participate in writing IEP goals and attending meetings.<br>— Set a goal related to interests or academics.<br>— Enroll in and complete core academic coursework.<br>— Enroll in electives related to career interests.<br>— Consider dual enrollment in courses at career technical school or community college.<br>— Align high school accommodations with expected postsecondary reasonable accommodations.<br>— Take ACT or SAT preparatory classes if planning to attend a 4-year college; request accommodations for the exams.<br>— Attend college and career fairs at high school, colleges/postsecondary settings.<br>— Visit postsecondary educational and training settings of interest.<br>   — Schedule meetings with admissions and disability support services, and take a tour.<br>   — Enroll in summer postsecondary education program.<br>— Meet with vocational rehabilitation counselor to determine eligibility for services.<br>— Apply for a part-time job to gain employment experience.<br>— Open checking or savings account to begin managing own finances. |

**Figure 9.2.**  Checklist of activities for the transition to postsecondary education and training. (*Sources:* Boyer-Stephens et al. [2010]; Kochhar-Bryant, Bassett, & Webb (2009); Shaw, Madaus, & Dukes [2010]).

*(continued)*

| | |
|---|---|
| | — Continue to update and improve organization, self-management, and study skills that best suit you.<br>— Expand technology/assistive technology to support academic skills.<br>— Begin taking charge of independent living at home (e.g., laundry, meals, car maintenance, cleaning).<br>— Participate in extracurricular clubs, sports, and activities. |
| 12th grade | — Develop portfolio of transition assessment results, documentation of disability, and accommodations.<br>— Meet with counselor/case manager to prepare for graduation and transfer of information to postsecondary settings.<br>— Discuss various scholarship, grant opportunities with counselor.<br>— Apply to postsecondary settings.<br>   — If an institution requires a written essay, ask English teacher or case manager to assist.<br>   — Get letters of recommendation from teachers, coaches, etc.; provide them with the college's forms.<br>— Apply for financial aid.<br>— Apply for vocational rehabilitation services to support career goals.<br>— Self-direct senior year IEP and summary of performance.<br>— Learn about Section 504 of the Rehabilitation Act and the ADA; laws that govern college supports.<br>— Enroll in electives related to career interests.<br>— Consider dual enrollment in courses at the career/technical school or local community college.<br>— Retake ACT or SAT if a better score is desired; request accommodations for the exams.<br>— If attending community college, take placement exams.<br>   — Note: Most community colleges only require high school diploma/GED and completion of placement exams.<br>— Revisit the postsecondary programs that accepted application.<br>— Schedule meetings with department chair and disability support services when on campus.<br>— Choose the postsecondary setting you will attend.<br>— Send a final transcript showing graduation to the institution.<br>— Apply for housing on campus or select living arrangements off campus if available.<br>— Continue working a part-time job.<br>— Continue managing budget and finances.<br>— Continue using organization, self-management, and study skills.<br>— Independently manage daily needs (e.g., laundry, meals, transportation, cleaning).<br>— Participate in extracurricular clubs, sports, and activities. |
| Summer after 12th grade | — Attend orientation and schedule meeting with disability services.<br>— Attend first-year activities at postsecondary setting.<br>— Enroll in enrichment courses as needed.<br>— Consider taking reading, math, or written language enrichment courses to continue to practice skills in areas of need.<br>— If planning to play a sport or participate in band or choir, research whether the college has any summer camps for conditioning and practice.<br>— Continue part-time job to meet college expenses other than tuition, room, and board (e.g., books, housing supplies, transportation).<br>— Take community college placement exams.<br>   — If you haven't already taken these exams in the spring of your senior year, set up an appointment. Your score will determine the level of course for which you are best prepared. |

**WHAT YOU CAN DO RIGHT NOW:**
**Putting Ideas Into Action**

Helping your students prepare for college and success as they continue their education after high school may seem like a daunting responsibility. Yet the various strategies, practices, and tips provided in this chapter can make a successful transition to college possible. Figure 9.2 provides a time line of important transition activities related to postsecondary education, organized over 4 years of high school, that can provide you with a way to begin tracking each of your student's progress. You can use this checklist to help keep yourself grounded on what to do and when. It can be used to help you organize learning activities that can be embedded in classes or during individual advisement with students, and it can be a guide in ensuring that appropriate transition services are provided to facilitate the transition to postsecondary education and training. This checklist is comprehensive, with some items repeating each year (e.g., meet with case manager, update transition assessments, enroll in core coursework). These steps are ongoing, and it is helpful for students and families to recognize the repetition and consistency of certain activities during high school. In addition, the checklist also includes activities for the summer after senior year, which can also be very important in helping students be prepared for postsecondary education. Many community colleges and local universities provide enrichment courses, summer camps, and orientation activities throughout the summer that can position students for success in the fall. There may be enrichment courses on the postsecondary campus that focus on an area of need, such as math, reading, written language, or technology, that will better prepare students with learning challenges for the transition to postsecondary education (Burgstahler, Crawford, & Acosta, 2001; NCSET, 2010).

Moving from high school to postsecondary education and training requires greater levels of collaboration, and you will want to seek out those within your high school and community who can assist students in the transition. This is a time when families and students must take the lead in determining such important next steps, but you can provide support and guidance along the way. The suggestions and ideas in this chapter may be the catalyst you and your students need to start thinking and planning for postsecondary education and training and will help the dream of college become a reality.

# 10

# Preparing for Independent Living and Inclusion in the Community

with Dawn Rowe and Ryan Kellems

Esmeralda is a 17-year-old with an intellectual disability. She has been receiving special education services since she was 4 years old. She currently lives with her parents, has very little interaction with her peers at school with any regularity, and has next to no interactions outside of school. During her latest IEP meeting, her parents discussed their vision for Esmeralda's future, which included her regularly participating in community activities and living in a supported living situation. When the special education teacher asked if Esmeralda had the skills necessary to live independently, both parents just looked each other and said, "We have not really thought about that; we have been focusing on getting by from day to day. She knows what *you* all have taught her here at school." How would you explain the different and important roles of the family and the school in preparing Esmeralda for community living? If Esmeralda's parents' goal is for her to live in a supported living environment, what can the family and school do now to prepare her for this transition?

## GETTING STARTED:
## Why Should Community Living Be Considered an Important Postsecondary Outcome?

As practitioners, one of our main objectives is to prepare our students to live fulfilling, productive lives. What exactly this life entails will be different for each individual, but living a meaningful, productive life includes being included in the community to the fullest extent possible. It is important to understand that all people, including individuals with disabilities, have a basic civil right to the community, which includes opportunities for full inclusion in social, economic, sporting, and/or cultural life.

Typically, when "inclusion" is referred to, educators and families may limit the term solely to educational settings and narrow its definition to whether students are participating in the general curriculum with their same-age peers (Agran, Alper, & Wehmeyer, 2002). However, inclusion extends past educational settings and should encompass all aspects of life. Inclusive experience in school can also extend to other dimensions of adulthood, such as going out to eat with friends or attending a high school football game with peers without disabilities. Unfortunately, we know that even when students spend their school day integrated with peers who are nondisabled, they may still spend their nonschool time alone or in segregated settings (Trainor, Morningstar, Murray, & Kim, 2013). It is important to understand that the ultimate goal is to facilitate full integration in both school and community settings for students while they are still in school, as well as when they transition to post-school environments.

There are many factors that need to be considered in supporting individuals with disabilities to be fully included and engaged in their communities, including making personal choices, accessing interesting places, feeling safe, and having the freedom to fully participate in community life. Successful community living occurs when people have independence, safety and security, freedom of mobility, access to a mode of communication, affordable and accessible housing and transportation, and access to health care and long-term supports (National Council on Disability, 2011).

## TIP FOR TRANSITION: Consider Independent Living Skills Throughout the Lifespan

Families can play an instrumental role in helping students learn important skills, such as learning to get up by themselves, prepare simple meals, manage money, shop for groceries and necessities, and engage in other tasks of daily life. This will make independent living skills easier to apply when living at college or on their own. Provide increasing independence for your student and begin taking more of a "back-seat" or "cheerleader" role. Students with significant disabilities will need a longer transition period to ensure they are as independent as possible.

Community living is a broad concept that means different things to different people. What may be appropriate for one person may not be appropriate for another. It is therefore important to view community living from the perspective of your students and families while paying attention to the values and customs of the community. Positive community living includes joy and happiness, health and safety, hopes and dreams, meaningful activities, intimate relationships with family and friends, having a home, transportation, work, money (bank accounts), and the ability to contribute to family and community (Ankeny, Wilkins, & Spain, 2009; Geenen, Powers, & Lopez-Vasquez, 2001).

Research has established positive outcomes related to living and participating in the community. Outcomes include 1) having an established network of family, friends, co-workers, support service providers, and other supporters; 2) cultivating intimate relationships; 3) being an active member of the community; 4) pursuing interests, hobbies, and leisure activities; 5) graduating from postsecondary education, and 6) obtaining gainful employment (Newman et al., 2011). As your students transition, they will assume many different adult roles (e.g., employee, husband/wife, friend, parent). For example, Esmeralda wants to work after high school. As an employee, Esmeralda will have to answer to a boss and follow the rules and regulations as established by her employer, rules she does not have to abide by when she is at home. This is but one of many roles that Esmeralda will be expected to navigate, as she and her family have numerous other post-school goals beyond employment. Esmeralda's family envisions her engaging in many positive community experiences after high school. They want her to have choices about her daily activities (e.g., swimming at the YMCA, going shopping, spending time with friends, working). They also expect her to live in a setting in which she has access to the individualized supports she needs to make choices and contribute to her community, whether as an employee, friend, consumer, neighbor, or volunteer.

As with many transition concepts, there is not a single comprehensive community living curriculum available to meet all of your students' needs. Most often, you will have to develop your own curriculum based on the individual IEP goals of your students. To ensure quality, teachers should follow the principles of instructional design (Coyne, Kame'enui, & Carnine, 2007). Ensuring quality of instruction starts with two key questions:

1. What should we teach?

2. How should we teach it?

A concept map is one way to get organized and answer the question "What should we teach?" Figure 10.1 provides a concept map that illustrates many essential components to be included in a community living curriculum. Each component may be broken down into several subcomponents, or you may find additional areas to include based on student need. The concept map provided is just a starting place for developing individualized curricula for your students.

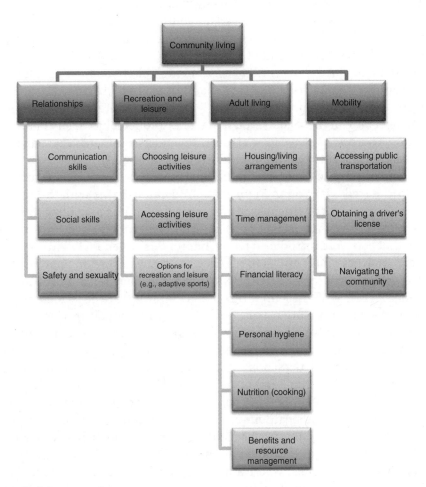

**Figure 10.1.**   Community living concept map.

### TIP FOR TRANSITION: Offer a Transition Class

Offer a transition class for high school juniors and seniors. The curriculum for this course can include self-advocacy, community resources, and daily living skills (e.g., opening a bank account, renting an apartment, buying a car). Guest speakers from postsecondary institutions as well as community agencies can provide information about adult services.

## MAKING IT HAPPEN:
## Preparing Youth for Community Living

Now that you have an understanding of why community living is an important transition outcome and how decisions made during the transition years can have an impact on a youth and his or her family for years to come, what are the strategies you can use to support students as they transition from school to the community? If Esmeralda is to have choices about the daily activities in which she participates, live in a place she chooses, and contribute to her community, what services and supports will she need? In this section, we will share approaches for assessing students' skills for successful community living (e.g., person-centered planning, ecological assessments) and providing instruction to ensure community inclusion (e.g., teaching social/communication skills, independent living skills). We will also share ideas for how to address the needs of culturally diverse youth and families as they transition.

It is essential to first assess the needs of youth as well as the community environments in which they will be included to determine what skills a student needs to successfully transition to the next stage of life (Neubert & LeConte, 2013; Walker, Kortering, Fowler, Rowe, & Bethune, 2013). Transition assessments help to determine appropriate community environments for current and future activities. In addition, you will want to identify opportunities to meet your students' preferences and interests for community engagement. To meet both of these goals, you will want to consider a variety of unique assessment approaches. There are several formal and informal assessments that can be used to assess a range of skills related to community living (see Table 10.1).

Remember the Independent Living Postsecondary Goal IEP Team Decision Assistance Form shared with you in Figure 2.2? You can use this with families, students, and the IEP team to identify critical skills for instruction. It is also important to bring all the right people to the table to assist in planning for community engagement. One approach to planning that you were introduced to in Chapter 2 is called PCP. This process can be used to support students and families to plan for the future using an approach that focuses on strengths and preferences (O'Brien & O'Brien, 2000). Four of the most common approaches to PCP (e.g., PATH, MAP, Essential Lifestyles Planning) are described in Figure 10.2.

More specific information regarding PCP can be found in Chapter 2, along with a resource list of methods and approaches. Using PCP strategies can especially help when planning for community involvement because the focus starts with what the student is interested in, and then the PCP team brainstorms all the ways these student preferences can be a community focus. For example, because Esmeralda really likes country music, her PCP team brainstormed a variety of community opportunities she could be involved in: square dancing, taking music lessons at the local guitar store, joining a jam session, and so forth. Keep in mind that while Esmeralda is still in high school, she can participate in both formal and informal musical opportunities (e.g., chorus, band, country music club, jamming with a band).

Once you have identified where and what your students are interested in, you can then identify the community liaisons that can provide supports and help increase opportunities for participation. In many ways, your role becomes more than just a "teacher of independent living skills"; you also assume the position of "facilitator" in that you will be supporting

**Table 10.1.**  Sample assessments related to independent living

| Name of Assessment | URL |
| --- | --- |
| **Assessment area: academic achievement** | |
| Key Math (Connolly, 2007) | www.pearsonclinical.com/education/products/100000649/keymath3-diagnostic-assessment.html |
| Easy CBM (Alonzo & Tindall, 2011) | http://riversidepublishing.com/products/easycbm/index.html |
| ACT WorkKeys | www.act.org/products/workforce-act-workkeys/ |
| **Assessment area: self-determination** | |
| AIR Self-Determination Assessment (Wolman, Campeau, Du Bois, Mithaug, & Stolarski, 1994) | www.ou.edu/zarrow/sdetermination.html |
| ARC Self-Determination Assessment (Wehmeyer & Kelchner, 1995) | www.beachcenter.org (downloads, books, manuals, reports, full pubs) |
| Self-Determination Assessment Internet (Hoffman, Field, & Sawilowsky, 2014) | http://www.ealyeducation.com |
| **Assessment area: career interests and aptitude** | |
| O*NET Career Interest Inventory (U.S. Department of Labor, 2002) | www.onetonline.org |
| Career Key (Jones, L.K., 2014) | www.careerkey.org |
| Brigance Transition Skills Inventory | www.curriculumassociates.com/products/detail.asp?title=BrigESI&Type=&CustId |
| **Assessment Area: Life Skills** | |
| Casey Life Skills (Casey Family Programs, 2012) | www.caseylifeskills.org |
| Enderle-Severson Transition Rating Scale (Enderle & Severson, 2003) | www.estr.net/publications.cfm |
| Checklist of Adaptive Living Skills (CALS) | www.riverpub.com/products/cals/pricing.html |

From: Walker, A.R., Kortering, L., Fowler, C.H., Rowe, D.A., & Bethune, L. (2013). *Age-Appropriate Transition Assessment Guide (2nd ed.)*. National Secondary Transition Technical Assistance Center: University of North Carolina at Charlotte.

others in the community to support your students. When using PCP, Esmeralda, her family, and those who know her best can develop a plan for community living that includes where she wants to live, work, and have fun. Knowing this information can assist her team to map out the community to determine available resources, supports, and opportunities for Esmeralda to be fully included. It allows the team to identify appropriate people to help facilitate her participation in the community. For example, Esmeralda's parents may play an important role in building Esmeralda's network of supports and facilitating Esmeralda's initial involvement in community social events (e.g., concerts in the park). The PCP team may designate the job coach as the person to facilitate full integration into the employment setting.

## TIP FOR TRANSITION: Identify the Student's Interests and Gifts

When planning how to support a student to increase his or her community connections, you can use the results of a PCP to identify shared interests, gifts, talents, and abilities. Ask questions such as, "What are the things the student does well?" and "How can he or she contribute to others?" Identify community organizations, memberships, and associations pertaining to particular interests and talents. You can identify one-to-one connections as well as membership in existing groups of similar interests.

While students are in school, you can provide them with access to instruction, transition services, and both formal and informal supports that research has shown lead to a higher likelihood of positive community living outcomes (Mazzotti et al., 2016). Skills such as self-determination, independent living, and social skills are important ones to focus on to promote community inclusion.

| PATH | MAPS | Essential lifestyle planning | Personal futures planning |
|---|---|---|---|
| • Requires either that the person can clearly describe his or her dream for the future or, if he or she does not use words to speak, that the others present know the person well enough to describe it for him or her<br><br>• Focuses first on the dream and works back from a positive and possible future, mapping out the actions required along the way<br><br>• Good for refocusing an existing team that is encountering problems or feeling stuck, and mapping out a change in direction | • Used as a starting point with individuals who feel comfortable with dreaming and who already have a few people around them to support them working toward their dreams<br><br>• More of a picture building style than PATH<br><br>• Goes over the person's history at the beginning of the process<br><br>• Allows people to express both their hopes for the future and their fears about the future | • Helps people find out who and what is important to the person and what support the person needs to have a good quality of life<br><br>• Does not focus on a desirable dream for the future<br><br>• Specifies the way that support is to be provided on a day-to-day basis | • Helps people to build on areas of their lives that are working well now and to move toward their desirable futures<br><br>• Provides an overview from which areas of concern can be considered |

**Figure 10.2.** Four common approaches to person-centered planning. (*Source:* O'Brien & O'Brien, 2000.)

## Teach Self-Determination Skills

Recall from Chapter 3 that self-determination skills involve making choices, solving problems, setting goals, evaluating options, taking initiative, and accepting the consequences of one's actions (Rowe et al., 2015). Students who exhibit strong self-determination skills are much more likely to achieve positive post-school employment, education, and community living outcomes (Berry, Ward, & Caplan, 2012; Carter et al., 2012; Chiang, Cheung, Hickson, Xiang, & Tsai, 2012). To ensure students leave high school with skills to access the community, you must systematically instruct in self-determination using either a structured curriculum that has been proven to be successful (see Table 3.2 in Chapter 3) or an evidence-based instructional strategy. Don't forget that systematic instruction must be paired with guided practice in natural school and community-based settings if you want to be successful (Rowe et al., 2015; Test et al., 2009). Guided practice in natural and community-based settings helps to promote generalization of skill across settings, people, or materials.

Self-determination can be addressed within the general education curriculum by creatively working with academic teachers. For example, the Common Core State Standards (CCSS) include anchor standards that specifically address components of self-determination (Common Core State Standards Initiative, 2012). Because of the focus of most schools on the CCSS (if you are teaching in a state that has not adopted the CCSS, check your own state standards), there are ample opportunities to teach self-determination throughout the school year using the standards. As an example, let's look at CCSS, ELA-Literacy.W.9-10.2, which requires students to write informative/explanatory texts to examine and convey complex ideas, concepts, and information clearly and accurately through the effective selection, organization, and analysis of content (National Governors Association Center for Best Practices & Council of Chief State School Officers, 2010).

To embed self-determination into this standard, you might require your students to convey personal goals and objectives in writing and have them include plans to achieve these goals. Such an assignment would require them to analyze complex concepts in writing, such as their own skillset, and the requirements of the environment in which they are required to perform these skills (e.g., classroom, community). While teaching or encouraging self-determination skills, it is important to remember that you should work with related services staff to ensure that students have an appropriate and functional means of communicating so they can demonstrate their acquired self-determination skills (Rowe et al., 2015). In fact, for students with significant disabilities, having access to a means of communication is an essential component of achieving "supported" self-determination, as is learning how to make choices and having adults who are responsive to both symbolic and nonverbal communication attempts (Morningstar, 2017).

Unfortunately, most of the self-determination curricula and interventions do not specifically address the communication and response needs of students with significant disabilities. Therefore, how to support students to be self-determined requires thinking outside the box. Wehmeyer (2005) has argued that self-determination should not be considered a set of skills because this may be limiting for students with significant disabilities. Supported self-determination specifically addresses how students with significant disabilities express their needs and affect their worlds. To ensure support for self-determination you may need to work closely with speech and language personnel as well as assistive technology coordinators to guarantee that students with significant disabilities have been appropriately assessed and have access to a means for communication, including augmentative devices.

As an example that demonstrates how to weave both self-determination skills into academic content and ensure that students with disabilities have ways of demonstrating these skills, consider the following activity conducted in Esmeralda's 11th grade English class. The class is currently reading the novel *Of Mice and Men* by John Steinbeck. The students have had several discussions related to setting goals that tied to the novel. For instance, they talked about Lennie and George's goals to own their own farm one day and the steps the characters were taking to get there. Esmeralda's teacher then asked the class to apply lessons learned from *Of Mice and Men* to their own lives and had each student set post-school goals and then write steps for achieving those goals. In this assignment, Esmeralda was to use speech-to-text software as one form of assistive technology to write her personal goals. For other examples of evidence-based practices and curricula to teach self-determination skills, see links to web sites and further resources found in the online resources list at the end of this chapter.

## Teach Independent Living Skills

Independent living skills are defined as "skills necessary for management of one's personal self-care and daily independent living, including the personal management skills needed to interact with others, daily living skills, financial management skills, and the self-management of health care/wellness needs" (Rowe et al., 2015, p. 121). Independent living skills are certainly needed for successful community inclusion (Carter et al., 2012). Regardless of whether they have a disability label, all adolescents have needs related to independent living. In order for some students to acquire independent living skills, you must identify services or instruction based upon their transition assessment results. The team may need to focus on areas of independent living such as 1) financial planning and budgeting, 2) self-care, 3) cooking, 4) home maintenance, 5) using public and/or private transportation, 6) clothing care, 7) accessing community services (e.g., banks, post office), 8) organizational skills such as time management, 9) adult roles/citizenship, 10) community and peer relationships, and 11) critical thinking and social problem solving.

Because there may not be a specific class for community living for all students in high school, it will be important to embed independent living skills instruction into academic coursework and throughout school environments to help students connect academic skills to post-school goals (Rowe et al., 2015; Test et al., 2009). For example, Esmeralda's post-school goal is to live in an apartment with the supports she needs. She will need to learn to develop a budget and make financial decisions. Instruction in these areas can extend the learning taking place in her general education math class, Probability and Statistics, where she has been working with probability to make decisions. Specifically, her class has been addressing the following Common Core standard for math content: CCSS Math Content HSS.MD.B.5: Evaluate and compare strategies on the basis of expected values (National Governors Association Center for Best Practices & Council of Chief State School Officers, 2010). Esmeralda can work toward performance of this standard while learning budgeting and financial skills related to her independent living goal.

To illustrate, Esmeralda has a monthly budget of $400 and is required to purchase renters' insurance for her apartment; however, she must also consider sufficient funds for other utilities (e.g., water, power), her meals, transportation, and recreational activities. Esmeralda will need to work with an insurance agent to determine the most practical renter's insurance policy to meet her needs. She has to examine high-deductible (e.g., $2,000) vs. low-deductible (e.g., $500) renters' insurance policies, considering various circumstances that could occur (e.g., theft, fire, flood). If she chooses a higher deductible, it means more money out of pocket at the time of an incident; however, the policy will be cheaper over the year. A lower deductible means less money out of pocket if an incident occurs, but a higher monthly rate. She must consider and problem-solve the consequences of buying the policy with the higher deductible and the ramifications this will have on her budget for the month—an example of evaluating and comparing strategies based on expected values. Thus, a general education math class can be an ideal place for students like Esmeralda to work on the skills they will need to be able to weigh outcomes and make informed financial decisions.

Other life skills might be addressed in Esmeralda's Career Technical Education (CTE) classes. For example, to support her post-school goal of living independently, she will need to learn other life skills such as cooking, washing clothes, and cleaning house. Family and Consumer Science classes are intended to prepare students for independent living and the workforce to promote personal and community well-being. Some schools offer specific courses in food and nutrition, human development, and life management. Esmeralda's family also plays an important role in helping Esmeralda develop these critical life skills. As Esmeralda grows older and gains more autonomy, her parents will allow her to take on more responsibilities at home. For example, they may make her responsible for all her own laundry or for making her own meals.

## Evidence-Based Practices: Purchasing Skills

There are several evidence-based practices for teaching purchasing skills. The "one-more-than" strategy is one practice that you can use (Denny & Test, 1995). This strategy involves teaching students to pay one more dollar than requested. For example, for an item costing $3.29, the student learns to gives $4.00. Some of the instructional strategies you might use include describing and modeling the concept, role-playing purchasing skills, and providing systematic prompting and reinforcement. Students should have plenty of opportunities to practice both in simulated settings as well as in the community. For additional examples of evidence-based practices to teach independent living skills, follow the links to web sites and resources found at the end of the chapter.

## Teach Social Skills

Often, it is necessary for you to explicitly teach social skills so that students not only acquire new skills, but also understand the rules and contextual factors underlying social behaviors. Direct instructional approaches and curricula can be used to teach skills such as social communication and problem solving, maintaining interpersonal relationships, reciprocal conversations, conflict resolution, and group or team skills, all important for community living. As would be expected, you should facilitate specific skills within the natural contexts in which they are most likely to occur. Given that the levels of social competence will vary among the students with whom you work, you will want to consider how critical skills can be addressed throughout the general curriculum as an extension of the CCSS. For example, ELA-Literacy.SL.11-12.1b (Speaking and Listening) focuses on working with peers to promote civil, democratic discussions and decision making, setting clear goals and deadlines, and establishing individual roles as needed (National Governors Association Center for Best Practices & Council of Chief State School Officers, 2010). A speaking and listening content standard is a prime opportunity to teach social skills and provide opportunities for students to practice social and interpersonal engagement (Rowe et al., 2015; Test et al., 2009).

For example, in Esmeralda's 11th grade English class, she was assigned to a group to complete a service learning project. The goals of the project were for groups to demonstrate understanding of a critical issue that has an impact on their community (e.g., recycling, civil rights) and then design an activity to create awareness of the issue for students in a neighborhood middle school. This activity required Esmeralda's group to have democratic discussions and come to consensus on their final stand. It also required them to assign roles in order to complete the project in a timely manner. Esmeralda was assigned the role of reflector in her group. She listened to what others had to say and then repeated it back to the group in her own words. She would then ask the original speaker if her interpretation was correct. Esmeralda was assigned a peer mentor to assist her in this role. The peer mentor was trained to use promoting strategies (e.g., least-to-most prompting) to elicit a response from Esmeralda at the right time in the conversation. Esmeralda was able to successfully engage with the group and practice some very valuable social skills (e.g., reciprocal turn-taking, listening, acknowledging another speaker).

An important aspect of community living is having the knowledge and ability needed to build positive and enduring relationships (Amado, 2013; Heal, Khoju, Rusch, & Harnish, 1999). Individuals should understand that there are a variety of relationships, including romantic, intimate, social, professional, financial, and family relationships. Each relationship comes with a unique set of social rules, challenges, and rewards. Some students will be able to develop positive relationships naturally, while others may need support with certain social expectations and pragmatics associated with developing and sustaining relationships.

Social and interpersonal skills, sometimes referred to in school as the "hidden curriculum," are often acquired over time and may never be explicitly taught (Myles,

Trautman, & Schelvan, 2004). One strategy to overcome this challenge is to explicitly teach students about different types of relationships and their corresponding skills and contextual rules. The underlying principle to keep in mind is that contributing to one's family and community are important aspects of living a happy fulfilling life that should be directly addressed as part of an individual's transition planning process (Virginia Department of Behavioral Health and Developmental Services, 2009). Chapter 11 delves more deeply into how the transition specialist can teach and support social skills and prepare students for the interpersonal relationships of adulthood.

## Support Participation in Community Experiences

In preparing your students for community experiences, you may need to consider how to balance inclusion in academic classes with opportunities to participate in community experiences (Wehman & Kregel, 2012). Community experiences are defined as "activities occurring outside of the school setting, supported with in-class instruction, where students apply academic, social, and/or general work behaviors and skills" (Rowe et al., 2015, p. 120). Figure 10.3 maps out important areas to inventory in the community, including employment industries, recreational and leisure activities, support groups, and community and adult services. When you inventory your community, you identify key places the student is interested in and the supports available so that students can access the community to meet their post-school community living goals. Familiarity with key locations and environments will lead you to more robust knowledge of the community, which is helpful when you focus on transition planning and how to support students in acquiring the skills needed for community participation.

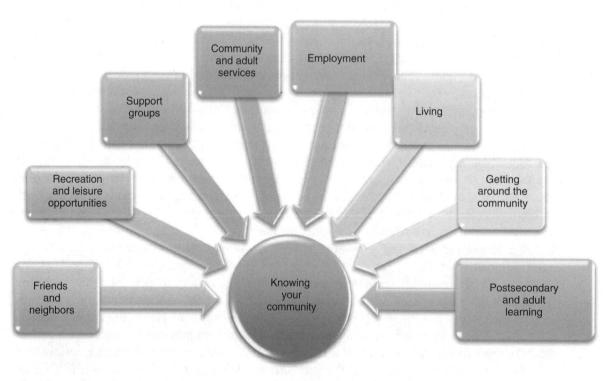

**Figure 10.3.**  Areas of the community to inventory.

Once applicable community opportunities and supports have been identified, it is important to conduct an ecological inventory to determine particular skills needed for these various community environments. An ecological inventory involves carefully examining environments where activities normally occur. An ecological inventory will help you to identify the subenvironments, activities, and skills required to be successful in the community location. You can use the results to teach students to acquire the skills needed for community participation.

As an example, Esmeralda wants to use the local YMCA after she leaves high school for swimming, to work out on the exercise machines, and also to join a volleyball team. This is a recreational activity the whole family likes to do, and she and her family hope to expand her engagement at the YMCA. To complete the ecological inventory, Esmeralda and her teacher went to the YMCA and took notes about all of the different subenvironments found there (e.g., the registration desk, the locker room, the pool, the gym, the snack bar). Then within each sub-environment, the teacher can identify all of the essential activities occurring there (e.g., checking in, using the locker room, using the exercise equipment). Esmeralda and her teacher observed the different areas of the YMCA, making notes about all tasks Esmeralda would be required to complete to independently access and use the YMCA (e.g., in the locker room—changing clothes, showering, using the restroom), and the skills needed in those areas (e.g., organization, safety, sanitation, hygiene). To support Esmeralda in conducting the inventory, her teacher asked her questions like: "Where are we?" "What are people doing here?" "What things do you see?" "What skills do you think you need to be able to access this space?" See Figure 10.4 for an example of an ecological inventory completed for Esmeralda (blank copies of the assessment and task analysis are found in the Chapter 10 Appendix).

Once the ecological inventory has been completed, the next step is to determine what specific skills Esmeralda needs to learn and how she can be supported to successfully participate to her fullest extent possible in the different activities and environments of the YMCA. A task analysis, in which the steps of activities or tasks are broken down and analyzed, can aid in identifying these skills and supports, and is most often used for instruction. Figure 10.5 depicts a completed task analysis for Esmeralda. (See the Chapter 10 Appendix for blank versions of the Ecological Inventory and Task Analysis forms that you can use to support your students' participation in community activities.)

For some students, instruction in community activities may occur outside of the school day and involve support from family members, friends, and community service providers. In other circumstances, community-based instruction incorporated into the student's school day may be needed (Rowe et al., 2015; Test et al., 2009). Oftentimes, there is a strong focus on community experiences for students with disabilities age 18 to 21 who continue to receive special education services, particularly focused on transition skills and experiences needed to be successful post-school. For these students, community experiences become a natural and inclusive part of their day.

---

## Evidence-Based Practices: Community-Based Instruction

Community-based instruction (CBI) is used to learn skills in natural, nonschool environments so students can access a range of community experiences. CBI occurs on a regularly scheduled basis (i.e., weekly, twice weekly, daily) and must be specifically related to transition IEP goals. Walker, Richter, Uphold, and Test (2010) conducted a comprehensive literature review of

| Environment | Subenvironments | Activities or tasks | Skills needed |
|---|---|---|---|
| 1. YMCA | 1. Registration desk | 1. Check in. | 1. Greet desk clerk. |
| | | | 2. Give desk clerk membership card. |
| | | 2. Take towel. | 3. Locate towels. |
| | | | 4. Choose between large or small towels. |
| | | 3. Check out/ return equipment. | 5. Ask for specific equipment needed. |
| | | | 6. Provide membership card for check out. |
| | 2. Locker room | 1. Change into workout clothes. | 1. Find a closed area (cubicle/ shower cubicle). |
| | | | 2. Remove street clothes and shoes. |
| | | | 3. Put on workout clothes and sneakers. |
| | | 2. Keep personal belongings in locker. | 4. Find available locker large enough for personal belongings. |
| | | | 5. Lock locker using passcode. |
| | | 3. Take a shower. | 6. Bring necessary items into shower area (clothes, soap, etc.). |
| | | | 7. Close shower curtain before showering. |
| | | | 8. Shower and dry off. |
| | | 4. Use the restroom. | 9. Find available cubicle, lock cubicle door. |
| | | | 10. Flush after use. |
| | | | 11. Wash hands. |
| | 3. Exercise room | 1. Use exercise equipment. | 1. Read and follow picture or instruction on how to use equipment. |
| | | | 2. Ask for assistance from employee if needed. |
| | | | 3. Adjust equipment to own strength and height. |
| | | | 4. Stop when tired or if does not match physical strength. |
| | | 2. Clean the equipment before and/or after use. | 5. Find cleaning spray bottle and towel. |
| | | | 6. Spray sanitation liquid on cleaning towel and wipe equipment. |
| | | 3. Re-rack weights. | 7. Remove weights from bar. |
| | | | 8. Place weights back in labeled weight area. |

**Figure 10.4.** Sample ecological assessment.

**Task:** Check-in

**Expected Student Outcome:**

Provide membership card to desk clerk at YMCA gym before entering

| Steps: | Date | | | | | | | | | |
|---|---|---|---|---|---|---|---|---|---|---|
| **1.** Greet desk clerk | | | | | | | | | | |
| **2.** Give the desk clerk membership card | | | | | | | | | | |
| **3.** Wait for clerk to clear/approve the membership card | | | | | | | | | | |
| **4.** Clerk nods/says "you are good to go": take card from clerk | | | | | | | | | | |
| **5.** Say "thank you" to clerk | | | | | | | | | | |
| **6.** Push metal entrance bars to enter | | | | | | | | | | |
| **7.** | | | | | | | | | | |
| **8.** | | | | | | | | | | |
| **9.** | | | | | | | | | | |
| **10.** | | | | | | | | | | |

After completion of the task analysis, briefly review to make sure it meets certain basic requirements.

1. Are all of the steps stated in observable, measurable terms?

2. Are any critical steps omitted? If so, add additional steps.

3. Can learner perform the major skill after mastering all the steps?

4. Are all of the steps relevant to the skill?

5. Are any of the steps so minute as to be unnecessary? Can any be combined without losing information?

6. Are the steps arranged in logical order?

**Figure 10.5.** Task analysis worksheet.

interventions using CBI to teach adult life skills. Their review included CBI interventions to improve skills of students with disabilities across grade levels (i.e., elementary, middle, high). Skills taught included, but were not limited to, vocational skills, laundry skills, purchasing items, and banking skills. Findings indicated that using CBI as an instructional strategy resulted in increased acquisition of the target skill. Generalization of the newly learned skill to new places, people, or materials was measured in many of the studies, most of which found that students could generalize to other settings. The steps to conducting CBI include:

- Communicate with students and parents about the student's preferences, interests, talents, and contributions.
- Inventory a range of community settings of interest to the student that would make a good match.
- Complete an ecological inventory and task analysis of each community setting.
- Collect baseline assessment data using the task analysis.
- Plan instruction to learn skills and provide access to supports and accommodations to the environment.
- Teach and assess in the classroom, school, and community.
- Evaluate the process based on student performance.

In summary, to prepare their students for full community living and participation, transition specialists must develop a thoughtful transition plan that includes assessment and person-centered planning, instruction of essential skills, and access to supports and services. Esmeralda, her parents, and her teachers worked together to develop a transition plan that included full inclusion in school and post-school environments. She engaged in many instructional activities that enhanced her self-determination skills, independent living skills, and social skills. She also participated in community experiences to prepare her for the next stage in life while she was in high school. As a result, a few years later Esmeralda is now living a fully included life. With the help of her parents, Esmeralda lives in an apartment in the same city. She has three roommates, one of whom also has a disability. Esmeralda has a support person from the local developmental disability agency come visit her once a week. During this weekly visit, this person provides additional independent living support (e.g., helping her create a grocery list; monitoring her overall financial, physical, social, and emotional well-being). While Esmeralda is physically close to her parents and they can assist when needed, she typically only visits with them once a week. Esmeralda enjoys being around other individuals and is actively involved in her community. She volunteers once a week at the library, assisting with story time for 3 to 5 year olds. Esmeralda also accesses community-based education offered by her city (e.g., culinary classes, photography classes). Like Esmeralda, with the appropriate efforts and supports, each of your students can achieve a fulfilling future and lead an inclusive adult life.

## WHAT YOU CAN DO RIGHT NOW:
### Putting Ideas Into Action

Given the multitude of skills needed to prepare for community living, this preparation can be overwhelming. It requires you to listen, observe, and help the family and student prioritize skills needed based on what is required in the next environment. It also requires you to know how to assess students' skills for community living; identify evidence-based practices to teach self-determination, independent living, and use of social skills; and provide a variety of community experiences. You can use the resources provided throughout this chapter and in the appendix to plan instruction addressing all of the different facets of community living, identify a PCP approach appropriate for each student's needs, and help each student prepare for the particular environments and activities he or she finds most engaging.

Remember, both the family and the school play important roles in helping to ensure that each student leads a quality life. Of course, a happy and fulfilling adult life means something different to every student and should be based on the individual's personal wishes, desires, passions, and preferences. However, regardless of a student's vision for the future, he or she has a fundamental right to meaningfully contribute to and be fully included in his or her community.

## ONLINE RESOURCES

National Autism Professional Development Internet Modules: www.autisminternetmodules.org/

National Technical Assistance Center for Transition (NTACT): www.transitionta.org

Transition Coalition: http://transitioncoalition.org/transition/

Zarrow Center: www.ou.edu/content/education/centers-and-partnerships/zarrow/ transition-education-materials.html

# Ecological Inventory and Task Analysis Forms

# Ecological Inventory

| Environment | Subenvironments | Activities or tasks | Skills needed |
|---|---|---|---|
| 1. | 1. | 1. | 1. |
| | | | 2. |
| | | 2. | 3. |
| | | | 4. |
| | | 3. | 5. |
| | | | 6. |
| | | 4. | 7. |
| | | | 8. |
| | 2. | 1. | 1. |
| | | | 2. |
| | | 2. | 3. |
| | | | 4. |
| | | 3. | 5. |
| | | | 6. |
| | | 4. | 7. |
| | | | 8. |
| 2. | 1. | 1. | 1. |
| | | | 2. |
| | | 2. | 3. |
| | | | 4. |
| | | 3. | 5. |
| | | | 6. |
| | | 4. | 7. |
| | | | 8. |
| | 2. | 1. | 1. |
| | | | 2. |
| | | 2. | 3. |
| | | | 4. |
| | | 3. | 5. |
| | | | 6. |
| | | 4. | 7. |
| | | | 8. |

**Task:** _____

**Expected Student Outcome:**

_____

_____

| Steps: | Date: | | | | | | | | | |
|--------|-------|--|--|--|--|--|--|--|--|--|
| 1. | | | | | | | | | | |
| 2. | | | | | | | | | | |
| 3. | | | | | | | | | | |
| 4. | | | | | | | | | | |
| 5. | | | | | | | | | | |
| 6. | | | | | | | | | | |
| 7. | | | | | | | | | | |
| 8. | | | | | | | | | | |
| 9. | | | | | | | | | | |
| 10. | | | | | | | | | | |

After completion of the task analysis, briefly review to make sure it meets certain basic requirements.

1. Are all of the steps stated in observable, measurable terms?

2. Are any critical steps omitted? If so, add additional steps.

3. Can learner perform the major skill after mastering all the steps?

4. Are all of the steps relevant to the skill?

5. Are any of the steps so minute as to be unnecessary? Can any be combined without losing information?

6. Are the steps arranged in logical order?

# 11

# Preparing for Interpersonal Engagement

Josh is a junior at a large suburban high school. He has a very energetic and exciting personality, which draws people to him. He participates in school and community activities such as the Boy Scouts of America and video gaming club, and he works out at a local fitness club. He has struggled, however, in classroom and nonstructured environments with using expected and mature behaviors to maintain friendships. Josh plans to attend the local community college and pursue a career in video game design. He has shown an interest in pursuing a part-time job, but has not yet completed any applications. His teacher is concerned that his social, behavioral, and organizational challenges are going to make it difficult for him to be successful at college. What would you do to support Josh in increasing his positive social interactions and achieving his future goals?

All of the important adult outcomes for youth—employment, postsecondary education, independent living, and community participation—involve and require social skills and interpersonal relationships. Social skills are not only needed for success after high school, but are also an essential part of the school experience. As you may remember from Chapter 6, students who reported having positive social engagement in school exhibited higher levels of academic achievement and were more likely to remain engaged in school. Interpersonal interactions, such as chatting and hanging out with friends, are often some of the most motivating and memorable moments of the school day for teenagers like Josh. Teenagers with and without disabilities rated visiting with friends and family and engaging in social activities as their second highest preferred free time activity, which means that opportunities to learn and use interpersonal skills for teenagers would seem to be quite high (Repetto et al., 2011). However, even students with a strong desire to socialize may need support to establish and engage in positive relationships.

Developing skills to establish and maintain friendships can be challenging for students with disabilities. Specifically, some students may have difficulty with starting conversations, responding to others during a conversation, engaging in new social encounters, and interpreting nonverbal cues (Winner, 2007b; Bellini, 2006). Studies have linked students with poor social skills to more negative outcomes, including engaging in risky behaviors, dropping out of school, depression and anxiety, substance abuse, and being arrested (Maag, 2006; Murray & Greenberg, 2006; Otten & Tuttle, 2011). On the other hand, supporting students to develop strong interpersonal skills can lead to positive outcomes and prepare students to achieve future goals. We know that students with disabilities who have had positive social opportunities and experiences during high school are two to three times more likely to be employed after high school, and they were more actively engaged in communities, families, and friendships as adults (McConnell et al., 2013). Skills such as communication, empathy, social awareness, respect for others, and personal responsibility have been associated with college and career readiness skills for students with disabilities (Morningstar, Lombardi, Fowler, & Test, 2015).

As far as employment is concerned, positive social interactions between employees with disabilities and co-workers are also associated with greater job retention for employees with certain types of disabilities (Roberts et al., 2010). Hanley-Maxwell and Izzo (2012) identified foundational skills for preparing students with disabilities for the 21st century workforce, and social skills were found to be crucial to success. Ju, Zhang, and Pacha (2012) identified critical "employability" skills influencing employment that were not job-specific: following instructions, showing respect for others, and demonstrating personal integrity. These skills are similar to what have come be known as 21st century, or soft skills (Office of Disability Employment Policy, n.d.). Twenty-first century skills are an essential consideration of career readiness for all students, regardless of plans to pursue a 2- or 4-year degree or vocational training, or enter directly into the workforce. Most recently, employers and community members have identified skills such as dependability, teamwork, and persistence as cornerstones for success in career settings (Neuenswander & Watson, 2015). The research is clear: social and emotional skills and interpersonal engagement are all necessary components of a successful transition to adult life.

## GETTING STARTED:
## Interpersonal Engagement and the Impact on Student Success

With its frequent opportunities for social interaction, the high school environment is the logical place to teach social-emotional skills that are valued on the job, in postsecondary settings, and throughout a person's adult life (Ryndak, Alper, Hughes, & McDonnell, 2012). However, in order to teach these skills most effectively, first you must understand the different levels of interpersonal engagement occurring in secondary schools.

## Understanding Multiple Levels of Secondary School Engagement

Secondary schools have been described as multi-level systems that start with classrooms, where positive teacher-student interactions are considered to be important predictors of student academic performance. Positive engagement with peers is also essential. When students report they are listened to, involved in decisions, and accepted by peers, they are more likely to be motivated to perform in school (Pianta, La Paro, & Hamre, 2008). Positive interactions with adults and peers in secondary schools work best when embedded within daily curriculum and explicitly connected to other school activities (Greenburg et al., 2003). Learning interpersonal skills and having opportunities to practice them are equally important, and educators have confirmed that practice of interpersonal skills should be included throughout a student's day to successfully prepare him or her for the future (Bridgeland, Bruce, & Hariharan, 2013). Essential skills needed for interpersonal engagement include collaborating and communicating with parents, adults, and peers, as well as social awareness and empathy (e.g., treating others with respect and understanding the feelings of others) (Morningstar, Lombardi et al., 2015).

The diversity of students in today's schools means that we need to teach not only social, emotional, and character development skills, but also adaptability, acceptance, and respect for individual differences. It is possible to address these skills in the general education classroom; in fact, the CCSS include essential skills, such as participating in conversations, collaborating with diverse partners, problem solving, and critical thinking (www .corestandards.org/about-the-standards/frequently-asked-questions/#faq-2323). The skills outlined in these standards enhance and enrich core academic content, allowing students with disabilities access to the general education curriculum along with opportunities to further prepare for college and careers, where social interactions and interpersonal skills will be key (Villa, Thousand, & Nevin, 2013). Therefore, essential social and interpersonal skills should be embedded in the general education curriculum and incorporated into classroom activities, with specialized supports provided to individual students as needed.

In addition to positive teacher-student and peer interactions at the classroom level, systems-level factors influence middle and high school performance and social adjustment. Systems-level, school-wide approaches help establish positive school climates through efforts like promoting positive, supportive relationships; ensuring consistent goals and norms; enhancing collaboration; and maintaining a safe school environment. A systematic approach to creating a positive school environment leads to positive student outcomes that include decreased absenteeism, reduced suspensions, and improvements in academic achievement (Thapa, Cohen, Guffey, & Higgins-D'Alessandro, 2013). Positive school climates encourage interpersonal engagement and allow students to feel a sense of safety and security. For the most part, schools emphasize a systems approach to developing positive pro-social interactions and social engagement while utilizing interventions to teach social skills to individual students (Furlong & Christenson, 2008). For students in need of more targeted social supports, well-planned interventions cannot only improve individual social skills, but also increase the pro-social behaviors needed for successful transition outcomes (Allwell & Cobb, 2009).

## Effective Practices for Teaching Interpersonal Skills

While research has long supported embedding opportunities for learning interpersonal skills into general education, this practice has not always occurred, especially in core academic classes. It seems that secondary special educators and transition coordinators are inconsistent in determining the most highly valued interpersonal skills and selecting valid skills for instructional focus (Agran, Hughes, Thoma, & Scott, 2014). Some states have adopted specific standards targeting social-emotional learning, and there are several exemplary school- or district-wide evidence-based programs, curricula, and targeted interventions. Effective practices often fall into two categories: 1) curriculum with scripted lessons, units, scope and sequence, and enrichment activities; and 2) school-wide programs that outline specific instructional practices and expectations (CASEL Guide, 2015).

Among the various programs and curricula, some consistent skills and competencies have emerged that all teachers can teach and reinforce in the classroom. The Collaborative for Academic, Social, and Emotional Learning (CASEL) outlined five competency areas for social-emotional success: self-awareness, self-management, social awareness, interpersonal skills, and responsible decision making (Durlak, Weissberg, Dymnicki, Taylor, & Schellinger, 2011). Social skills related to these competency areas can be learned directly through teacher- or peer-mediated instruction, as well as through incidental learning and peer modeling (Sargent, Perner, & Cook, 2012). Of course, the best place to learn and practice social skills is in natural settings where adolescents learn, socialize, and work. Students with disabilities who spend their time in inclusive settings are much more likely to be engaged with same-aged peers without disabilities, and so naturally have more opportunities to learn, practice, and engage in interpersonal skills (Bauminger et al., 2008).

### TIP FOR TRANSITION: Promote Social-Emotional Learning

*The 2015 CASEL Guide, Effective Social and Emotional Learning Programs—Middle and High School Edition,* describes programs promoting social emotional learning (www.casel.org/middle-and-high-school-edition-casel-guide). The guide includes curricula with lessons teachers can use. Descriptions of school-wide practices to increase positive school culture are also included. For example, student success skills offers lessons to teach goal setting, stress reduction, emotion management, and cognitive skills.

This chapter's Making It Happen section will outline beneficial strategies to support your students' social and interpersonal skills as they prepare for life after high school. It is a guide for providing specially designed instruction related to social-emotional learning within the context of the general education curriculum, promoting a positive school and classroom climate, and helping your students develop the relationships needed for success. You'll also find helpful tips and activities for your students that provide practical experiences with social-emotional skills.

## MAKING IT HAPPEN:
### Increasing Interpersonal Engagement

Schools can help students develop appropriate interpersonal competence through three different approaches: 1) establishing systems-level practices to create school climates supportive of interpersonal engagement, 2) embedding instruction within the academic curriculum, and 3) directly teaching skills to students (CASEL Guide, 2015). These strategies are not mutually exclusive and work best when implemented together. For this chapter, we will describe ways to ensure positive school climates, as well as how to embed, teach, and reinforce specific skills in inclusive settings.

### Creating Positive School Climates

To better promote interpersonal engagement, begin by ensuring that your classroom, school, and programs have a strong sense of community, with an emphasis on respecting others and diversity, helping and working cooperatively, having high expectations, and maintaining a positive school climate (Sargent, Perner, & Cook, 2012). As defined by the National School Climate Center (www.schoolclimate.org/climate), school climate refers to the quality and character of school life based on student, parental, and school staff experiences. A positive school climate reflects several critical elements:

- The school's norms, values, and expectations for positive and respectful relationships

- Teaching practices that nurture and emphasize positive engagement and learning

- Organizational structures promoting collaboration and input from all stakeholders

School-based efforts to improve school climates are designed to promote positive peer interactions, teach relationship building skills to students, and provide opportunities for students to use and generalize skills (Murray & Greenburg, 2006).

When teaching and supporting the development of social skills, remember that effective social skill instruction is more likely to be found in classrooms and settings that structure a variety of learning groups, including whole-class instruction and cooperative learning exhibiting flexible groupings (e.g., grouping students by interests, mixed abilities, and so forth). Table 11.1 describes various learning groups that support social interaction among a diverse group of students.

Based on ideas from Sargent, Perner, and Cook (2012), the following steps are some ways you can help your school or program build social skills:

1.  Provide time for students to socially interact.

2.  Encourage and reinforce cooperative learning and behaviors.

3.  Offer less structured whole-group teaching activities and design units focused on cooperative and project-based learning.

4.  Modify instruction so that all students can participate in the learning process using mixed-ability groupings.

5.  Model and reinforce class/program expectations for appropriate social interactions on a regular basis.

6.  Provide opportunities for students to practice and reinforce positive interpersonal skills, including video feedback.

7.  Use peer-mediated approaches to support and learning.

School-wide initiatives to improve social engagement likely align with plans to implement PBIS or dropout prevention programs (see Chapter 6). A large component of PBIS is school-wide support of appropriate social-emotional learning for all students. Having a school-wide program that aligns with PBIS, as well as smaller programs targeting interpersonal engagement, will prepare all students with the social, emotional, and behavioral skills needed to develop social relationships throughout their lives. Implementing school-wide efforts associated with interpersonal engagement for all students ensures that all staff are responsible for teaching and promoting interpersonal engagement. In this way, essential competencies such as social awareness, self-management, and interpersonal skills will be explicitly supported. As a transition specialist, you should be included in supporting your school's programs and curricula for social skill development.

## Identifying Students Requiring Targeted Social Interventions

Working at the school and program level to increase positive relationships for students is but one critical element of supporting your students. You may also be required to implement more explicit interventions for students needing targeted or intensive supports. Determining which students in the building need more systematic support for interpersonal engagement requires teachers to use screening and diagnostic assessments. Brief screening instruments allow staff to quickly identify students exhibiting initial social challenges so they can acquire a more in-depth understanding of why these challenges are occurring and how to address them. Table 11.2 reviews three screeners that can be used in secondary schools.

**Table 11.1.**   School-based approaches to learning groups and their effect on social skill development

| Learning group | Description | Considerations for social skill development | Example |
|---|---|---|---|
| Whole class instruction | The teacher leads the whole class in instruction. This often occurs at the beginning of a lesson through a short lecture with visuals (presentation or video) to introduce content and concepts. Teachers often end a class session back in whole groups, to summarize and have students reflect on their learning. | Whole class instruction allows teachers to build classroom community, establish class routines, quickly introduce new units, and develop common experiences for all students. It requires consideration of class diversity so that all students are included and interacting. Direct instruction on class expectations and behaviors is incorporated at the beginning and end of whole class instruction. | The life science teacher begins the class session on seed germination by presenting a short, 15-minute PowerPoint lecture introducing key concepts, reviewing the learning objectives, and identifying critical vocabulary words. She then provides an overview of the lab, reviews class rules for appropriate behavioral and social expectations, and divides the class into teams where they must then self-monitor team behaviors and interactions. |
| Small-group instruction/ cooperative learning groups | Often referred to as cooperative learning groups, these small groups consist of approximately three to six students who collaboratively work on a class project during class time and often outside of class. The teacher supports student groups by rotating around the room providing feedback, guidance, and redirection. Within each small group, students are often assigned specific roles (e.g., notetaker, time keeper) to ensure consistent and organized performance. | Small-group instruction allows opportunities for practicing social and communication skills. The teacher can determine groups or students can self-select. Groups should not extend beyond a single project or unit, to ensure students have opportunities to work with all classmates. Students develop collaboration, communication, and problem-solving skills. Because projects may take longer than a single class period, levels of student independent work are also supported and evaluated through this method. Groups with students from various ability levels work best when students are assigned specific tasks for the project. Students can serve as role models and receive assistance from each other. Everyone contributes based on individual needs and abilities. | In a U.S. Civics class, small groups of four students must develop a newscast that demonstrates social and economic conditions related to a teacher-developed list of ongoing domestic or foreign issues (e.g., gun control, immigration, civil rights, voting rights, free trade). The news team must address historical/social contexts impacting the policy decisions and outcomes. Critical communication and problem-solving skills are addressed and reinforced by the teacher throughout the small group work. |
| Paired groups | Pairs of students work collaboratively to complete required assignments. Paired groups may be formed to offer peer feedback and review of individual work, or for purposes such as peer tutoring, in which students provide additional academic and social supports to each other. | Pairs can be based on a variety of factors (abilities, interests, skills). Pairs may be teacher-directed or student-selected. Often, students are assigned to pairs based on mixed ability levels so that students can form collaborative helping relationships. Peer tutoring is a form of paired groupings and offers opportunity for practicing social and communication skills. Other times, pairs may be based on specific student interests or capabilities, with high-achieving students working together on extension activities, while the others complete required core learning objectives. | In a ninth-grade English Language Arts class related to persuasive writing, the teacher has divided students into pairs to work together. First, they discuss the topic of texting as a form of communication and the advantages and disadvantages of texting versus face-to-face communication. Then pairs individually draft their arguments using the established class rubric for persuasive writing. During the last part of the class, the pairs come back together and review each other's work, providing edits and feedback with the rubric. |

| Learning group | Description | Considerations for social skill development | Example |
|---|---|---|---|
| Cluster and flexible groups | Clusters of students may be organized into specific groups for specific instructional goals or educational purposes, such as reading or math groups. Teachers provide needed modifications and adaptations or extension activities to meet the unique needs of students in the room. Typically, students remain in the group for a specific period of time or until the learning objectives are met. | Students are organized into more homogeneous groups within a classroom based on abilities or unique learning differences related to a specific academic area (i.e., low-achieving, high-achieving). Using cluster groups allows teachers to differentiate the curriculum to meet the needs of a diverse set of learners. Keeping the focus on short-term instructional groups is best, so that all students move in and out of groupings according to their interests, abilities, and pace of learning, thereby avoiding stigmatizing groupings. | During an Algebra 1 class, the algebra teacher and the paraprofessional divide the class into flexible groups to provide more explicit instruction during the content focused on graphing linear equations. For some advanced students, extension activities are the focus, and they are working in a small group primarily independently, while most of the class is working on grade-level standards, learning how to graph equations with an actual dataset. The teacher is rotating around the class, checking on student work. For the small group of students who need additional supports, the paraprofessional is re-teaching a lesson that has been adapted to meet their needs. This includes focusing on the essential components of linear relationships using some modified materials and activities. |

*Source:* Sargent, Perner, & Cook (2012).

Formal diagnostic assessments are also available for students with identified social and behavioral challenges. Two predominant diagnostic assessments are:

- *The Social Skills Improvement System Rating Scales* (SSIS) (Gresham & Elliott, 2008), which enables targeted assessment of individuals and small groups to help evaluate social skills (communication, cooperation, assertion, responsibility, empathy, engagement, self-control), competing problem behaviors (externalizing, bullying, hyperactivity, internalizing, autism spectrum), and academic competence (reading, math, motivation to learn). Teachers, parents, and students complete the assessment, which develops a comprehensive picture across school, home, and the community.

- *Behavior Assessment System for Children* (BASIC-3) (Reynolds & Kamphaus, 2015), an evaluation process that can be used with children and adolescents and includes a set of rating scales and forms completed by teachers, parents, and students; a formal student observation system; and a structured developmental history approach to understand background information. The outcomes include a comprehensive evaluation of student behavior patterns, emotions, and feelings, and a profile of social, psychological, developmental, medical, and educational history.

Diagnostic scales can help you and the IEP team identify specific and in-depth needs regarding a student's challenging behavior. You can also use observational data to determine

**Table 11.2.**   Three screening tools validated for use in secondary schools that assess social and behavioral challenges

| Points to consider | SRSS-IE | BASC 2 – BESS | SAEBRS |
|---|---|---|---|
| Grade levels | K–12 | Pre-K–12 | K–12 |
| Behaviors measured | Externalizing behaviors. Internalizing behaviors. | Externalizing behaviors. Internalizing behaviors. Adaptive skills. School problems. | Social behavior. Emotional behavior. Academic behavior. |
| Description | Rating scale focusing on specific negative behaviors. | Rating scale targeting positive behavioral characteristics as well as negative behaviors. | Rating scale of positive behaviors (social, emotional, academic) as well as negative behaviors. |
| Who administers? | Teachers. | Teachers. Parents. Students (11–17 years old). | Teachers. |
| Cost? | No. | Yes—see web site. | No. |
| Time to complete | 10–15 minutes per class. | 5–10 minutes per student. | 1–3 minutes per student. |
| Online/computer-based option | Yes. | Yes. | No. |
| Intervention component? | No. | Yes. | No. |
| How to find instrument | CI3T web site: www.ci3t. org/measures. html#srss-ie | Pearson Educational Products: www .pearsonclinical. com/ | University of Missouri: http://ebi.missouri.edu/ wp-content/uploads/ 2014/ 03/EBA-Brief-SAEBRS.pdf |

*Source:* Lane, Menzies, Oakes, & Kalberg (2012).

*Key:* BASC 2 - BESS, BASC-2 Behavioral and Emotional Screening System; SAEBRS, Social, Academic, and Emotional Behavior Risk Screener; SRSS-IE, Student Risk Screening Scale – Internalizing and Externalizing

which students are struggling with interpersonal engagement, as well as analyze office disciplinary referrals, teacher observations, and students' participation in extracurricular activities. Figure 11.1 is an example of an observation sheet that can be used to collect behavioral data regarding social interactions and classroom behaviors. Using all three approaches—screeners, formal assessments, and anecdotal observations—will help your team identify students who may need more targeted interventions.

## Effective Interventions and Strategies for Improving Interpersonal Engagement

Let's think back to Josh, a student with identified social challenges. Josh has an energetic and humorous personality that helps him start friendships, but he struggles with staying positive, managing his emotions, and engaging in socially acceptable interactions. The team therefore will need to select appropriate interventions and supports to help Josh build and maintain positive relationships. Because of Josh's challenges, his teacher recognizes that he would benefit from learning how to identify and then problem solve which actions are causing him difficulty. She believes she can work with Josh to increase his ability to create positive social interactions and plans to help him identify and self-monitor a social communication goal.

Once schools and collaborative teams have identified students with or without disabilities who may need more structured or intense support, it will be helpful to have various targeted interventions to choose from that are based on proven research. It is important to note that the conceptual orientation toward teaching social skills includes research-based

Student name: _____ Date of observation: _____

Setting: _____

**Instructions:** Collect data on the presence of the identified behavior(s) in predetermined time periods. Tally each time you observe the behavior in the 5 minute interval of time. During breaks, take notes on what was observed during the previous 10-minute block. Choose a typically developing peer to observe as a comparison.

| Behavior: | 5 mins | 5 mins | break | 5 mins | 5 mins | break | 5 mins | 5 mins | break |
|---|---|---|---|---|---|---|---|---|---|
| Target Student | | | | | | | | | |
| Peer | | | | | | | | | |
| **Behavior:** | | | | | | | | | |
| Target Student | | | | | | | | | |
| Peer | | | | | | | | | |

Description of social interaction behaviors for focus:

Interventions classroom teacher used:

Effectiveness of interventions:

Suggestions for improvement:

**Figure 11.1.** Social interaction behavioral observation data sheet.

components (i.e., research has verified the importance of social skills instruction and investigated individual social skills needed for success), yet some social skills programs and interventions may not be evidence-based if rigorous, randomized studies have not yet been completed (Strawhun, O'Connor, Norris, & Peterson, 2014). Programs and strategies do exist, however, that are evidence-based and effective, and quite a bit of research has been completed in this area. Keep in mind some research results may not be conclusive for long-term generalization of skills to other settings. Nevertheless, many benefits of social skills instruction have been found, especially when instruction is frequent and embedded throughout the school day, and includes effective practices such as modeling, role playing, coaching, rehearsal, feedback, and reinforcement (Gresham, Sugai, & Horner, 2001).

If you are not working in a school where school-wide positive behavior supports and interventions are in place, having access to social, emotional, and behavioral interventions to use with your students will be vital. The interventions found at PBIS World (www .pbisworld.org), many of which are easy to use and embed in your daily interactions with students, include both research- and evidence-based interventions that can be helpful. (See "Tip for Transition: Find a Positive Behavior Intervention and Support that Works!" for more information). When deciding on a social skills curriculum or any teaching strategy, consider the following questions (Otten & Tuttle, 2011):

- How flexible is the program or curriculum for allowing the skills to be taught in large groups, small groups, or individually?

- What types of effective and evidence-based instructional methods are incorporated into the curriculum (e.g., modeling, direct instruction, role playing, practice, feedback)?

- Does the program identify different types of skills to be taught and offer strategies for each, particularly related to skill acquisition, performance, and/or fluency needs?

- Does the program lead to student self-management? Learning social skills using natural cues and avoiding external prompts should be an essential goal.

## TIP FOR TRANSITION: Find a Positive Behavior Intervention and Support That Works!

Two "go-to" web sites for understanding PBIS and finding a range of resources and strategies are:

- The PBIS Center (www.pbis.org), a technical assistance center funded by the U.S. Department of Education, includes a wide range of information and strategies for supporting students to develop effective pro-social behaviors. Resources found on this web site include evidence- and research-based practices, presentations, videos, and a range of training tools.

- PBIS World (www.pbisworld.com) offers a variety of interventions based on the behavior selected (lack of social skills, being out of one's seat, off-task behaviors, etc.); from there it provides appropriate interventions for that behavior at each level of support: Tier 1, Tier 2, and Tier 3. Some helpful strategies found here include using a 4:1 ratio of praise to correction, preparing visual schedules for students during class transitions, and developing social narratives for intensive social skills supports.

Teaching interpersonal engagement skills can be accomplished by embedding lessons within academic coursework to meet the needs of all adolescents. For example, before you break into a small group project or activity, you can remind students about a problem-solving strategy for brainstorming ideas that all members of the group can use. In other circumstances, you may need to target more specific skills and provide focused attention through a regularly scheduled session, such as during an advisory or guided studies class. Instruction on specific social skills typically starts by defining the expected social or emotional skill through class lecture, examples, and discussion. Then students practice the target skills, primarily through role playing, while receiving constructive feedback from the teacher (Reinke, Lewis-Palmer, & Martin, 2007). The following subsections detail some specific strategies for teaching and promoting interpersonal engagement.

***Improving Social Problem-Solving Skills*** Part of some students' limited ability to generalize social skills may be because they are taught isolated behaviors that are hard to transfer to other settings. A broader approach is to focus on developing cognitive-behavioral skills that help students develop a form of "self-talk" to modify underlying thoughts influencing social behaviors (Smith, 2002). A fundamental perspective of a cognitive-behavioral approach is that social behaviors can be changed and improved when students use cognitive strategies to think about and change how they interact and behave. Cognitive-behavioral interventions can be used to address areas such as social problem solving, coping techniques, and social functioning skills. Maag (2006) noted that cognitive-behavioral interventions typically incorporate behavioral strategies to teaching skills, such as modeling (including video modeling), role playing, self-evaluation, and positive reinforcement.

## TIP FOR TRANSITION: Social Thinking Curriculum

This research-supported curriculum uses cognitive-behavioral approaches to teach students with autism and learning disabilities how to modify and improve social skills by first examining the context of a social situation, and then thinking about the responses and reactions of others before they act. Rather than memorizing specific skills, *Social Thinking* (www.socialthinking.com) teaches students to become active social problem solvers. Students spend time understanding what people around them are doing, what they are expecting, and what the student desires from the social interaction. This approach helps students figure out how to interact in any given time or place and with different people.

Social problem-solving interventions often focus on how students communicate with peers and how to appropriately engage in social interactions across various school and community settings. Interpersonal interactions require students to be agile in listening and responding to others, as well as to problem solve what is occurring during a conversation (Winner, 2007a). Mastering the art of conversation can seem like a daunting task for some students, and explicitly teaching social communication skills (e.g., initiating and maintaining a conversation, engaging in small talk) can be taught through problem-solving strategies, opportunities to role play, and reinforcing the use of newly acquired skills in natural settings. A useful tool, *Social Behavior Mapping* (Winner, 2007b), teaches students a concrete approach to connecting their social actions with the emotions and consequences (both positive and negative) of these actions. Figure 11.2 is an example of a social behavior map for a student learning to understand the consequence of social behaviors during lunch time.

| Context: Eating lunch with friends Expected behaviors | | | |
|---|---|---|---|
| **Expected behaviors you do** | **How this makes others feel** | **Consequences you experience** | **How you feel about yourself** |
| Talking with others about TV shows they watched. | Comfortable. | People will keep talking with you. | Happy. |
| Listening to others when they talk. | Respected. | People will see you are interested in them. | Proud. |
| Looking at your friends when they talk. | Listened to and valued. | Friends will listen to you when you talk. | Part of the group. |
| **Unexpected behaviors** | | | |
| **Unexpected behaviors you do** | **How this makes others feel** | **Consequences you experience** | **How you feel about yourself** |
| Talking fast and eating with your mouth open. | Grossed out. | People may sit somewhere else. | Embarrassed. |
| Talking the whole time without letting others talk. | Frustrated. | Friends may not want to talk to you. | Depressed. |
| Talking about topics only you are interested in. | Bored. | Friends may ignore you or sit elsewhere. | Sad, lonely. |

**Figure 11.2.**   Example of a social behavior map. (*Source:* Winner, 2007.)

Other types of visual social problem-solving strategies found to be effective in improving and supporting students include:

- *Social Autopsy:* Developed by Richard Lavoie, this problem-solving strategy helps students find and correct social errors using the following steps: 1) identify social error, 2) determine who was harmed by error, 3) decide how to correct error, and 4) develop a plan. The goal of a social autopsy is to help the student understand a social situation and assist him or her to respond effectively in similar situations. Using pictures to support comprehension can enhance a social autopsy. For sample forms, see www.ocali.org/ project/resource_gallery_of_interventions/page/social_autopsy.

- *Social narratives:* These are visually represented stories that describe a social situation and socially appropriate responses and behaviors. Social narratives can be written, descriptive accounts or scripts designed to promote social understanding. Drawings, photographs, and cartoons have also been used to create stories told from the student's perspective.

Josh would benefit from using a social behavior map to help him think about challenging social situations and help him problem solve. For him, social challenges typically lead to his impulsive behaviors. This cognitive-behavioral approach could help him remember to listen to others and respond with supportive comments, which makes people feel comfortable and results in his peers continuing to engage with him.

**Role Playing Social Situations**    Role playing can be a helpful technique to engage students, allow them to practice newly acquired skills, and acquire specific feedback about their social performance. Having your student role play social situations with various peers and adults is an effective strategy for simulating a wide range of school, community, and workplace interactions. Role plays can be set up using the following steps:

1. Observe a student's social interactions across a range of settings (e.g., classrooms, cafeteria, hallways, with friends, with adults) and discuss with the student areas they find most challenging.

2. Identify specific social behaviors you think the student may need to acquire or perform with more fluency, such as starting and maintaining a conversation, understanding nonverbal communication, or joining a group.

3. Recreate scenarios addressing the social behaviors of concern, making sure to demonstrate both expected and unexpected ways to interact.

4. Video tape the role play and share with students afterwards.

5. Hold a structured discussion about the role play. Problem solve why different actions lead to both expected and unexpected outcomes.

6. Brainstorm possible solutions to improve skills, using visuals such as the social behavior map to connect actions with emotional responses and potential consequences.

**Using Multimedia to Teach Social Skills**    While research into the use of multimedia to teach social skills is fairly recent, there are a number of reasons to consider using technology such as video modeling to augment social skills instruction. Multimedia often meets the specific learning styles and preferences of students with disabilities (e.g., virtual environments, simulations, videos) who may be hands-on and visual learners (Odom et al., 2014). Many of the cognitive-behavioral strategies described previously work well with a variety of multimedia tools. When taught in authentic situations, activities such as role playing, social narratives, self-monitoring, observing others, and conducting social autopsies all can be augmented with the use of multimedia, especially digital video technologies. While commercially available software is available for teaching social skills, it is possible to create your own technologies that can be tailored to the specific needs of your students. For example, you can video tape students role playing or engaged in social interactions, and then use the video for discussion afterwards using the social autopsy steps. Photographs can be used to create a slideshow loaded onto a student's phone that he or she can use as a reminder prior to entering a specific social situation.

***Developing and Supporting Peer-Mediated Programs***     Over the years, there has been an increase in research on peer mentoring as an effective strategy to promote interpersonal engagement (DuBois, Portillo, Rhodes, Silverthorn, & Valentine, 2011). A peer mentorship allows students to establish authentic school relationships while also developing interpersonal skills. Peer mentoring programs offer many benefits, including learning and practicing social skills with peer mentors and developing acquaintances and friendships (Carter, Cushing, Clark, & Kennedy, 2005). Research has found that students with disabilities engaged in peer support programs have more frequent and positive social interactions (Carter, Cushing, & Kennedy, 2009). Peer-mediated programs come in different forms and offer a variety of social supports, including information, emotional support, companionship, and material and personal aids (e.g., physical help, sharing items, making decisions) (Janney & Snell, 2006). Most important, building positive relationships is reciprocal, with a balance of social and academic interactions occurring across all partners, meaning the student with disabilities is not always on the receiving end of the support, but contributes to supporting others (Carter et al., 2009). There are many different types of peer-mediated instruction and social interventions, with some of the most common approaches shared in Table 11.3.

- - - - - - - - - - - - - - - - - - - - - - - - - - - - - - - - - - - - - - - - - - - - - - - - - - - - - - - - - - - -

## Evidence-Based Practices: Peer Mentoring Programs

Developing peer support arrangements in general education classes and peer network strategies outside of class time for students with significant disabilities increases academic engagement, social interactions, and both in-school and out-of-school friendships in high school. Developing and supporting peer-mediated programs with fidelity leads to long-term social contacts and friendships (Carter et al., 2016).

- - - - - - - - - - - - - - - - - - - - - - - - - - - - - - - - - - - - - - - - - - - - - - - - - - - - - - - - - - - -

In addition to increasing social access and networks, peer-mediated programs can be used to increase academic, language/communication, and interpersonal skills. One essential guideline for designing your own peer-mediated program is to use sufficient but not excessive support structures. You will want to balance existing scheduled activities (e.g., lunch, extracurricular clubs) with more structured and specialized programs, such as a Best Buddies or a social skills class or club (Janney & Snell, 2006). Remember, as the structure increases, so does your and others' time and efforts to maintain it. Sometimes when creating a "specialized" type of program, peers may assume this is the only time to socially

**Table 11.3.**   Peer-mediated interventions and approaches

| Approach | Description |
| --- | --- |
| Peer modeling | Students learn appropriate social behaviors through observation and imitation. Often used with other methods such as peer tutoring or cooperative groups. Using videos to model behaviors and to provide natural feedback is an effective approach. |
| Peer training and monitoring | Often used with students with more significant disabilities, this approach requires specific training for peers who provide support to promote identified social and communication interactions. This approach is often used in conjunction with peer monitoring, where peers check the student's performance and provide feedback to a student with disabilities. |
| Peer networking | Developing supportive social environments for students with disabilities also has been shown to increase social and communication behaviors. Peer networks are designed to increase the frequency and quality of social interactions with peers through supportive friendship networks engaged in school and community activities. |
| Peer buddy | Peers support the inclusion of students with disabilities in high schools and are training to provide instructional and social supports. Peer buddies can provide academic supports during classes, reduce the need for adult supports, and offer instruction and social supports throughout the day. |
| Peer tutoring | Peer tutoring has been used extensively for students with and without disabilities to increase academic and social behaviors. It is beneficial to both students with and without disabilities, but requires additional training of the tutors and program time for the teacher during the initial set up. |
| Cooperative learning | Students work in groups to achieve a common academic goal. It requires positive interdependence, individual group member accountability, specific cooperative behaviors and interpersonal interactions, and student reflection and goal setting. |

*Source:* Sargent, Perner, & Cook (2012).

engage with students with disabilities. Consider embedding peer supports and mentor programs within existing activities first, and then enhancing programs and activities as needed. For example, rather than creating a club where the focus is only to increase social engagement for students with disabilities, you could work with an existing school club to add a component for including students with disabilities.

It is important to decide the overall purpose of the peer-mediated program. For example, it may be to establish a social network for the student with disabilities. In this case, your program can focus on creating friendship pairs or having small groups get together throughout the day and week to build opportunities to spend time together. Most often, you want to pair up groups with similar interests and enthusiasms. Your role may be to provide the needed support and guidance to the group to make sure it is positive and successful. For example, you may connect a small group of peers who all like sports to attend high school football games. Most likely, you will need to provide some training ahead of time, so the peer mentors understand their roles and have necessary information to provide effective supports. Being available before or during the event to provide onsite training and modeling and answer questions may be essential early on in the process, and then your assistance can gradually fade.

Other peer-mediated programs may be more specific to a social skills class. In this circumstance, you may be teaching an elective class for students with disabilities and peer mentors who can model effective and appropriate social skills. In other circumstances, peer-mediated programs involve community service learning, where students with and without disabilities experience increased social interactions through service to the broader community (e.g., food drive, volunteering at nursing home, recycling program). Finally, peer-mediated supports are often used to establish academic supports in classes, with peers providing increased supports and adaptations for academic learning. This often involves cooperative learning groups, peer tutoring, and other more academic approaches. Hughes and Carter (2008) describe a series of essential steps to setting up a peer mentoring program:

1.  Laying the groundwork. First, you must identify the goals of the program. Is it to develop a service learning class? Improve school climate? Increase inclusive education? Develop individual friendships? Provide information about the program you hope to establish? This often requires an ability awareness session that first focuses on providing information to peers about students with disabilities, emphasizing similarities of interests rather than deficits. This training also shares unique ways the student with disabilities may communicate or engage with others. The purpose is to introduce the idea of a peer mentoring program and establish positive expectations among students and the school environments. You can plan an ability awareness program for the entire school, which may take considerable time and planning, or you can embed smaller trainings within an existing class or activity.

2.  Recruiting participants. After you provide general ability awareness training through classes, clubs, and possibly school assemblies, you can select students most interested in and suited to peer mentoring programs. You will want to establish a way for interested students to sign up. This may be as simple as a sign-up sheet or may be a more detailed process, such as an application for and/or interview with the interested students. High school students may be interested in signing up as a teacher's assistant during a free period in their schedule. You can use these students as peer mentors or buddies, rather than as a more typical assistant in the class. A good match between peer mentors and students with disabilities is essential. It may be better to match a student with a network of peers (two to four students in a class) rather than just one mentor. This relieves some of the burden placed on a single student, and also introduces the student with disabilities to a broader network of potential friends and acquaintances.

3.  Developing procedures. Clearly articulating the roles and responsibilities of the adults and students in the program will help to establish a strong program. It is important to maintain communication with teachers, paraprofessionals, administrators, and other adults, as well as to set up regular meetings with the peer mentors. Establish expectations for the peer mentors, including the focus of interactions (e.g., academic supports, social interactions inside and outside of school, support during community service projects), when and how interactions will take place, and how peer mentors and students will be matched. Most programs start with orientation sessions providing an overview of the roles and expectations, as well as instructional strategies and supports.

4.  Supporting the mentors. Ongoing opportunities for peer mentors to ask questions and continue to learn about socially appropriate supports are necessary. Some programs are highly structured, with peer mentors turning in assignments and receiving grades, whereas others are more informal and individualized. As part of supervising the program, you and others will need to observe the peer mentors to identify additional areas for training. You can use checklists, such as the one developed by Carter et al. (2009) in Figure 11.3. Often, the areas of focus include how the peer mentors can provide supports during academic classes, such as making adaptations to the learning, or assist with providing social supports (e.g., modeling appropriate social interactions, treating student with respect and as a peer, including student in broader social circle).

| | | | | Checklist for Monitoring Peer Support Arrangements |
|---|---|---|---|---|

Class: _____ Student: _____

Teacher: _____ Team: _____

At various times during the class, reflect on each question and check the associated box when the answer is *yes*. If no boxes are checked for a question, use the space at the bottom of the chart to brainstorm ideas for addressing this item.

| Segment of class | | | | |
|---|---|---|---|---|
| **1** | **2** | **3** | **4** | **Reflection questions** |
| ❑ | ❑ | ❑ | ❑ | Is the student seated next to the peer(s) with whom he or she is paired? |
| ❑ | ❑ | ❑ | ❑ | Does the student have the same materials as his or her classmates (e.g., worksheets, books, lab materials, writing utensils, computers)? |
| ❑ | ❑ | ❑ | ❑ | Are the student and his or her peers *actively engaged* in ongoing instruction? |
| ❑ | ❑ | ❑ | ❑ | Is the work the student is doing *closely aligned* with work expected of the rest of the class? |
| ❑ | ❑ | ❑ | ❑ | Are interactions among the student and his or her peers *appropriate* given the context or the types of interactions other students have? |
| ❑ | ❑ | ❑ | ❑ | Are students completing class activities in a timely fashion or at a reasonable pace? |
| ❑ | ❑ | ❑ | ❑ | Are peers restating or clarifying directions? |
| ❑ | ❑ | ❑ | ❑ | Are peers giving appropriate prompts and feedback to the student? |
| ❑ | ❑ | ❑ | ❑ | Are peers summarizing activities? |
| ❑ | ❑ | ❑ | ❑ | Do the student and his or her peers appear to be enjoying working together? |
| ❑ | ❑ | ❑ | ❑ | Are students truly working *together* (rather than simply next to each other)? |
| ❑ | ❑ | ❑ | ❑ | Other: _____ |
| ❑ | ❑ | ❑ | ❑ | Other: _____ |

Ideas:

**Figure 11.3.** Checklist for monitoring peer support arrangements. (From Carter, E.W., Cushing, L.S., & Kennedy, C.H. [2009]. *Peer Support Strategies for Improving All Students' Social Lives and Learning* Baltimore, MD: Paul H. Brookes Publishing Co.; reprinted by permission.)

5. Implementing the program inside and outside of school. Many peer mentoring programs include an out of school component where students interact outside of school, such as on the weekends or in the evenings. This element will greatly enhance the skills and experiences of your students with disabilities, especially when they have had limited opportunities to socially engage outside of school. Some steps to implementing the program both inside and outside of school include 1) identify hobbies and activities your students are most interested in and pair peer mentors who have similar interests, 2) determine the activity requirements (fees, permission, etc.), 3) address logistical needs (ride, accommodations), 4) ensure appropriate supports and responsibilities are in place, 5) collaborate with family and supervisors of the activity, and 6) address any other potential challenges (e.g., health needs, accessibility, communication).

6. Evaluating, sustaining, and expanding. Periodically, you should evaluate the success of the peer mentoring program. Be sure to include feedback from peer mentors, your students with disabilities, school staff, and families. You can develop a student survey or use interviews and focus groups to solicit input. Carter et al. (2009) have developed surveys with reflective questions for all involved. You may want to expand the program to new school groups or across the district, and establishing an advisory board made up of students, parents, school staff, and community members ensures stability and sustainability over time.

Josh has participated in his high school's peer mentoring program and has been connected with peer mentors for the past 2 years, with considerable influence on his overall social skills. Now, when he is in stressful situations that would have elicited an inappropriate response in the past, more often than not he now uses problem-solving skills to identify a successful response. He has shown leadership by assisting other students in class with learning skills he used to struggle with. Although he still exhibits difficulties when faced with multiple stressors, overall observational and office disciplinary referral data has shown a marked decrease in oppositional and impulsive behaviors. More importantly, Josh talks about how much he has changed over the past 2 years. He feels more confident and knows that he has skills and a social network to turn to for support.

 **WHAT YOU CAN DO RIGHT NOW:**
**Putting Ideas Into Action**

Interpersonal engagement skills are necessary for every facet of your students' lives in high school, as well as at home and in the community, and these skills will be essential for a successful transition to adulthood. The strategies and approaches shared with you in this chapter provide a starting place for supporting, encouraging, and teaching these important skills. Table 11.4 provides a list of steps you can take to improve your overall school-wide efforts to promote positive behaviors and interpersonal engagement, as well as individual strategies you can implement right away. Resources for more information are also included.

Teaching social skills to students with disabilities has been a common element of an individualized education program for decades, which means there are well-established curricula and models you can use that best fit your students' needs. Emphasizing interpersonal skills within academic coursework provides a universal approach to preparing all students. Finally, providing opportunities to ensure positive and supportive school climates so students feel valued and connected will ensure positive outcomes.

**Table 11.4.**   Implementing strategies to improve interpersonal engagement

| Steps | Resources for more information |
|---|---|
| 1. Use evidence to guide the development of curriculum, instruction, and systems-wide improvements for social and interpersonal engagement. | • National Center on Intensive Interventions Updated Tools Charts for Behavioral Interventions: www.intensiveintervention.org<br>• Effective Social and Emotional Learning Programs-Middle and High School (2015, CASEL): www.casel.org/middle-and-high-school-edition-casel-guide |
| 2. Evaluate student academic and behavioral outcomes and use data to revise/enhance programs and interventions. | • Student grades, attendance, office referrals, etc.<br>• National Center on Student Progress Monitoring: www.studentprogress.org<br>• Center on Response to Intervention: www.rti4success.org |
| 3. Develop a student screening and selection process. | • CI3T web site: www.ci3t.org/measures.html#srss-ie<br>• BASC-2: www.pearsonclinical.com<br>• Social, Academic, and Emotional Behavior Risk Screener (SAEBRS): http://ebi.missouri.edu/wp-content/uploads/2014/03/EBA-Brief-SAEBRS.pdf |
| 4. Develop school and classroom expectations for behaviors and be explicit about reinforcing across all settings. | • National School Climate Center: www.schoolclimate.org<br>• School Safety Survey: www.pbisapps.org/Applications/Pages/PBIS-Assessment-Surveys.aspx#sss |
| 5. Review behaviors of teachers and other educators and adults to ensure consistent use of school and classroom expectations. | • Self-Assessment Survey (SAS): www.pbisapps.org/Applications/Pages/PBIS-Assessment-Surveys.aspx#sss |
| 6. Implement effective instructional models to teach specific social and interpersonal skills. | • Effective Social and Emotional Learning Programs-Middle and High School (2015, CASEL): www.casel.org/middle-and-high-school-edition-casel-guide<br>• PBIS World: www.pbisworld.com/ |
| 7. Plan for generalization of student skills and teacher behaviors/interventions across settings (e.g., school locations, classes, home), and teachers and other adults. | • Embedding Social Skills Instruction Throughout the Day (2007): www.pbis.org/common/cms/files/pbisresources/palmer0RPBS20307.ppt<br>• Multimedia Instruction of Social Skills, CITEd: www.cited.org/index.aspx?page_id=154 |
| 8. Train and support adults in building and using professional development (training + coaching). | • PBIS Center Training web site: www.pbis.org/training<br>• National Center on Intensive Interventions, Behavior strategies and Sample Resources: www.intensiveintervention.org/behavior-strategies-and-sample-resources<br>• OCALI Autism Internet Modules: www.autisminternetmodules.org |

## ONLINE RESOURCES

Social Thinking: www.socialthinking.com

Ohio Center for Autism and Low Incidence (OCALI) serves families, educators, and professionals. This online training focuses on social competence. See www.ocali.org/project/social_competence

Zones of Regulation: www.zonesofregulation.com

Model Me Kids: www.modelmekids.com/social-skills-curriculum.html

Collaborative Problem Solving: www.livesinthebalance.org

CI3T (Comprehensive, Integrated, Three-Tiered Model of Prevention): www.ci3t.org

Collaborative for Academic, Social, and Emotional Learning (CASEL): www.casel.org

Student Engagement Project: Strategy Briefs focusing on K-12 academic, social, behavioral engagement: http://k12engagement.unl.edu/strategy-briefs

Peer-Mediated Learning Strategies

Peer Assisted Learning Strategies: http://kc.vanderbilt.edu/pals

Promising Practices Network: http://promisingpractices.net

What Works Clearinghouse for Student Behavior: http://ies.ed.gov/ncee/wwc/topic .aspx?sid=15

# 12

# Working With Outside Agencies

## Implementing Practices to Promote Interagency Collaboration

with Monica L. Simonsen

Alicia Richter is a special education teacher in Somerville Bay, a rural school district. She spends half of her day teaching special education at the district's high school, and during the rest of her day she is responsible for coordinating the work-based learning program for students with disabilities. Somerville Bay doesn't have a district-level transition specialist, so Ms. Richter has assumed many of the program-level responsibilities related to transition services, especially for work experiences. She is often invited to district meetings related to transition, but she is not always able to attend because of her classroom teaching responsibilities. Ms. Richter knows that many of her students will need ongoing supports after they exit school, so she works hard to make sure that Somerville Bay students exit high school with work-based experiences and are referred to post-school services and agencies, including VR, mental health services, postsecondary educational programs supporting students with disabilities, and her community's intellectual disabilities agency. However, she is unsure of how to create strong linkages with these outside agencies. For instance, she has tried unsuccessfully to involve VR in attending her students' IEP meetings, and she doesn't know how to get community agencies more involved. What can Ms. Richter do to facilitate interagency collaboration in order to meet the needs of her students?

For adolescents with disabilities, ongoing support needs are often a common denominator of transition planning. These students will likely need some level of continued support after they leave high school, so it becomes necessary to coordinate with other agencies and organizations that can provide services to meet the needs of our young adults. Like Ms. Richter, when you are working with students and families to plan for successful employment, postsecondary education, and independent living outcomes, you may find that you are interacting with an ever-expanding range of community services and adult systems. It is no wonder, then, why transition planning can be a confusing time for everyone involved!

When it comes to working with outside agencies in your students' transition planning, think about a relay race and how important it is to smoothly hand off the baton to the next runner. For students transitioning to adulthood, effective interagency collaboration ensures the handoff is smooth and transition is seamless. This chapter begins by defining interagency collaboration and how it develops over time. The Making It Happen section will discuss multiple strategies linked with high rates of interagency collaboration, and resources and examples for embarking on, supporting, and sustaining collaborative interagency efforts.

## GETTING STARTED:
## Understanding Interagency Collaboration

As students with disabilities make the transition from school to the complexities of adulthood, their support needs will vary. Sometimes the support they need is short-term; for example, helping students find a job in a career in which they are interested. For others, collaboration with a range of community agencies and supports is ongoing and long term. Ms. Richter coordinates the hand off in services for most of the students in her rural district. She has to be familiar with time-limited services, such as the supports students with disabilities would receive while enrolled in postsecondary training and educational settings, as well as vocational rehabilitation services to help students prepare for and find jobs. In addition, she must connect with agencies that provide long-term supports and services, such as employment and residential services for students with significant disabilities. She must even understand federal programs, including community-based Medicaid waiver programs and supplemental security income (SSI). Several different agencies and services are referred to throughout this chapter, and Table 12.1 provides a snapshot of the major agencies with which students are often engaged.

Interagency collaboration can provide the support network necessary for ensuring a student participates in and achieves the outcomes he or she desires. Not surprisingly, no one agency or organization will be able to meet all student needs. Therefore, school personnel like Ms. Richter must help ensure that students with disabilities are connected with a network of formal and informal supports prior to leaving school. Before we can implement interagency collaboration, it is important to sufficiently understand how it works. A recent definition of interagency collaboration is: "Interagency collaboration is a clear, purposeful, and carefully designed process that promotes cross-agency, cross-program, and cross-disciplinary collaborative efforts leading to tangible transition outcomes for youth" (Rowe et al., 2015, p. 10). Interagency collaboration has been substantiated as a promising transition practice for some time (Kohler, 1993; Landmark, Ju, & Zhang, 2010; Noonan, Morningstar, & Erickson, 2008). More recently, emerging research has noted the importance of interagency collaboration for influencing positive post-school outcomes, especially when students are linked with services prior to exiting high school (Test, Mazzotti et al., 2009). The quality of interagency collaboration is largely determined on how well the established support network assists the student in accomplishing his or her post-school goals. Therefore, it is essential that you and your colleagues come together to improve the linkages between schools, outside agencies, and other forms of support to ensure your students achieve positive post-school outcomes—that's the true test of interagency collaboration!

Interagency collaboration will look different depending on your community and school, so who is at the table when it comes to collaborating will vary significantly.

**Table 12.1.**   Snapshot of community agencies and services to support transition

| | |
|---|---|
| Disability resources | Supported by the Office of Disability Employment Policy, this web site connects people with disabilities, their families, and their caregivers to helpful resources on a wide range of topics. It is a great place to start searching for services and resources, and to find organizations in your state and community. To learn more, visit www.dol.gov/odep/topics/disability.htm |
| Vocational rehabilitation (VR) | VR services are available through your state. Every state has a VR agency that receives funds from the federal government because of the original Rehabilitation Act of 1973 as amended and most recently administered through the Workforce Innovation and Opportunities Act (2015). The purpose of the VR program is to assess, plan, develop, and provide services to adults with disabilities who meet certain eligibility requirements. Services that can be provided using VR funding are based on the development of an individual plan of employment (IPE) that provides services to train and prepare individuals for employment, help find jobs and support them on the job, and increase independence and integration into the workplace and the community. Pre-employment transition services are now available through VR as part of transition planning. VR counselors and schools work together to support employment outcomes beginning as young as 14 years old for students with disabilities. To learn more about VR services in your state, visit http://askjan.org/. To learn more about pre-employment services go to: http://www.wintac.org |
| Social security supplemental security income (SSI) | SSI is administered through the Social Security Administration and provides monthly benefits to individuals with limited income who have disabilities. In most states, individuals receiving SSI are also eligible for Medicaid health insurance to pay for hospital stays, doctor bills, and other medical costs. To receive SSI, individuals with disabilities must apply at age 18 and complete a comprehensive eligibility process. It can be complicated and is not tied to special education; therefore, helping families to understand and correctly apply for SSI is one of the many tasks during transition planning. More recently, work incentive programs have been developed to support individuals who want to work to reduce their SSI benefits without losing often critical medical benefits. In this way, individuals with disabilities are able to move from depending on federal benefits to becoming more independent. To learn more about SSI, visit www.ssa.gov/ssi/text-understanding-ssi.htm. |
| Intellectual and developmental disabilities (IDD) services | The Developmental Disabilities Act legislates federal policies for individuals with intellectual and developmental disabilities. The Administration on Intellectual and Developmental Disabilities (AIDD) provides national guidance to state IDD programs and services, such as the state councils on developmental disabilities, state protection and advocacy systems, and the national network of University Centers for Excellence in Developmental Disabilities, as well as promoting projects of national significance. Most states also support programs and services for individuals with IDD; however, these are not funded with federal funds, but exclusively from state and county government funding. Therefore, every state IDD system can provide vastly different services. For more information on AIDD, visit www.acl.gov/Programs/AIDD/Index.aspx; to find your state's IDD agency and learn more about the IDD program, visit www.nasddds.org. |
| Parent training and information (PTI) centers | Every state has at least one PTI supported by the Office of Special Education Services at the U.S. Department of Education. These centers are supported to provide information and training to parents of children with disabilities, from birth through age 26. Most PTIs provide information, training, and advocacy services to parents. To find your state, learn more about PTIs, and access a range of parent-friendly information and resources, visit www.parentcenterhub.org. |
| Centers for independent living (CILs) | CILs are community-based, cross-disability, nonprofit organizations that are designed and operated by people with disabilities. CILs are unique in that they operate according to a strict philosophy of consumer control, wherein people with all types of disabilities directly govern and staff the organization. CILs provide the following: peer support, information and referral, individual and systems advocacy, and independent living skills training. Most CILs promote and support specific transition initiatives. To learn more about CILs and to find your state's centers, visit www.ncil.org. |
| Disability benefits specialist | Disability benefits specialists help answer questions and solve problems related to social security, SSI, Medicaid health insurance, and other public and private benefits for people with disabilities. Most states support disability benefits specialists through a variety of federal and state funding sources. There is not an established single web site tracking disability benefits specialists for each state. The best option is to search for the term "disability benefits specialist" with your state name included. |

*(continued)*

**Table 12.1.**  (*continued*)

| | |
|---|---|
| Disability services at postsecondary campuses | For students with disabilities enrolled in postsecondary settings, Section 504 of the Rehabilitation Act ensures access to programs through accommodations and services. A student must first disclose they have a disability to receive services. Each postsecondary setting is unique and the range of services offered to ensure access may differ; some services typically offered include note taking, accessible testing locations, speech-to-text software, priority class registration, sign language interpreters, and accessible transportation, among others. To learn more about disability services in a range of postsecondary settings, visit www.ahead.org. |
| Community mental health | Supported by federal law, community mental health services were established in all states and communities. Services are designed to keep individuals with mental illness in their communities, rather than in large psychiatric institutions.<br>To find out about community mental health services in your state, visit www.thenationalcouncil.org or the U.S. Substance Abuse and Mental Health Services Administration (SAMSHA) at www.samhsa.gov. |

In addition to formal agencies and organizations serving individuals with disabilities, remember that informal networks are important. In fact, promoting inclusive adult lives for your students includes blending formal and informal supports in the community to ensure that the supports meet the unique preferences of the student and his or her family. This challenges the notion that your students can be supported only by agencies specifically designed to serve adults with disabilities. In fact, research has shown that building networks of both formal and informal supports through a person-centered approach leads to positive and inclusive adulthoods (Povenmire-Kirk et al., 2015). In contrast, we have known for quite some time that if services are arranged or provided for the convenience of service providers, little change will be felt by students and families, and there may even be unnecessary barriers to transition (Morningstar, Kleinhammer-Tramill, & Lattin, 1999). Effective interagency collaboration is further outlined in laws related to transition planning.

## Interagency Collaboration and Federal Law

The importance of developing interagency linkages for students prior to exiting school is identified by the IDEA of 2004. The law states that other community agencies that are involved or most likely will be involved with a student should be invited to transition planning meetings. If during transition planning an outside agency agrees to provide or pay for a service (e.g., VR will pay for a functional vocational evaluation of a student in his or her last year of high school), then you will want to make note of this as a transition service in the student's IEP. The IDEA is clear that if an agency does not provide an agreed-upon service, the educational team must reconvene to determine a new course of action. Recall that you cannot drop the service or goal from the IEP, but you can delay the timeline for implementation or identify a new agency or organization to provide the service. Table 12.2 provides further information about other federal laws addressing interagency collaboration during transition planning.

## Stages Leading to Interagency Collaboration

It can take time and planning to fully achieve "true" collaboration in your students' transition planning. In fact, there are numerous stages to interagency collaboration, which usually start with networking. Then, as teams start working together, they move through cooperation and coordination before finally achieving collaboration. Figure 12.1 provides

**Table 12.2.**  Laws focusing on interagency collaboration

| Individuals with Disabilities Education Act (IDEA) 2004 Transition Requirements | Rehabilitation Act Reauthorization (2014) | Workforce Investment Opportunities Act (2015) |
|---|---|---|
| Transition services under the IDEA means: a coordinated set of activities to facilitate the movement from school to adult life:<br><br>• Education/training<br>• Employment<br>• Independent living<br><br>Individualized education program (IEP) teams must invite agencies to meetings if they are likely to be responsible for providing or paying for services. | Vocational rehabilitation (VR) services are designed to maximize employment, economic self-sufficiency, independence, and full integration into society.<br>VR roles during transition planning include:<br><br>• Sharing resources about VR services with families and students.<br>• Consulting with schools, families, and students about work-related skills.<br>• Providing technical assistance related to employment services.<br>• Participating in transition IEPs. | For youth with disabilities, there is greater flexibility in how VR services can be used for students during transition. Now, at least 15% of VR funds must be used for transition services for pre-employment transition services with students as young as 16 years old, which can include:<br><br>• Job exploration counseling<br>• Work-based learning experiences<br>• Counseling on postsecondary opportunities<br>• Workplace readiness training<br>• Training on self-advocacy<br><br>State VR must have formal interagency agreements with state Medicaid services and state Intellectual and developmental disabilities agencies. |

an overview of these four stages to interagency collaboration, describing the activities associated with each.

The first stage, networking, typically focuses on seeking out and sharing information. At this stage, you should be identifying the range of services in your community. Networking is the stage where schools and agencies are working together informally, with most communication occurring during the referral process. For example, Ms. Richter has collected brochures of the agencies in her county that provide services to adults with disabilities, and she shares this information with her students and parents during IEP meetings. She has also scheduled time to visit with agency staff when a student might need that particular service.

The next stage, coordination, is the process where the IEP team supports a student and family to access services, and the case manager or transition specialist helps with coordinating community resources. It requires greater involvement of school personnel to seek out services for the student and might mean staying involved during the referral process. Ms. Richter has attempted to coordinate planning by inviting the VR counselor to students' IEP meetings so students and families can learn about the VR services, the referral process, and the necessary paperwork to apply for services. In addition, when a student is formally involved with VR services, Ms. Richter remains in contact with the VR counselor to problem solve and track progress toward the student's identified employment outcomes.

During cooperation, schools and agencies interact on a regular but often short-term basis. It has been described as the stage where "like-minded organizations share information and expertise in loose arrangements that result in low-risk/low-reward outcomes" (Meadows, Davies & Beamish, 2014, p. 333). At this stage, examples of low-risk/low-reward outcomes might include: schools and agencies jointly schedule meetings and get together on a regular basis to identify needs and work on shared activities or, when either schools or agencies provide staff trainings about transition or adulthood services,

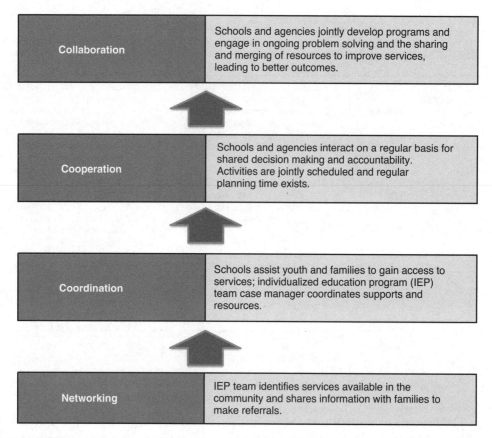

**Figure 12.1.** Moving from networking to collaboration during transition. (From Morningstar M.E. [2006]. *Moving from networking to collaboration during transition.* Presented at the KansTrans Transition Summit, Wichita, KS; reprinted by permission.)

outside groups are invited to attend. A community transition team is an example of the cooperation stage. These teams, described in detail later in this chapter, consist of critical transition stakeholders (schools, agencies, community organizations, parents, and student representatives) who meet regularly to improve programs and services. Ms. Richter has just returned from a state transition conference where she learned about forming a community transition team. She is interested to see if this might work in her community.

Finally, collaboration involves teams of school personnel and community agencies who jointly develop new programs to support improved outcomes. Well-established collaborative teams collectively identify needs within their community, and then problem solve and create new solutions to meet the needs of all community members. For example, in one community, a long-standing community transition team worked to develop a program to support work-based learning experiences leading to paid integrated employment. This involved a subcommittee made up of school vocational personnel, employment agencies, and members of the business community, who identified critical community needs and then developed a proposal for jointly funding the program to support improved employment outcomes.

As you can see, knowing about the services available in your community is an important first step to developing interagency collaboration. However, because schools are required to implement transition planning, not only must you know about the different agencies to call upon for assistance, but you should also develop positive working relationships with outside organizations. Students and families often rely upon teachers and other school professionals for information about what is available after high school, so offering families information and referrals will ensure better outcomes. Facilitating interagency collaboration can be an overwhelming undertaking if schools do not develop a systematic and multilevel approach. In the Making it Happen section, you will learn about effective strategies for developing positive and collaborative relationships with community agencies.

## MAKING IT HAPPEN:
## Building a Collaborative Approach to Transition Planning

Interagency collaboration doesn't just happen, you have to work hard to get it right. There are plenty of obstacles that can get in your way, so be sure to develop a solid set of proactive strategies to combat the barriers that may arise. Being knowledgeable about the strategies you can use to increase collaboration will improve your abilities to implement the strategies. This is important because teachers who believe they have control over certain interagency collaboration strategies are more likely to use them (Meadows et al., 2014). In this section, we have grouped the strategies for interagency collaboration into four different categories: 1) school-based strategies to support youth and families, 2) school programs promoting collaboration, 3) bridging-to-community strategies to ensure a positive handoff, and 4) community- and systems-level changes. Table 12.3 provides an overview of these different strategies and what they entail.

### Strategies for Supporting Youth and Families

As a transition specialist or a secondary special educator, you have a role in promoting and encouraging collaboration among schools, outside agencies, community organizations, and families and students. Many of the strategies shared here focus specifically on ways that secondary and transition educators can support students and families to be prepared for a smooth and seamless transition from school to adulthood, with the unique supports and services needed to be successful.

***Start Planning Early***    It's never too early to begin planning for the connections and linkages students and families will need. The first step toward developing the network of

**Table 12.3.**   Strategies to promote interagency collaboration

| Supporting youth and families | School-level changes | Bridging to the community | Community and systems change |
|---|---|---|---|
| • Start planning early.<br>• Use community resource mapping.<br>• Develop transition portfolios.<br>• Facilitate meetings with students, families and community agencies.<br>• Invite agencies to spend time in school. | • Identify personnel responsible for transition programs.<br>• Be flexible with scheduling and location of services.<br>• Establish a systematic planning process. | • Develop a community transition council.<br>• Work together to advocate for systems change.<br>• Jointly train staff.<br>• Disseminate information widely. | • Develop seamless transition models.<br>• Jointly fund rehabilitation counselors in schools.<br>• Support dual enrollment programs. |

support for students is the development of MPGs. As detailed in Chapter 2, postsecondary goals must clearly articulate the future goals of the student related to postsecondary education and training, integrated employment, and independent living. These goals are best developed using appropriate transition assessments focusing on PCP in which the youth and family are actively involved. See Chapters 2 to 5 for helpful resources and activities addressing MPGs, student and family engagement in transition planning, and transition assessment methods, including PCP.

***Use Community Resource Mapping***     After identifying the long-term outcomes for students, you can then begin to develop a community map of the formal and informal supports and services that the student and family may need. Community resource mapping is a process for identifying services in a community for youth with disabilities who are transitioning to adulthood. Some of you may be interested in a specific disability group (e.g., intellectual disabilities, emotional disabilities), whereas others will be developing maps that include a broader set of disability-related services. In addition to disability services, you will want to gather information about generic services (e.g., temporary employment agencies, public transportation, public housing) and informal community organizations (e.g., community arts center, churches, community bands and orchestras), as these are available to everyone. Figure 12.2 is a sample form you could use for community resource mapping with your students.

To get started, you should first check within your school or district for others who may have started this type of initiative, perhaps for groups of students who do not have disabilities but who also can be supported by the range of community organizations available (e.g., as part of dropout prevention and supporting low-income students, multicultural families, and so forth). In addition, you should check with educators who typically understand and have community resources at their fingertips, like school social workers and guidance and career counselors. Next, find out if any other community agencies have developed community resource directories. For example, when Ms. Richter decided to create a transition resource directory, she talked with her colleagues and found that the community mental health center had already compiled a resource directory that she could use as a starting point. She was able to use many of the resources, especially the community services that everyone could access, such as health care offices, banking services, and community recreation. In addition, because it was a mental health agency directory, several of the disability agencies that served youth and adults with mental illness were already included (e.g., VR, counseling services, social security and supplemental security information). Ms. Richer then added several that were specific to her students, such as services for students with intellectual disabilities, autism, and physical disabilities. Through this effort, Ms. Richter started connecting with organizations that she had not been familiar with, such as her county's center for independent living. Centers for independent living are federally supported and every state has at least one. Their primary mission is to provide information, training, referral, and advocacy services to anyone with a disability. The county independent living center partnered with Ms. Richter to compile the directory so they could use it with families and youth with whom they worked.

***Develop Comprehensive Transition Portfolios***     Creating transition portfolios is an easy way to facilitate positive connections with outside agencies. A transition portfolio is an excellent strategy for collecting the most relevant information about a student's movement toward his or her postsecondary goals. Most often, transition portfolios include

| Community Resource Mapping Tool: Defining Resources |
|---|
| **Task:** Identify and define each resource. |
| **Process:** |
| *Step 1:* Identify the geographic region for your map (city, county, region of state). |
| *Step 2:* Consider the disability groups with whom you are most concerned to help narrow your mapping. |
| *Step 3:* Use the table to find information about the different organizations. Use the definitions below for clarification. |
| **Definitions:** |
| *Purpose:* Identify the purpose of the community organization or agency. Is it mandated by legislation? How is operated in your community? |
| *Funding source:* Identify who sponsors or funds the organization. Are there costs associated with the services offered by the agency? |
| *Target population/number served:* Identify types of youth served, and information on the number of youth served. |
| *Activities and services:* List the activities or services provided by this organization or agency (e.g., work experiences, mentoring, leadership training, counseling, transportation). |
| *Partnering agencies:* Identify other agencies and organizations that partner with the organization. |
| *Expected outcomes:* Indicate what this organization hopes to achieve; identify its strengths in meeting the needs of youth you are concerned about. |
| *Other:* Identify other relevant information about each organization (e.g., funding sources, planning cycles, contact information). |

| Identifying resources | | | | |
|---|---|---|---|---|
| **Name of community organization** | | | | |
| Purpose | | | | |
| Funding for services | | | | |
| Target population served/number served | | | | |
| Activities/services offered | | | | |
| Partnering agencies | | | | |
| Expected outcomes | | | | |
| Other | | | | |

**Figure 12.2.** Community resource mapping tool: Defining resources.

information about the student that has been collected as a part of the transition experiences completed while in school. For example, the portfolio might include a resume, examples of activities from past work experiences, certificates of completion for trainings or other experiences, extracurricular activities and awards, results of a comprehensive transition assessment, and finally, the student's SOP (that you learned about in Chapters 1 and 2). While a portfolio can be used for a variety of purposes, they all uniquely summarize and communicate the student's strengths, preferences, and interests related to their post-school outcomes. Organizing a portfolio by the three major domains of transition planning (postsecondary education, employment, and independent living) with subcategories for each will organize students' experiences, track progress, and also communicate to outside agencies critical information needed to provide ongoing services. In this day and age of technology, it is easy to develop online transition portfolios. Several links to sample transition portfolios are found in the online resources at the end of the chapter.

Similar to the SOP described in Chapter 2, transition portfolios can be used to identify appropriate linkages to informal supports and formal services. Once you know where the student is headed and what services and supports are available, you can develop a plan for linking the student with these supports and services. Keep in mind that when the services and agencies available in your community are not a good match for your student and his or her family, more systems-level change will be required (see the strategies for building bridges to the community discussed later in this chapter).

***Facilitate Meetings with Students, Families, and Community Agencies***     While we often think about how to involve outside agencies in meetings, research has noted that developing interagency collaboration is most likely to occur outside of the formal IEP meeting (Noonan & Morningstar, 2012). As a transition specialist, you will need to facilitate more informal and student-specific meetings to ensure students and families are connecting with the right agencies and services. These meetings should not be limited to a standard menu of agencies from your community; instead, you should organize meetings with a diverse group of community agencies and informal supports based on the needs and post-school goals of each student.

At times, facilitating meetings with community agencies may simply require sharing information about the referral, application, and eligibility requirements; the student and family will take the lead on connecting with services. However, for many students and families, you are likely to be more involved. You may have to actively engage with some students and families early on so they fully understand the many requirements for determining eligibility for different community services. This may mean, for example, organizing visits to the disability services office of your local community college and taking students and families to meet with staff on campus, or scheduling meetings for students at your local work force investment to make sure they apply for the range of employment services available.

### TIP FOR TRANSITION: Take Parents and Students on Field Trips!

Transition specialists often set appointments for groups of parents to meet and tour adult agencies and postsecondary settings. This is an especially effective approach in rural communities, where services are more limited and spread farther apart. By organizing a group visit, you can save more time than with individual visits. Doing this well before the student will graduate is critical so that parents are connected with community services.

***Invite Adult Community Agencies to Spend Time in School***      Developing early and ongoing relationships with outside agencies will solidify the necessary connections with students and families. Some highly collaborative schools invite community agency staff to have an ongoing presence in the high school (Noonan, Morningstar, & Erickson, 2008). In particular, this approach is used by the CIRCLES project, a successful model of interagency collaboration that uses school level teams (SLTs) made up of those community agency staff members most likely to be contacted by teachers and invited to IEP meetings (Povenmire-Kirk et al., 2015). Rather than having community agencies attend individual IEP meetings, the schools invite community organizations to a monthly meeting where the SLT meets with multiple students for the sole purpose of identifying possible adult services and supports. Prior to the meeting, school personnel prepare students to individually present information about themselves and their goals for the future using a student-centered planning approach (see Chapter 3). The presentation usually lasts about 5 minutes and allows students to talk about their strengths, areas of needed support, and goals for the future. Then, the SLT spends about 20 to 30 minutes talking with the students and their families, the special education staff, and one another to determine the best way to support each student into adulthood.

The CIRCLES approach allows students and families (and school personnel) to connect with a wide range of community agencies to answer questions and schedule follow-up appointments. In addition, it lets families describe needs that may be affected during their child's transition, thereby offering a holistic family approach to transition support. Finally, it allows agency staff to problem solve barriers to services and negotiate funding solutions as a collaborative group, which is not possible when they are meeting individually with students at the IEP meeting. The end result of each meeting is what the IEP team then uses when developing their transition plan. Preliminary results show that schools and agencies buy in to this approach once they see the benefit to their students, families, and themselves (usually after the first SLT meeting has occurred). For more information about this model and the logistical procedures for setting it up, visit http://circles.uncc.edu. It is important to remember that interagency collaboration is about more than just disability-specific agencies. You can be very successful if you work to also facilitate informal supports and organizations, thereby developing a broader support network for students.

## School-Level Changes

Even with all of your individualized work with students and families, if you want to develop true collaboration, you will need to work with your school and advocate for changes. School-level changes often require that you reach out to administrators in your building or district. Having administrator support for programmatic changes is essential. While you may not be able to implement all of the necessary changes on your own, knowing about what is needed will help you to better advocate for new practices. Changes that we know lead to more positive outcomes for students and significantly improve interagency collaboration include identifying school staff responsible for transition, allowing flexible schedules for transition staff, and developing a school-wide systematic planning process.

***Identify Personnel Responsible for Transition Program Coordination***      Many strategies for increasing interagency collaboration and improving outcomes fall to the transition specialist, or other personnel for whom systems-level transition activities are a large part of their role, such as a district coordinator, department chair, or administrator (Rowe et al., 2015; Test, Mazzotti et al., 2009). It is clear that the primary role of classroom teachers

is to focus on preparing students to be college and career ready. While secondary teachers significantly contribute to supporting students and families during transition planning
and have a student-centered role in promoting interagency collaboration, they do not have
the time or flexibility to sufficiently focus on systems-level changes. Rather, program- and
systems-level changes are best implemented by educators whose daily responsibilities
include transition-related coordination (Morningstar & Clavenna-Deane, 2014).

In order to achieve effective transition linkages, transition specialists are responsible
for developing opportunities to build long-term relationships with adult agencies. Given the
positive effects of interagency collaboration on student post-school outcomes, if staffing is
inadequate in your school, or it is unclear who is responsible for transition coordination, you
are encouraged to advocate for changes to better support interagency collaboration. This
might include requesting that the school create a new transition coordinator position. At
the very least, you can make a case for your district to help an existing school administrator,
department chair, or district-level secondary transition specialist carve out more time to
focus on transition and interagency collaboration.

***Be Flexible with Scheduling, Staffing, and the Location of Services***     Flexible scheduling
and adequate staffing in schools create the foundation for interagency collaboration. As
one transition specialist described it, "There is no way you can sit in a classroom and teach
*and* coordinate and network in the community. You can't do both, and that's why your transition specialist serves a role different than a classroom teacher" (Noonan, Morningstar,
& Erickson, 2008, p. 136). One of the transition specialist's primary responsibilities is to
work closely with a range of community agencies and organizations to initiate and secure
the formal and informal supports needed for youth with disabilities prior to exiting high
school. To make this happen, specialists need to have adequate time to connect with outside agencies and organizations, as well as flexible time to meet with parents.

Strong interagency collaboration cannot be sufficiently developed within a typical
school schedule or day. School staff responsible for transition programs must be very clear
about their responsibilities and tasks related to interagency collaboration, but have flexibility in their work schedule (e.g., working in the evenings) and the ability to meet with
agencies outside of school throughout their day. This allows classroom teachers to do what
they do best: prepare and support students and families for successful transitions.

Another area where schools can work to make program-level changes is to create
flexibility in where services are located. This may mean that school personnel work
outside of the schools or that community agencies and organizations are invited into
schools. The CIRCLES approach to inviting agency staff in for a monthly meeting with
students and families is an excellent example of being flexible in terms of services. In
other districts and states, jointly funded programs offer this level of flexibility. It could
be that the school and a local mental health agency have joined together to implement
dropout prevention supports for at-risk adolescents. Or, perhaps the state department of
education is collaborating with VR services, supporting VR counselors to be housed in
schools to aid in career development and work-based learning programs. While you may
not be able to implement such high levels of change on your own, being knowledgeable
about what is possible, and working to advocate for change within your administration,
are essential first steps.

***Establish Systematic Planning Structures***     Encouraging outside agencies to participate in
IEP meetings is important when you know that an agency is providing or paying for specific

transition services. However, for most agencies, collaboration is less about attending IEP meetings and more about the opportunities to network and plan with schools, students, and families. Given this, as you are developing your systematic plan for transition, consider how best to engage outside and community agencies. Think about who, when, where, and how to build relationships. Some strategies you can use include:

1. Develop a timeline for transition planning that includes when to make connections with outside agencies.

2. Complete a community resource map of your community. Be sure to include disability-specific services, generic services, and informal networks of support.

3. From your community map, develop a user-friendly resource directory that you can share with families and the student.

4. Support students and families while in school to expand their network of support (formal and informal) so that a strong safety net is in place when students exit school.

5. Establish regular times to meet with agencies and be sure to invite them into schools to meet with students and families.

6. Develop more formal agreements (this type of agreement is sometimes called a memorandum of understanding or MOU) with outside agencies regarding how they will be involved during transition planning.

7. Communicate with families and students about their future plans. The *New Parent Transition Survey* is one example of how to help families start planning early (www. transitioncoalition.org/transition/section.php?pageId=72).

School support for interagency collaboration is critical, and in the best circumstances your district administration will be on board and have systematic planning strategies in place. As you consider ways to advocate for change, think about linking your efforts to other initiatives your school or district may already be implementing. For example, your district may be working to increase graduation rates and support students at risk of dropping out of school. Oftentimes, the interventions related to dropout prevention include connecting with community agencies and supports. This is a great way to get involved to promote collaboration. Or, consider your district's CTE programs. Many CTE programs have established ties with business groups and are implementing career development internships for youth without disabilities. Expanding the work of the businesses and employment organizations to include youth with disabilities can make your job easier.

Connecting with existing school initiatives can help you build a network of community organizations that are involved with a wider and more diverse range of students (e.g., CTE, at-risk youth). Talk to other school staff involved in these initiatives and ask them to participate. Keep in mind that the first step to collaboration is to seek out others with whom you can work. This will include the wide range of educational staff, as well as a broad array of community organizations, members, and adult services staff.

## Bridging to the Community

A student-focused planning process guides you in identifying formal and informal community supports. As you identify agencies that provide services and the linkages needed to support your students to reach their post-school goals, your own professional network will grow. As a teacher or transition specialist, you can take action to collaborate with community partners. The strategies presented next can lead to strong connections with community agencies, leading to positive changes.

***Developing a Community Transition Council***    One strategy for building relationships with community agencies is to establish a committee or work group of community partners, frequently called a community transition council. Transition councils are designed to build bridges to support youth as they transition from school to work or postsecondary education. Transition councils often meet regularly (i.e., monthly) to identify school and community needs, share resources, and resolve barriers to ensure seamless transitions. You may find that the makeup of your community transition councils will vary depending on the size of your district and the organizations that are available within a close driving distance.

If you want to start a transition council, your first step should be to identify the organizations and agencies that should be represented (e.g., school programs, VR, community employment providers, postsecondary education representatives). Use your community resource map to identify the most critical community personnel to have on your team. Think about the people you already know who are likely to be committed to making systems-level changes for transition. Ideally, members should be able to make decisions on behalf of their organization. However, even if they are not the final decision makers, they often are able to advocate for changes. At the initial meeting, it is critical to establish practices that will encourage people to remain engaged with the team. Developing an agenda, adhering to the start and end times of the meeting, and making sure that everyone has a chance to participate are excellent strategies for increasing collaboration. Furthermore, identifying leaders who will chair or co-chair the council is an essential step to ensure the team will maintain focus and momentum.

## TIP FOR TRANSITION: Highlight One Organization Each Month

Highlight one organization at your monthly transition council meetings. The organization can describe the scope of their service, eligibility requirements, and contact information. This way the participants always learn something new, which keeps people coming back!

While regular meetings provide council members frequent opportunities to interact, it is essential that the meetings move beyond information sharing and networking events. Rather, the purpose of the group is to identify community transition-related issues influencing specific student outcomes (e.g., to increase access to paid internships, to increase enrollment at the local community college). Keep in mind current levels of collaboration and brainstorm how you can continue to move your council toward greater levels. In order to ensure that Somerville Bay's newly formed community transition team focuses on outcomes, Ms. Richter, who is co-chairing the team along with the local VR counselor, begins each meeting by sharing relevant data, such as 1) percentage of students with open vocational rehabilitation cases, 2) percentage of students with paid jobs, and 3) percentage of students enrolling in postsecondary education. The transition council can then collectively work toward improving these numbers, seeking to achieve a measurable, outcome-oriented goal. In addition, each month the partners discuss individual student cases to identify the status of post-school linkages. One month, it was determined that a student really wanted to study animal husbandry. One of the community providers knew the owner of a local horse farm and offered to help the student obtain an internship to see if she wanted to pursue this field in college.

Focusing on student-level issues may be appropriate at meetings, but the real focus of the council is to implement systems-level changes. The level of follow-through and focus on making change is critical to the effectiveness of the transition council. Research shows that councils that have focused on implementing change were more likely to improve student outcomes than councils that have only focused on the process of sharing information and networking (Fabian, Dong, Simonsen, & Leucking, 2016).

***Advocacy and Systems Change***     One of the major functions of a transition council is to address community- and system-level barriers to seamless transitions by creating new programs and approaches for youth with disabilities. In order to prioritize needs, transition councils often conduct a self-assessment of transition programs, services, and activities to identify gaps in services and improve outcomes. One useful tool is the *Quality Indicators of Exemplary Transition Programs Survey-2* found at www.transitioncoalition.org (Morningstar, Gaumer-Erickson, Lattin, & Lee, 2015). This online survey is designed for teams to evaluate the quality of their transition programs and services. It is divided into eight domains aligned to evidence-based transition practices and predictors. It can be filled out by school personnel, families, outside agencies, and students. Using the data from the QI-2 allows teams to identify priority areas and develop plans for improving services. It can then be used to track program improvements.

Because collaboration takes time and effort to develop, it is important to evaluate the quality of the collaboration among team members to address potential issues, strengthen partnerships, and sustain the momentum of the group. The *Levels of Collaboration Scale* (LoCs) (Frey, Lohmeier, Lee, & Tollefson, 2006) was adapted by Fabian and colleagues (in press) to help assess the stages of collaboration achieved by community transition teams. It was used to determine how interagency collaboration contributed to successful employment outcomes. It helps to measure how teams operate and what level of collaboration the team has achieved within the following range: 0 = no integration, 1 = networking, 2 = cooperation, 3 = coordination, 4 = coalition, and 5 = collaboration. These researchers found that greater levels of collaboration lead to better employment outcomes for students (Fabian et al., in press).

After assessing transition programs, services, and activities, the next step is to develop an action plan by setting goals, objectives, and target dates for the activities the team identifies as important. It is usually helpful to have one or two members of the community team who lead this process and monitor progress on identified goals. As an example, Ms. Richter asked each of the transition council members to complete the *Quality Indicators of Exemplary Transition Programs Survey-2* and then compiled the results. Based on the data, family engagement was identified as an area in need of improvement for the community transition council. The transition council then developed an action plan that included specific goals related to family engagement, including the development of family transition workshops.

***Jointly Training Staff***     If you are committed to learning more about the organizations in your community—their eligibility requirements, vocabulary, and processes—you should consider attending a training or conference hosted by a community partner. Your participation will likely foster some mutual learning opportunities. For instance, Ms. Richter registered for a 1-day training about the ADA that was hosted by a community employment agency. She learned a lot about the rights and responsibilities of adults with disabilities in the workplace and made a few new contacts. One of the other participants was a newly hired job developer, who Ms. Richter invited to join the transition council. Community transition councils can even facilitate joint training opportunities. In Somerville

Bay, the transition council decided that the fear of losing certain disability benefits was a major barrier for many of the families in the district. The council asked a benefits specialist, someone trained to understand the most current disability benefits (see Table 12.1) to host a workshop about work incentives and disability benefits management. The participants learned not only about work incentives, but also heard from their colleagues from other organizations about the common challenges they face and the strategies they were engaged in to solve community-wide problems. By sharing both the challenges they have in common, as well as the unique characteristics of community organizations, relationships among the members of the transition council were strengthened. They all had a better understanding of what all members had in common and what distinct pressures faced certain organizations, and as a team they could problem solve and plan for improvements.

### TIP FOR TRANSITION: Sharing Calendars

Create a shared calendar of events and trainings across transition council organizations. This way, everyone knows what is going on and can make efforts to attend their partner's fundraisers, special events, and trainings.

***Disseminate Information Widely***     In order to help build community awareness of transition-related issues and develop a shared vision of high expectations for student outcomes, it is important to disseminate information to community stakeholders. After the initial transition council meeting, find ways to publicly thank the participating members and their organizations. You might send a group e-mail to all members thanking each for their unique contributions or send out thank-you cards. This helps the members to have shared ownership in the success of the group and raises the community's awareness of the group. As the group proceeds to address transition issues, make sure to share these issues, resources (e.g., sample brochures, training materials, resource directories), and lessons learned with others. You might start each meeting with a round robin from each agency about a new initiative or situation that has emerged, then time can be spent brainstorming ideas and solutions. Frequent communication of the group's activities also helps to ensure that school and agency administrators are informed. Ms. Richter wrote a blog post on the school system's web site about transition council activities. Within a few days, the post was linked to each of the organizations' web pages. The transition council also shares important e-mail announcements about upcoming training events with each other, so that each organization can distribute the information to their own listservs and e-mail lists.

## Community and Systems Change

All of the strategies discussed so far have focused on actions that you as the secondary educator can do with your families and students, and that the transition specialist can spearhead to increase community collaboration. These activities can be the building blocks for systems change that occurs when transition partners (schools and community agencies) share in the development and cost for transition activities, services, and programs. This section will focus on several innovative systems-level programs that are the results of high levels of interagency collaboration. Knowing about these types of programs will support your ability to advocate for changes.

***Seamless Transition Models***     Seamless transition refers to a model of transition services that ensures that students do not experience an interruption in services after exiting school. In other words, students leave school with a job and/or enrolled in postsecondary education with all the necessary linkages and supports. The major features of a seamless transition model include 1) multiple work experiences throughout secondary school, 2) employment in integrated settings, 3) adult agency employment specialists working alongside school personnel to support the youth before school exit, 4) resource and cost sharing among various systems (including district, VR, services for intellectual/developmental disabilities, and mental health agencies), and 5) an outcome of paid work and/or postsecondary enrollment (Simonsen, Stuart, Luecking & Certo, 2013). By sharing the costs and responsibilities for ensuring student success, the agencies reduce duplication of services and improve outcome data required to be reported by schools and VR services. For example, schools must annually report the post-school outcomes of their students who graduate or exit special education services and VR services must report the number of jobs their clients obtain (Simonsen et al., 2013).

### TIP FOR TRANSITION: Designing the First Day After School

Try to make sure that the first day after high school graduation looks just like the day before. Early referrals to VR and other agencies help ensure that students will already have the necessary supports in place when they exit school. In some cases, the schools contract directly with the service providers. For example, some schools pay community employment agencies to provide job coaching to students working in afterschool jobs.

***Jointly Funded Rehabilitation Counselors in Schools*** As stressed throughout this chapter, creating early linkages with adult agencies is an effective way to ensure that students have supports in place before they exit school. Because of funding restrictions, it is sometimes difficult to engage VR early. Luckily, recent legislation called the Workforce Innovation Opportunities Act promotes strong collaboration between schools and VR. Many more pre-employment transition services will be available for students still in school to ensure the transition to integrated employment. Some states have addressed this issue by funding transition-focused services with a combination of school and VR funds. This model paves the way for the VR counselor to begin working with the youth while they are still in school. This high level of collaboration helps to prevent eligible students from "falling through the cracks" after high school. Students are enrolled in VR while they are still in school and participate in the necessary career assessments, training, and job development activities before they exit school. A funded VR counselor can serve as a bridge for the student and his or her family to help cross from school and VR systems, and provide consistent case management services to the students and their families. The school-based VR counselor's continued involvement after the students exit school also helps schools collect follow-up data.

### Evidence-Based Practices: What You Can Do to Improve Employment Outcomes

To improve employment outcomes for young adults with disabilities, you must seek out services and assistance from outside employment agencies, such as VR, mental health agencies, and developmental disabilities services, before your students exit high school. Research shows that students who receive assistance from multiple agencies prior to leaving high school are more likely to be employed. In addition, developing work-based learning models jointly funded by schools, VR, and employment agencies have been shown to lead to higher rates of employment for youth with intellectual and developmental disabilities.

**Characteristics of Interagency Collaboration Assessment**

Mark whether this characteristic is evident in your community. If not, you may want to prioritize this as an area to improve. If you are not certain about a characteristic, mark that you need to learn more about it.

1. Identify members for an interagency team, terms of service, procedures for replacing members, orientation of new members, and online and print member directories.

| Evident in our community ☐ | Learn more about this ☐ | Notes: |
|---|---|---|

2. Develop teams across disability and nondisability agencies that have a focus on transition related services.

| Evident in our community ☐ | Learn more about this ☐ | Notes: |
|---|---|---|

3. Clearly define roles and responsibilities of organizations within an interagency agreement.

| Evident in our community ☐ | Learn more about this ☐ | Notes: |
|---|---|---|

4. Develop formal and informal agreements with agencies responsible for delivering transition services.

| Evident in our community ☐ | Learn more about this ☐ | Notes: |
|---|---|---|

5. Develop procedures for how services will be delivered and shared among school and community agencies.

| Evident in our community ☐ | Learn more about this ☐ | Notes: |
|---|---|---|

6. Implement a state-wide plan that addresses gaps, includes strategies for funding, streamlines the transition process, and eliminates repetitive service delivery.

| Evident in our community ☐ | Learn more about this ☐ | Notes: |
|---|---|---|

7. Create a vision and mission for transition services and programs in the community.

| Evident in our community ☐ | Learn more about this ☐ | Notes: |
|---|---|---|

8. Create a toolkit with information about all of the community agencies that are available to youth in your area.

| Evident in our community ☐ | Learn more about this ☐ | Notes: |
|---|---|---|

9. Schedule regular planning times for interagency team meetings

| Evident in our community ☐ | Learn more about this ☐ | Notes: |
|---|---|---|

10. Develop procedures to include students, families, and agencies in the transition process.

| Evident in our community ☐ | Learn more about this ☐ | Notes: |
|---|---|---|

11. Decide how information sharing and communication will take place across agencies.

| Evident in our community ☐ | Learn more about this ☐ | Notes: |
|---|---|---|

12. Provide continuing professional development opportunities for all interagency team members.

| Evident in our community ☐ | Learn more about this ☐ | Notes: |
|---|---|---|

13. Develop a set of procedures to help problem solve when you encounter barriers.

| Evident in our community ☐ | Learn more about this ☐ | Notes: |
|---|---|---|

**Figure 12.3.** Characteristics of interagency collaboration assessment. (*Source:* Rowe, Alverson, Unruh, Fowler, Kellems, & Test, 2015.)

# WHAT YOU CAN DO RIGHT NOW:
## Putting Ideas Into Action

Programs that are jointly funded by community transition partners epitomize true collaboration. Developing these programs and services requires teams to move beyond relationship building and resource sharing, and work together to create new opportunities for youth with disabilities. Such models can provide ideas, inspiration, and strategies for collaborating with community partners. While developing these programs certainly requires the buy-in from your administrators and the leadership from community agencies, learning more about system-level collaboration models enables you to advocate for new programs in your own community and be a catalyst for change.

As secondary educators and transition specialists, you can work to ensure that students have necessary supports and linkages in place when they exit school by utilizing the strategies reviewed in this chapter to 1) support youth and families, 2) promote school-level collaborative practices, 3) connect with community organizations, and 4) advocate for community systems change. Understanding what it takes to facilitate meaningful interagency collaboration is a critical first step. As you prioritize strategies, it is important to remain focused on the important outcomes for transition: successful employment, postsecondary education, and independent living. You may want to first identify the strategies that are easiest to implement, while focusing on building relationships with important community partners. To evaluate the levels of interagency collaboration in your community and begin prioritizing where change is most needed, use the Characteristics of Interagency Collaboration Assessment shown in Figure 12.3 (Rowe et al., 2015). This assessment provides a checklist of 13 collaborative activities and asks you to mark whether each activity is evident in the community or is an area that you need to learn more about, with a space to write notes and ideas or brainstorm further strategies.

Be sure to share information with your administration and community about the importance of strategies to foster effective interagency collaboration. This may go a long way in ensuring their support of system-level collaboration (e.g., seamless transition models, dual enrollment models). Finally, be patient, but not complacent. Remember that true collaboration takes time—but it has to start somewhere!

# References

Agran, M., Alper, S., & Wehmeyer, M.L. (2002). Access to the general curriculum for students with significant disabilities: What it means to teachers. *Education and Training in Mental Retardation and Developmental Disabilities, 37*(2), 123–133.

Agran, M., Hughes, C., Thoma, C.A., & Scott, L.A. (2014). Employment social skills: What skills are really valued? *Career Development and Transition for Exceptional Individuals,* 2165143414546741.

Allen, I.E., & Seaman, J. (2015, February). *Grade level: Tracking online education in the United States.* Babson Park, MA: Babson Survey Research Group.

Allen, S.K., Smith, A.C., Test, D.W., Flowers, C., & Wood, W.M. (2001). The effects of "self-directed" IEP on student participation in IEP meetings. *Career Development for Exceptional Individuals, 24*(2), 107–120.

Allensworth, E., & Easton, J. (2007). *What matters for staying on-track indicator and graduating in Chicago public high schools.* Chicago, IL: Consortium on Chicago School Research.

Allwell, M., & Cobb, B. (2009). Social and communicative interventions and transition outcomes for youth with disabilities: A systematic review. *Career Development for Exceptional Individuals, 32*(2), 94–107.

Amado, A.N. (2013). *Friends: Connecting people with disabilities and community members.* Minneapolis: University of Minnesota, Institute on Community Integration, Research and Training Center on Community Living.

American Council on the Teaching of Foreign Languages. (2015). *National Standards Collaborative Board releases world-readiness standards for learning languages.* Retrieved from www.actfl.org/news/press-releases/national-standards-collaborative-board-releases-iworld-readiness-standards-learning-languagesi

America's Promise Alliance. (2014, May). *Don't call them dropouts: Understanding the experiences of young people who leave high school before graduation.* Retrieved from http://gradnation.org/report/dont-call-them-dropouts

Anctil, T.M., Ishikawa, M.E., & Scott, A.T. (2008). Academic identity development through self-determination: Successful college students with learning disabilities. *Career Development for Exceptional Individuals, 31*(3), 164–174.

Anderson, D., Kleinhammer-Tramill, P.J., Morningstar, M.E., Lehmann, J., Bassett, D., & Kohler, P., et al. (2003). What's happening in personnel preparation in transition? A national survey. *Career Development for Exceptional Individuals, 26*(2), 145–160.

Ankeny, E.M., Wilkins, J., & Spain, J. (2009). Mothers' experiences of transition planning for their children with disabilities. *Teaching Exceptional Children, 41*(6), 28–36.

Appleton, J.J., Christenson, S.L., & Furlong, M.J. (2008). Student engagement with school: Critical conceptual and methodological issues of the construct. *Psychology in the Schools, 45*(5), 369–386. doi:10.102/pits.20303

Archambault, I., Janosz, M., Morizot, J., & Pagani, L. (2009). Adolescent behavioral, affective, and cognitive engagement in school: Relationship to dropout. *Journal of School Health, 79*(9), 408–415.

Armstrong, K.H., Dedrick, R.F., & Greenbaum, P.E. (2003). Factors associated with community adjustment of young adults with serious emotional disturbance: A longitudinal analysis. *Journal of Emotional and Behavioral Disorders, 11*(2), 66–91.

Baer, R.M., Flexer, R.W., Beck, S., Amstutz, N., Hoffman, L., Brothers, J., & Zechman, C. (2003). A collaborative follow up study on transition service utilization and post-school outcomes. *Career Development for Exceptional Individuals, 26*(1), 7–25.

Balduf, M. (2009). Underachievement among college students. *Journal of Advanced Academics, 20*(2), 274–294.

Balfanz, R., Bridgeland, J.M., Fox, J.H., Depaoli, J., Ingram, E.S., & Maushard, M. (2014, April). *Building a grad nation: Progress and challenge in ending the high school dropout epidemic.* Baltimore, MD: Civic Enterprises, Johns Hopkins University.

Balfanz, R., Byrnes, V., & Fox, J. (2012). *Sent home and put off-track: The antecedents, disproportionalities, and consequences of being suspended in the ninth grade.* Unpublished manuscript. Center for Civil Rights Remedies national conference: Closing the School Research Gap: Research to Remedies.

Balfanz, R., Herzog, L., & Mac Iver, D.J., (2007). Preventing student disengagement and keeping students on the graduation path in urban middle-grades schools: Early identification and effective interventions. *Educational Psychologist, 42*(4), 23–235. doi:10.1080/00461520701621079

Balli, S. (2011). Pre-service teachers' episodic memories of classroom management. *Teaching and Teacher Education, 27*(2), 245–251.

Balli, S. (2014). Pre-service teachers' juxtaposed memories: Implications for teacher education. *Teacher Education Quarterly, 41*(3), 105–120.

Banerjee, M. (2010). Technology trends and transition for students with disabilities. In S.F. Shaw, J.W. Madaus, & L.L. Dukes (Eds.), *Preparing students with disabilities for college success: A practical guide to transition planning* (pp. 115–136). Baltimore, MD: Paul H. Brookes Publishing Co.

Barrera, I., & Corso, R.M. (2005). Cultural competency as skilled dialogue. *Topics in Early Childhood Special Education, 22*(2), 103–113.

Bauminger, N., Solomon, M., Aviezer, A., Heung, K., Brown, J., & Rogers, S.J. (2008). Friendship in high-functioning children with autism spectrum disorder: Mixed and non-mixed dyads. *Journal of Autism and Developmental Disorders, 32,* 1211–1229.

Belfield, C., & Levin, H.M. (2007). *The price we pay: Economic and social consequences of inadequate education.* Washington, DC: Brookings Institution Press.

Bellini, S. (2006). *Building Social Relationships.* Shawnee Mission, KS: Autism Asperger Publishing Company.

Benitez, D., Morningstar, M.E., & Frey, B. (2009). Transition service and delivery: A multi-state study of special education teachers' perceptions of their transition competencies. *Career Development for Exceptional Individuals, 32*(1), 6–16.

Berry, H.G., Ward, M., & Caplan, L. (2012). Self-determination and access to postsecondary education in transitioning youths receiving supplemental security income benefits. *Career Development and Transition for Exceptional Individuals, 35,* 68–75.

Blackorby, J., & Wagner, M. (1996). Longitudinal postschool outcomes of youth with disabilities: Findings from the National Longitudinal Transition Study. *Exceptional Children, 62*(5), 399–413.

Blalock, G., Kleinhammer-Tramill, P.J., Morningstar, M.E., & Wehmeyer, M. (2003). Introduction to the special issue on personnel preparation in transition. *Career Development for Exceptional Individuals, 26*(2), 125–130.

Blue-Banning, M.J., Turnbull, A.P., & Pereira, L. (2000). Group action planning as a support strategy for Hispanic families: Parent and professional perspectives. *Mental Retardation, 38*(3), 262–275.

Boethel, M. (2003). *Diversity: School, family, & community connections.* National Center for Family and Community Connections with Schools. Retrieved from www.sedl.org

Boone, R.S. (1992). Involving culturally diverse parents in transition planning. *Career Development for Exceptional Individuals, 15*(2), 205–221.

Boyer-Stephens, A., Hruska, C.F., Edwards, J., Matthews, S., Felsen, C., & Tutoli, E. (2010). *Missouri AHEAD college guidebook.* Retrieved September 21, 2015 from http://moahead.org/guidebook.html

Bradshaw, C.P., O'Brennan, L.M., & McNeely, C.A. (2008). Core competencies and the prevention of school failure and early school leaving. *New Directions for Child and Adolescent Development, 2008*(122), 19–32.

Brewer, D. (2006). *Transition quality indicators.* Ithaca, NY: Cornell University. Retrieved October 1, 2008 from www.ilr.cornell.edu/edi/transqual

Bridgeland, J., Bruce, M., & Hariharan, A. (2013). *The missing piece: A national teacher survey on how social and emotional learning can empower children and transform schools.* Washington, DC: Civic Enterprises and Hart Research Associates.

Bridgeland, J.M., DiIulio, J.J., & Morrison, K.B. (2006). *The silent epidemic: Perspectives of high school dropouts.* Washington, DC: Civic Enterprises.

Brozo, W.G. (2009). Response to intervention or responsive instruction? Challenges and possibilities of response to intervention for adolescent literacy. *Journal of Adolescent & Adult Literacy, 53*(4), 277–281. doi:10.1598/JAAL.53.4.1

Bryant, D.P., Bryant, B.R., & Ok, M.W. (2014). Assistive technology for individuals with learning disabilities. In G. Lancioni & N.N. Singh (Eds.), *Assistive technologies for people with diverse abilities* (pp. 251–276). New York, NY: Springer.

Bui, Y.N., & Turnbull, A. (2003). East meets west: Analysis of person-centered planning in the context of Asian American values. *Education and Training in Developmental Disabilities, 38*(1), 18–31.

Bullis, M., Davis, C., Bull, B., & Johnson, B. (1995). Transition achievement among young adults with deafness: What variables relate to success? *Rehabilitation Counseling Bulletin, 39*(2), 130–150.

Bullock, C.C., & Mahon, M.J. (1992). Decision making in leisure: Empowerment for people with mental retardation. *Journal of Physical Education, Recreation & Dance, 63*(8), 36–40.

Burgstahler, S., Crawford, L., & Acosta, J. (2001). Transition from two-year to four-year institutions for students with disabilities. *Disability Studies Quarterly, 21*(1), 25–38.

Cardillo, R., Freiberg, J.A., & Pickeral, T. (2013, April). *School climate and engaging students in the early grades.* New York: National School Climate Center (NSCC). Retrieved from www.schoolclimate.org/publications/documents/sc-brief-engaging-students.pdf

Carter, E.W., Austin, D., & Trainor, A. (2012). Predictors of postschool employment outcomes for young adults with severe disabilities. *Journal of Disability Policy Studies, 23*(1), 50–63.

Carter, E.W., Asmus, J., Moss, C.K., Biggs, E.E., Bolt, D.M., Born, T.L., & Fesperman, E. (2016). Randomized evaluation of peer support arrangements to support the inclusion of high school students with severe disabilities. *Exceptional Children, 8*(2), 209–233. doi:0014402915598780

Carter, E.W., Austin, D., & Trainor, A.A. (2012). Predictors of postschool employment outcomes for young adults with severe disabilities. *Journal of Disability Policy Studies, 23*(1), 50–63. doi:10.1177/1044207311414680

Carter, E.W., Cushing, L.S., Clark, N.M., & Kennedy, C.H. (2005). Effects of peer support interventions on students' access to general education and social interactions. *Research and Practice for Persons with Severe Disabilities, 30*(1), 15–25.

Carter, E.W., Cushing, L.S., & Kennedy, C.H. (2009). *Peer support strategies for improving all students' social lives and learning.* Baltimore, MD: Paul H. Brookes Publishing Co.

Chiang, H.M., Cheung, Y.K., Hickson, L., Xiang, R., & Tsai, L.Y. (2012). Predictive factors of participation in postsecondary education for high school leavers with autism. *Journal of Autism and Developmental Disorders, 42*(5), 685–596.

Children's Defense Fund. (2014). *The state of America's children.* Washington, DC. Retrieved from www.childrensdefense.org

Cho, S.J., & Gannotti, M.E. (2005). Korean-American mothers' perception of professional support in early intervention and special education programs. *Journal of Policy and Practice in Intellectual Disabilities, 2*(1), 1–9.

Christenson, S.L., Thurlow, M.L., Sinclair, M.F., Lehr, C.A., Kaibel, C.M., Reschly, A.L., & Pohl, A. (2008). *Check & connect: A comprehensive student engagement intervention manual.* Minneapolis, MN: Institute on Community Integration.

Clark, G. (2007). *Assessment for transitions planning* (2nd ed.). Austin, TX: PRO-ED.

Clark, G.M. & Patton, J.R (2014). *Transition planning inventory* (2nd Ed.). Austin, TX: PRO-ED.

Collaborative for Academic, Social, and Emotional Learning (CASEL, 2015). *2013 CASEL Guide: Effective Social and Emotional Learning Programs.* Chicago, IL: Collaborative for Academic, Social, and Emotional Learning. Retrieved from: http://secondaryguide.casel.org/casel-secondary-guide.pdf

Common Core State Standards Initiative. (2012). *Common core state standards initiative: Preparing America's students for college and career.* Retrieved from www.corestandards.org

Common Core State Standards Initiative. (2014). *About the standards.* Retrieved from www.corestandards.org/about-the-standards

Conley, D.T. (2010). *College and career ready: Helping all students succeed beyond high school.* San Francisco, CA: Jossey-Bass.

Connell, J.P. (1990). Context, self, and action: A motivational analysis of self-system processes across the life-span. In D. Cicchetti (Ed.), *The self in transition: Infancy to childhood* (pp. 61–97). Chicago, IL: University of Chicago Press.

Council for Exceptional Children. (2015). Advanced specialty set: Special education transition specialist. *What every special educator must know: Professional ethics and standards.* Arlington, VA: CEC.

Coyne, M.D., Kame'enui, E.J., & Carnine, D.W. (2007). *Effective teaching strategies to accommodate diverse learners* (3rd ed.). Upper Saddle River, NJ: Pearson Education.

Crone, D.A., Hawken, L.S., & Horner, R.H., (2010). *Responding to problem behavior in schools: The behavior education program* (2nd ed.). New York, NY: The Guilford Press.

Danielson, L., Roberts, G., & Scala, J. (2010, February). *The high school tiered interventions initiative: The implementation of tiered interventions and RTI in high schools.* Retrieved from www.rti4success.org/index.php?option=com_content&task=blogcategory&id=27&Itemid=149

Decker, M.M., & Buggey, T. (2014). Using video self- and peer modeling to facilitate reading fluency in children with learning disabilities. *Journal of Learning Disabilities, 47*(2), 167–177.

Denny, P.J., & Test, D.W. (1995). Using the one-more-than technique to teach money counting to individuals with moderate mental retardation: A systematic replication. *Education and Treatment of Children, 18*(4), 422–432.

DePaoli, J.L., Balfanz, R., & Bridgeland, J. (2016). *Building a grad nation: Progress and challenge in raising high school graduation rates.* Civic Enterprises and the Everyone Graduates Center at the School of Education at John Hopkins University. Retrieved from http://civicenterprises.net/MediaLibrary/Docs/civic_2016_full_report_FNL.pdf

Dinham, S., Cairney, T., Craigie, D., & Wilson, S. (1995). School climate and leadership: Research into three secondary schools. *Journal of Educational Administration, 33*(4), 36–58.

Dinnebeil, L.A., Hale, L.M., & Rule, S. (1996). A qualitative analysis of parents' and service coordinators' descriptions of variables that influence collaborative relationships. *Topics in Early Childhood Special Education, 16*(3), 322–347.

Duckworth, A.L., & Seligman, M.E. (2005). Self-discipline outdoes IQ in predicting academic performance of adolescents. *Psychological Science, 16*(12), 939–944.

DuBois, D. L., Portillo, N., Rhodes, J.E., Silverthorn, N., & Valentine, J. C. (2011). *How Effective Are Mentoring Programs for Youth: A Systematic Assessment of the Evidence.* Retrieved from: https://www.psychologicalscience.org/publications/journals/pspi/mentoring.html#.WTItJBPytSw.

DuFour, R., & Eaker, R. (1998). *Professional learning communities at work: Best practices for enhancing student achievement.* Bloomington, IN: National Educational Service.

Durlak, J.A., Weissberg, R.P., Dymnicki, A.B., Taylor, R.D., & Schellinger, K.B. (2011). The impact of enhancing students' social and emotional learning: A meta-analysis of school-based universal interventions. *Child Development, 82*(1), 405–432.

Dweck, C. S. (2008). Can personality be changed? The role of beliefs in personality and change. *Current Directions in Psychological Science, 17*(6), 391–394.

Dynamic Learning Maps Consortium (n.d.). *What is a learning map model?* Lawrence, KS: University of Kansas. Retrieved from http://dynamiclearningmaps.org/about/model#essential-elements

Dynamic Learning Maps Consortium. (2013). *Dynamic Learning Maps essential elements for English language arts.* Lawrence, KS: University of Kansas.

Dynarski, M., Clarke, L., Cobb, B., Finn, J., Rumberger, R., & Smink, J. (2008). *Dropout prevention: A practice guide (NCEE 2008-4025).* Washington, DC: National Center for Education Evaluation and Regional Assistance, Institute of Education Sciences, U.S. Department of Education. Retrieved from http://ies.ed.gov/ncee/wwc

Ellis, B. (2013). Class of 2013 grads average 35,200 in total debt. *CNN Money.* Retrieved from http://money.cnn.com/2013/05/17/pf/college/student-debt/index.html

Enderle, S., & Severson, J. (2003). *Enderle Severson transition rating scale.* Moorhead, MN: ESTR Publications. Retrieved from: https://www.estr.net/index.cfm

Epstein, J.L. (2001). *School, family, and community partnerships: Preparing educators and improving schools.* Boulder, CO: Westview Press.

Evers, T., Beckman, M.A., & Owens, L. (2012). *Opening doors to employment: Planning for life after high school. A handbook for students, school counselors, teachers, transition coordinators, parents and families.* Madison, WI: Wisconsin Department of Public Instruction. Retrieved from www.witc.edu/stusvcscontent/docs/accommodations/Opening-Doors-to-Employment.pdf

Fabian, E., Dong, S., Simonsen M., & Leucking, R. (2016). *Service system collaboration in transition: An empirical exploration of its effects on rehabilitation outcomes for students with disabilities. Journal of Rehabilitation, 82*(3), 3–10.

Farrington, C.A., Roderick, M., Allensworth, E., Nagaoka, J., Keyes, T.S., Johnson, D.W., & Beechum, N.O. (2012). *Teaching adolescents to become learners. The role of noncognitive factors in shaping school performance: A critical literature review.* Chicago, IL: University of Chicago Consortium on Chicago School Research.

Ferguson, D.L., & Ferguson, P.M. (2011). *The promise of adulthood.* In M.E. Snell & F. Brown (Eds.), *Instruction of students with severe disabilities* (7th ed.) (pp. 612–641). Boston, MA: Pearson.

Field, S.L., & Hoffman, A. (1996). *Steps to self-determination.* Austin, TX: PRO ED.

Field, S.L., & Hoffman, A. (2002). Lessons learned from implementing the steps to self-determination curriculum. *Remedial and Special Education, 23*(2), 90–98.

Finn, J.D., & Rock, D.A. (1997). Academic success among students at risk for school failure. *Journal of Applied Psychology, 82*(2), 221–234.

Flexer, R.W., Baer, R.M., Luft, P., & Simmons, T.J. (2013). *Transition planning for secondary students with disabilities* (4th ed.). Boston, MA: Pearson.

Flexer, R.W., Daviso, A.W., Baer, R.M., Queen, R.M., & Meindl, R.S. (2011). An epidemiological model of transition and post-school outcomes. *Career Development for Exceptional Individuals, 34*(2), 83–94.

Fredricks, J., Blumenfeld, P.C., & Paris, A.H. (2004). School engagement: Potential of the concept, state of the evidence. *Review of Educational Research, 74*(1), 59–109.

Fredricks, J., McColskey, W., Meli, J., Mordica, J., Montrosse, B., & Mooney, K. (2011). *Measuring student engagement in upper elementary through high school: A description of 21 instruments.* (Issues & Answers Report, REL 2011–No. 098). Washington, DC: U.S. Department of Education, Institute of Education Sciences, National Center for Education Evaluation and Regional Assistance, Regional Educational Laboratory Southeast. Retrieved from http://ies.ed.gov/ncee/edlabs

Frey, B.B., Lohmeier, J.H., Lee, S.W., & Tollefson, N. (2006). Measuring collaboration among grant partners. *American Journal of Evaluation, 27*(3), 383–392.

Fuchs, D., Fuchs, L.S., & Stecker, P.M. (2010). The "blurring" of special education in a new continuum of general education placements and services. *Exceptional Children, 76*(3), 301–323.

Fuchs, L.S., Fuchs, D., & Compton, D.L. (2010). Rethinking response to intervention at middle and high school. *School Psychology Review, 39*(1), 22–28.

Furlong, M.J., & Christenson, S.L. (2008). Engaging students at school and with learning: A relevant construct for all students. *Psychology in the Schools, 45*(5), 365–368. doi:10.1002/pits.20302

Gaumer-Erickson, A.S., Morningstar, M.E., Lattin, D.L., & Cantrell, L. (2008). *Transition assessment planning form.* Lawrence, KS: University of Kansas, Transition Coalition.

Gaumer, A., Morningstar, M.E., & Clark, G. (2004). Status of community-based transition programs: A national database. *Career Development for Exceptional Individuals, 27*(2), 131–149. doi:10.1177/088572880402700202.

Geenen, S., Powers, L.E., & Lopez-Vasquez, A. (2001). Multicultural aspects of parent involvement in transition planning. *Exceptional Children, 67*(2), 265–282.

Geenen, S., Powers, L.E., & Lopez-Vasquez, A. (2005). Barriers against and strategies for promoting the involvement of culturally diverse parents in school based transition planning. *Journal for Vocational Special Needs Education, 27*(3), 4–14.

Geenen, S., Powers, L., Lopez-Vasquez, A., & Bersani, H. (2003). Understanding and promoting the transition of minority adolescents. *Career Development for Exceptional Individuals, 26*(1), 27–46.

Getzel, E.E., & Briel, L.W. (2013). Pursuing post-secondary education opportunities for individuals with disabilities. In P. Wehman (Ed.), *Life beyond the classroom: Transition strategies for young people with disabilities* (pp. 363–376). Baltimore, MD: Paul H. Brookes Publishing Co.

Getzel, E.E., & Thoma, C.A. (2008). Experiences of college students with disabilities and the importance of self-determination in higher education settings. *Career Development for Exceptional Individuals, 31*(2), 77–83.

Good Day Plan. (n.d.). In *I'm determined: Virginia Department of Education self-determination project.* Retrieved from www.imdetermined.org/good_day_plan

Greenberg, M.T., Weissberg, R.P., O'Brien, M.U., Zins, J.E., Fredericks, L., Resnik, H., & Elias, M.J. (2003). Enhancing school-based prevention and youth development through coordinated social, emotional, and academic learning. *American Psychologist, 58*(6&7), 466–474.

Greene, G. (2011) *Transition planning for culturally and linguistically diverse youth.* Baltimore, MD: Paul H. Brookes Publishing Co.

Gresham & Elliott (2008). *Social skills improvement system* (SSIS). San Antonio, TX: Pearson.

Gresham, F.M., Sugai, G., & Horner, R.H. (2001). Interpreting outcomes of social skills training for students with high-incidence disabilities. *Exceptional Children, 67*(3), 331–344.

Grigal, M., & Hart, D. (2010). *Think college.* Baltimore, MD: Paul H. Brookes Publishing Co.

Gugerty, J., Foley, C., & Frank, A. (2008). Developing and operating school based enterprises that empower special education students to learn and connect classroom, community, and career-related skills. *The Journal for Vocational Special Needs Education 31*(1–3), 19–56.

Guy, B. A., Sitlington, P. L., Larsen, M. D., & Frank, A. R. (2009). What are high schools offering as preparation for employment?. *Career Development for Exceptional Individuals, 32*(1), 30–41.

Hamblet, E.C. (2011). *7 Steps for success: High school to college transition strategies for students with disabilities.* Arlington, VA: Council for Exceptional Children.

Hammer, M.R. (2004). Using the self-advocacy strategy to increase student participation in IEP conferences. *Intervention in School and Clinic, 39*(5), 295–300.

Hanley-Maxwell, C., & Izzo, M.V. (2012). Preparing students for 21st century workforce. In M.L. Wehmeyer & K.A. Webb (Eds.), *Handbook of adolescent transition for youth with disabilities* (pp. 139–155). New York, NY: Routledge.

Hanley-Maxwell, C., Whitney-Thomas, J., & Pogoloff, S.M. (1995). The second shock: A qualitative study of parents' perspectives and needs during their child's transition from school to adult life. *Journal of the Association for Persons with Severe Handicaps 20*(1), 3–15.

Hanson, E.W., & Lynch, M.J. (2011). *Developing cross-cultural competence: A guide for working with children and their families* (4th ed.). Baltimore, MD: Paul H. Brookes Publishing Co.

Hanson, M.J., & Lynch, E.W. (2013). *Understanding families: Supportive approaches to diversity, disability and risk* (2nd ed.). Baltimore, MD: Paul H. Brookes Publishing Co.

Haring, K.A., & Lovett, D.L. (1990). A follow-up study of special education graduates. *The Journal of Special Education, 23*(4), 463–477.

Hart, D., Mele-McCarthy, J., Pasternack, R.H., Zimbrich, K., & Parker, D.R. (2004). Community college: A pathway to success for youth with learning, cognitive, and intellectual disabilities in secondary settings. *Education and Training in Developmental Disabilities 39*(1), 54–66.

Harvard Family Research Project. (2011). *Family engagement for high school success toolkit.* Cambridge, MA.

Hasazi, S.B., Johnson, R.E., Hasazi, J.E., Gordon, L.R., & Hull, M. (1989). Employment of youth with and without handicaps following high school outcomes and correlates. *The Journal of Special Education, 23*(3), 243–255.

Heal, L.W., Khoju, M., Rusch, F. R., & Harnisch, D. L. (1999). Predicting quality of life of students who have left special education high school programs. *American Association on Mental Retardation, 104*(4), 305–319.

Henderson, A.T. (2009. Feb. 10). *Engaging families in the pathway to college: Solutions to the dropout crisis.* National Dropout Prevention Center/Network, Clemson, SC: Clemson University. Retrieved from: http://www.dropoutprevention.org/webcast/11-engaging-families-pathway-college

Henderson, A.T., & Mapp, K.L. (2002). *A new wave of evidence: The impact of school, family, and community connections on student achievement.* Austin, TX: National Center for Family and Community Connections in Schools, SEDL.

Hetherington, S.A., Durant-Jones, L., Johnson, K., Nolan, K., Smith, E., Taylor-Brown, S., & Tuttle, J. (2010). The lived experiences of adolescents with disabilities and their parents in transition planning. *Focus on Autism and Other Developmental Disabilities, 25*(3), 163–172.

Higher Education Opportunity Act. (2008). Pub. L. No. 110-315. 20 U.S.C. §§ 1001 et. seq.

Holland, J. L. (1997). *Making vocational choices: A theory of vocational personalities and work environments.* Lutz, FL: Psychological Assessment Resources.

Hoover-Dempsey, K.V., & Sandler, H.M. (2005, March 22). *Final performance report for OERI Grant #R305T010673: The social context of parental involvement: A path to enhanced achievement.* Retrieved from www.vanderbilt.edu/peabody/family-school/Reports.html

Hu, M. (2001). *Preparing preservice special education teachers for transition services: A nationwide web survey.* Unpublished doctoral dissertation. Kansas State University.

Hughes & Carter (2008). *Peer buddy programs for successful secondary school inclusion.* Baltimore, MD: Paul H. Brookes Publishing Co.

Hughes, C., & Carter, E.W. (2012). *The new transition handbook: Strategies secondary school teachers use that work.* Baltimore, MD: Paul H. Brookes Publishing Co.

IDEA Partnership (n.d.). *Creating dialogue.* Retrieved from www.ideapartnership.org/using-tools/dialogue-guides.html

Individuals with Disabilities Education Act of 2004. 20 U. S. C. §1400 et seq. (2004).

Jameson, J.M., Riesen, T., Polychronis, S., Trader, B., Mizner, S., Martinis, J., & Hoyle, D. (2015). Guardianship and the potential of supported decision making with individuals with disabilities. *Research and Practice for Persons with Severe Disabilities, 40*(1), 36–51.

Janney, R., & Snell, M.E. (2006). *Social relationships & peer supports (2nd ed.)* Baltimore, MD: Paul H. Brookes Publishing Co.

Johnson, M.D., Bullis, M., Benz, M.R., & Hollenbeck, K. (2004). *WAGES: Working at gaining employment skills: A job-related social skills curriculum for adolescents.* Longmont, CO: Sopris West.

Johnson, C., & Walker, B. (n.d.). *Positive behavior support & transition services* [PowerPoint slides]. Retrieved from www.ncesd.org/cms/lib4/WA01000834/Centricity/Domain/33/T2%20%20Positive%20Behavior%20Support%20and%20Transition%20Services.pdf

Ju, S., Zhang, D., & Pacha, J. (2012). Employability skills valued by employers as important for entry-level employees with and without disabilities. *Career Development and Transition for Exceptional Individuals, 35*(1), 29–38.

Kalyanpur, M., & Harry, B. (2012). *Culture in special education: Building reciprocal family-professional relationships.* Baltimore, MD: Paul H. Brookes Publishing Co.

Karpur, A., Clark, H.B., Caproni, P., & Sterner, H. (2005). Transition to adult roles for students with emotional/behavioral disturbances: A follow-up study of student exiters from Steps-to-Success. *Career Development for Exceptional Individuals, 28*(1), 36–46.

Kellems, R., & Morningstar, M.E. (2009). *Tips for transition.* Lawrence, KS: The Transition Coalition, University of Kansas. Retrieved from www.dlc-ma.org/_manual/Additional%20Resources/08-Tips%20for%20Transition.pdf

Kellems, R.O., & Morningstar, M.E. (2012). Using video modeling delivered through iPods to teach vocational tasks to young adults with autism spectrum disorders. *Career Development for Exceptional Individuals, 35*(3), 155–167.

Kena, G., Aud, S., Johnson, F., Wang, X., Zhang, J., Rathbun, A., & Kristapovich, P. (2014). *The condition of education 2014.* NCES 2014-083. Washington, DC: National Center for Education Statistics.

Kennelly, L., & Monrad, M. (2007). *Approaches to dropout prevention: Heeding early warning signs with appropriate interventions.* Washington, DC: American Institutes for Research.

Keyes, M.W., & Owens-Johnson, L. (2003). Developing person-centered IEPs. *Intervention in School and Clinic, 38*(3), 145–152.

Keyes, W. (Producer), & Sureshkumar, V. (Director). (2007). *Dropout nation* [Motion picture]. United States: Aum Films.

Kim, K.H., & Morningstar, M.E. (2005). Transition planning involving culturally and linguistically diverse families. *Career Development for Exceptional Individuals, 28*(2), 92–103.

Knab, J., Pleet, A., & Brito, C. (2000). *Parent involvement checklist.* Parent Partnerships. The NTA Resource Bulletin. Retrieved from http://ici.umn.edu/ncset/publications/nta/bulletins/july_2000.htm

Kochhar-Bryant, C., Bassett, D., & Webb, K. (2009). *Transition to postsecondary education for students with disabilities* (pp. 108–113). Thousand Oaks, CA: Corwin Press.

Kochhar-Bryant, C., & Greene, G. (2009). *Pathways to successful transition for youth with disabilities: A developmental process.* Upper Saddle River, NJ: Pearson Education.

Kohler, P.D. (1993). Best practices in transition: Substantiated or implied? In P.D. Kohler, J.R. Johnson, J. Chadsey-Rusch, & F. Rusch (Eds.), *Transition from school to adult life: Foundations, best practices, and research directions* (pp. 31–54). Champaign-Urbana: Transition Research Institute at Illinois, University of Illinois.

Kohler, P.D. (1996). Preparing youths with disabilities for future challenges: A taxonomy for transition programming. In *Taxonomy for transition programming: Linking research and practice* (pp. 9–72). Champaign-Urbana: University of Illinois.

Kohler, P.D., & Fields, S. (2003). Transition-focused education: Foundation for the future. *Journal of Special Education, 37*(3), 174–183.

Kohler, P.D., & Greene, G. (2004). Strategies for integrating transition-related competencies into teacher education. *Teacher Education and Special Education: The Journal of the Teacher Education Division of the Council for Exceptional Children, 27*(2), 146–162.

Kohler, P.D., & Rusch, F.R. (1996). Secondary education programs and transition perspectives. In M.C. Wang, M.C. Reynolds, & H.J. Walberg (Eds.), *Handbook of special and remedial education: Research and practice* (2nd ed.) (pp. 107–130). Tarrytown, NY: Elsevier Science.

Kortering, L.J., McClannon, T.W., & Braziel, P.M. (2008). Universal design for learning: A look at what algebra and biology students with and without high incidence conditions are saying. *Remedial and Special Education, 29*(6), 352–363.

Landmark, L.J., Ju, S., & Zhang, D. (2010). Substantiated best practices in transition: Fifteen plus years later. *Career Development for Exceptional Individuals, 33*(3), 165–176.

Lane, K.L., Menzies, H.M., Oakes, W.P., & Kalberg, J.R. (2012). *Systematic screenings of behavior to support instruction.* New York, NY: Guilford Press.

Lane, K.L., Oakes, W.P., Jenkins, A., Menzies, H.M., & Kalberg, J.R. (2014). A team-based process for designing comprehensive, integrated, three-tiered (CI3T) models of prevention: How does my school-site leadership team design a CI3T model? *Preventing School Failure: Alternative Education for Children and Youth, 58*(3), 129–142.

Lane, K.L., Oakes, W.P., & Menzies, H.M. (2014). Comprehensive, integrated, three-tiered models of prevention: Why does my school—and district—need an integrated approach to meet students' academic, behavioral, and social needs? *Preventing School Failure: Alternative Education for Children and Youth, 58*(3), 121–128.

Leake, D., & Black, R.S. (2005). *Cultural and linguistic diversity: Implications for transition personnel* (Essential Tools Monograph Series). Minneapolis, MN: National Center for Secondary Education and Transition.

Leake, D., & Cholymay, M. (2004). Addressing the needs of culturally and linguistically diverse students with disabilities in postsecondary education. *NCSET Information Brief: Addressing Trends and Developments in Secondary Education and Transition, 3*(1). Retrieved November 10, 2009 from www .ncset.org.publications

Lee, S. (2013). *Household debt and credit: Student debt.* PowerPoint presentation retrieved from www .newyorkfed.org/newsevents/mediaadvisory/2013/Lee022813.pdf

Lee, Y., Wehmeyer, M.L., Palmer, S.B., Williams-Diehm, K., Davies, D.K., & Stock, S.E. (2010). Examining individual and instruction-related predictors of the self-determination of students with disabilities: Multiple regression analyses. *Remedial and Special Education, 33*(3), 0741932510392053.

Lehr, C.A., & McComas, J. (2005, Spring). Students with emotional/behavioral disorders: Promoting positive outcomes. *Impact, 18*(2), 2–3; 37.

Leucking, R.G. (2009). *The way to work: How to facilitate work experiences for youth in transition.* Baltimore, MD: Paul H. Brookes Publishing Co.

Li, J.Y., Bassett, D.S., & Hutchinson, S.R. (2009). Secondary special educators' transition involvement. *Journal of Intellectual and Developmental Disability, 34*(2), 163–172.

Lindstrom, L., Dorien, B., & Meisch, J. (2011). Waging a living: Career development and long-term employment outcomes for young adults with disabilities. *Exceptional Children, 77*(4), 423–434.

Liptak, J.J. (1994). *Leisure/work search inventory: LSI.* Indianapolis, IN: JIST Works, Inc.

Lynch, E.W., & Hanson, M.J. (2011). *Developing cross-cultural competence: A guide for working with children and their families.* Baltimore, MD: Paul H. Brookes Publishing Co.

Maag, J.W. (2006). Social skills training for students with emotional and behavioral disorders: A review of reviews. *Behavioral Disorders, 32*(1), 4–17.

Mac Iver, M.A., & Mac Iver, D.J. (2009). *Beyond the indicators: An integrated school-level approach to dropout prevention.* Arlington, VA: The Mid-Atlantic Equity Center, The George Washington University Center for Equity and Excellence in Education.

Martin, J.E., Hennessey, M., McConnell, A., Terry, R., & Willis, D. (2015). *TAGG technical manual.* Retrieved from https://tagg.ou.edu/tagg

Martin, J.E., Marshall, L.H., Maxson, L.M., & Jerman, P. (1996). *Self-directed IEP.* Longmont, CO: Sopris West. Retrieved from www.zarrowcenter.ou.edu

Martin, J.E., Marshall, L.H., & Sale, P. (2004). A 3-year study of middle, junior high, and high school IEP meetings. *Exceptional Children, 70*(3), 285–297.

Martin, J.E., Portley, J., & Graham, J.W. (2010). Teaching students with disabilities self-determination skills to equalize access and increase opportunities for postsecondary education success. In S.F. Shaw,

J.W. Madaus, & L.L. Dukes (Eds.), *Preparing students with disabilities for college success: A practical guide to transition planning* (pp. 65–81). Baltimore, MD: Paul H. Brookes Publishing Co.

Martin, J.E., Van Dycke, J.L., Christensen, W.R., Greene, B.A., Gardner, J.E., & Lovett, D.L. (2006). Increasing student participation in IEP meetings: Establishing the self-directed IEP as an evidenced-based practice. *Exceptional Children, 72*(3), 299–316.

Martin, J.E., & Williams-Diehm, K. (2013). Student engagement and leadership of the transition planning process. *Career Development and Transition for Exceptional Individuals, 36*(1). doi:2165143413476545

Mazzotti, V.L., Rowe, D. A., Sinclair, J., Poppen, M., Woods, W.E., & Shearer, M.L. (2016). Predictors of post-school success: A systematic review of NLTS2 secondary analyses. *Career Development and Transition for Exceptional Individuals, 39*(4), 196–215.

McCarney, S.B., & Arthaud, T. J. (2012). *Transition behavior scale (3rd ed)*. Columbia, MO: Hawthorne Educational Services.

McConnell, A.E., Martin, J.E., Juan, C.Y., Hennessey, M.N, Terry, R.A., el-Kazimi, N.A., Pannells, T.C., & Willis, D.M. (2013). Identifying nonacademic behaviors associated with post-school employment and education. *Career Development for Exceptional Individuals, 36*(3), 174–187.

McEvoy, A., & Welker, R. (2000). Antisocial behavior, academic failure, and school climate: A critical review. *Journal of Emotional and Behavioral Disorders, 8*(3), 130–140. doi:10.1177/106342660000800301

McGoldrick, M., Carter, B., & Garcia-Preto, N. (2010). *The expanded family life cycle: Individual, family, and social perspectives*. Old Tappan, NJ: Prentice Hall.

Meadows, D., Davies, M., & Beamish, W. (2014). Teacher control over interagency collaboration: A roadblock for effective transitioning of youth with disabilities. *International Journal of Disability, Development and Education, 61*(4), 332–345.

Michaels, C.A., & Ferrara, D.L. (2005). Promoting post-school success for all: The role of collaboration in person-centered transition planning. *Journal of Educational and Psychological Consultation, 16*(4), 287–313.

Migliore, A., Mank, D., Grossi, T., & Rogan, P. (2007). Integrated employment or sheltered workshops: Preferences of adults with intellectual disabilities, their families, and staff. *Journal of Vocational Rehabilitation, 26*(1), 5–19.

Mithaug, D., Wehmeyer, M.L., Agran, M., Martin, J., & Palmer, S. (1998). The self-determined learning model of instruction: Engaging students to solve their learning problems. In M.L. Wehmeyer & D.J. Sands (Eds.), *Making it happen: Student involvement in educational planning, decision-making and instruction* (pp. 299–328). Baltimore, MD: Paul H. Brookes Publishing Co.

Moore, R.J., Cartledge, G., & Heckaman, K. (1995). The effects of social skill instruction and self-monitoring on game-related behaviors of adolescents with emotional or behavioral disorders. *Behavioral Disorders, 20*(4), 253–266.

Morningstar, M.E. (1997). Critical issues in career development and employment preparation for adolescents with disabilities. *Remedial and Special Education, 18*(5), 307–320.

Morningstar, M.E. (2006). *Quality indicators of exemplary transition programs needs assessment instrument*. Lawrence: University of Kansas.

Morningstar, M.E. (2006). *Moving from networking to collaboration during transition*. Presented at the KansTrans Transition Summit, Wichita, KS.

Morningstar, M.E. (2008). *Job analysis form*. Lawrence: University of Kansas.

Morningstar, M.E. (2013). *What's in your toolkit? Building a transition assessment toolkit*. Lawrence: University of Kansas, Transition Coalition.

Morningstar, M.E. (2015). *MTSS and CCR: Are we ready?* [PowerPoint slides]. Retrieved from http://transitioncoalition.org/wp-content/uploads/2016/07/MTSSandCCR-UMTSS-2015.pdf

Morningstar, M.E. (2017). Transition to adulthood for youth with severe and multiple disabilities. In F.P. Orelove, D. Sobsey, & D. Gilles (Eds.), *Educating students with severe and multiple disabilities: A collaborative approach* (5th ed.). Baltimore, MD: Paul H. Brookes Publishing Co.

Morningstar, M.E., Bassett, D.S., Kochhar-Bryant, C., Cashman, J., & Wehmeyer, M.L. (2012). Aligning transition services with secondary education reform: A position statement of the Division on Career Development and Transition. *Career Development and Transition for Exceptional Individuals, 35*(3), 132–142.

Morningstar, M.E., & Benitez, D.T. (2013). Teacher training matters: The results of a multistate survey of secondary special educators regarding transition from school to adulthood. *Teacher Education and Special Education: The Journal of the Teacher Education Division of the Council for Exceptional Children, 36*(1), 51–64.

Morningstar, M.E., & Clavenna-Deane, B. (2014). Preparing secondary special educators and transition specialists. In P.T. Sindelar, E.D. McCray, M.T. Brownell, & B. Lignugaris (Eds.), *Handbook of research on special education teacher preparation* (p. 405). New York, NY: Routledge.

Morningstar, M.E., Frey, B.B., Noonan, P.M., Ng, J., Clavenna-Deane, B., Graves, P., & Williams-Diehm, K. (2010). A preliminary investigation of the relationship of transition preparation and self-determination for students with disabilities in postsecondary educational settings. *Career Development for Exceptional Individuals, 33*(2), 80–94.

Morningstar, M.E., Gaumer-Erickson, A., Lattin, D.L., & Lee, H.J. (2015). *Quality indicators of exemplary transition programs survey-2.* Lawrence, KS: University of Kansas, Transition Coalition, www.transition-coalition.org.

Morningstar, M.E., Gaumer-Erickson, A., Lattin, D.L., & Wade, D.K. (2008). *Best practices in planning for transition.* Lawrence, KS: University of Kansas, Department of Special Education, Transition Coalition web site: www.transitioncoalition.org.

Morningstar, M.E., Gaumer-Erickson, A., Lattin, D., & Wilkerson, D. (2012). *Enhancing career readiness and improving employment outcomes: School and work-based actions.* Lawrence: University of Kansas, Transition Coalition.

Morningstar, M.E., Gaumer-Erickson, A., Lattin, D., & Wilkerson, D. (2012). *Enhancing employment outcomes for youth with disabilities.* Lawrence: University of Kansas, Center for Research on Learning. Retrieved from www.transitioncoalition.org

Morningstar, M.E., Gaumer, A.E., & Noonan, P.M. (2009). *Transition and multi-tiered systems of support: How does it all fit together?* Presentation at the KansTran Summit. Wichita, KS.

Morningstar, M.E., Kleinhammer-Tramill, P.J., & Lattin, D.L. (1999). Using successful models of student-centered transition planning and services for adolescents with disabilities. *Focus on Exceptional Children, 31*(9), 1–19.

Morningstar, M.E., Knollman, G., Semon, S., & Kleinhammer-Tramill, J. (2012). Metrics for what matters: Using postschool outcomes to build school and community renewal. In L.C. Burrello, W. Sailor, & J. Kleinhammer-Tramill (Eds.), *Unifying educational systems: Leadership and policy perspectives* (pp. 158–167). Florence, KY: Routledge, Taylor & Frances Group.

Morningstar, M.E., Lattin, D., & Sarkesian, S. (2009). *It's more than just the law: People make it happen.* Lawrence, KS: University of Kansas, Transition Coalition.

Morningstar, M.E., Lee, H., Lattin, D.L., & Murray, A.K. (2015). An evaluation of the technical adequacy of a revised measure of quality indicators of transition. *Career Development and Transition for Exceptional Individuals, 39*(4), 227–236. doi:2165143415589925

Morningstar, M.E., Lombardi, A., Fowler, C.H., & Test, D.W. (2015). A college and career readiness model for secondary students with disabilities. *Career Development and Transition for Exceptional Individuals.* doi:10.1177/2165143415589926

Morningstar, M.E., Trainor, A.A., & Murray, A.K. (2015). Examining outcomes associated with adult life engagement for youth adults with high incidence disabilities. *Journal of Vocational Rehabilitation 43*(3), 195–208. doi:103233/JVR-150769

Morningstar, M.E., & Turnbull, A.P. (2002). *What makes families unique: Understanding the concepts related to a family systems framework in promoting and supporting self-determination.* Detroit, MI: Wayne State University.

Morningstar, M.E., Turnbull, A.P., & Turnbull, H.R. (1995). What do students with disabilities tell us about the importance of family involvement in the transition from school to adult life? *Exceptional Children, 62*(3), 249–260.

Munandar, V. (2016, May). *Efficacy of video modeling in improving job interviewing skills for two college students with autism.* Unpublished manuscript. Lawrence, KS: University of Kansas.

Murray, C., & Greenberg, M. T. (2006). Examining the importance of social relationships and social contexts in the lives of children with high-incidence disabilities. *The Journal of Special Education, 39*(4), 220–233.

Myles, B.S., Trautman, M.L, & Schelvan, R.L. (2004). *The hidden curriculum: Practical solutions for understanding unstated rules in social situations.* Shawnee Mission, KS: Autism Asperger Publishing Company.

National Alliance for Secondary Education and Transition. (2010). *Career preparatory experiences.* Retrieved from: http://nasetalliance.org/careerprep/index.htm.

National Center and State Collaborative, www.ncscpartners.org.

National Center for Education Statistics. (2013). *Digest of educational statistics.* Washington, DC: U.S. Department of Education. Retrieved from http://nces.ed.gov/programs/digest/2013menu_tables.asp

National Center for Education Statistics. (2016). *Public high school graduation rates.* Washington, DC: U.S. Department of Education. Retrieved from https://nces.ed.gov/programs/coe/indicator_coi.asp

National Center on Secondary Education and Transition, Institute on Community Integration. (NCSET, 2010*). Post-secondary education and students with disabilities webpage.* Retrieved from www.ncset.org/websites/postsecondary.asp

National Collaborative on Workforce and Disability for Youth. (n.d.). *Work-based learning jump start.* Retrieved from www.ncwd-youth.info/work-based-learning

National Council on Disability. (2011). *National disability policy: A progress report.* Retrieved from www.ncd.gov/progress_reports/Oct312011

National Dissemination Center for Children with Disabilities. (2010, September). Supports, modifications and accommodations for students. Retrieved from: http://www.parentcenterhub.org/repository/accommodations/#part1

National Governors Association Center for Best Practices & Council of Chief State School Officers. (2010). Common Core State Standards. Retrieved from www.corestandards.org

National School Climate Center. (n.d.). *School climate.* Retrieved from www.schoolclimate.org/climate

National Secondary Transition Technical Assistance Center. (2011). *Tool for universal design for learning and secondary transition planning for students with disabilities: 101.* David W. Test & Audrey Bartholomew.

National Secondary Transition Technical Assistance Center. (2011). *Predictors of in-school and post-school success.* Charlotte, NC: University of North Carolina, Charlotte. Retrieved from www.nsttac.org

National Secondary Transition Technical Assistance Center. (2013). *In-school predictors of post-school success in secondary transition.* Charlotte, NC: University of North Carolina, Charlotte. Retrieved from www.nsttac.org/sites/default/files/assets/pdf/InschoolPredictorsofPostSchoolSuccess.pdf

National Secondary Transition Technical Assistance Center. (2013). *Summary of predictor categories, outcome areas, level of evidence, descriptions, and student populations.* Retrieved July 10, 2014 from www.nsttac.org/sites/default/files/assets/pdf/pdf/ebps/SummaryOfPredictorsCategories.pdf

National Secondary Transition Technical Assistance Center. (2013). *Examples of infusing secondary transition skills into college and career ready standards in English Language Arts.* Retrieved January 2017 from www.transitionta.org/sites/default/files/Transition_Skills_and_CCSS_in_ELA_2013.pdf

National Technical Assistance Center on Transition (NTACT, 2015). *Effective practices and predictors.* Retrieved from www.transitionta.org/effectivepractices.

Neubert, D.A., & Leconte, P.J. (2013). *Age-appropriate transition assessment: The position of the Division on Career Development and Transition.* Career Development and Transition for Exceptional Individuals, 36(2), 72–83. doi:2165143413487768

Neuenswander, B. & Watson, R. (2015). *What does a 24-Year old KansanlLook like? Themes from community leaders, businesses, educators, and families.* Presented at Statewide Leadership Conference, Wichita, KS.

Newman, L. (2004). *Family involvement in the educational development of youth with disabilities.* A special topic report from the National Longitudinal Transition Study-2 (NLTS2). Menlo Park, CA: SRI International.

Newman, L. (2005). *Family involvement in the educational development of youth with disabilities.* A special topic report from the National Longitudinal Transition Study-2 (NLTS2). Online submission.

Newman, L., Wagner, M., Cameto, R., & Knokey, A.M. (2009). *The post-high school outcomes of youth with disabilities up to 4 years after high school.* A report of findings from the National Longitudinal Transition Study-2 (NLTS2) (NCSER 2009-3017). Menlo Park, CA: SRI International. Retrieved from www.nlts2.org/reports/2009_04/nlts2_report_2009_04_complete.pdf

Newman, L., Wagner, M., Cameto, R., Knokey, A., & Shaver, D. (2010). *Comparisons across time of the outcomes of youth with disabilities up to 4 years after high school.* A report of findings from the National Longitudinal Transition Study (NLTS) and the National Longitudinal Transition Study-2 (NLTS2). Washington, DC: National Center for Special Education Research, NCSER 2010–3008.

Newman, L., Wagner, M., Knokey, A.M., Marder, C., Nagle, K., Shaver, D., & Wei, X., with Cameto, R., Contreras, E., Ferguson, K., Greene, S., & Schwarting, M. (2011). *The post-high school outcomes of young adults with disabilities up to 8 years after high school.* A report from the National Longitudinal Transition Study-2 (NLTS2) (NCSER 2011-3005). Menlo Park, CA: SRI International. Retrieved from www.nlts2.org/reports

Next Generation Science Standards. (n.d.). *Next generation science standards.* Retrieved from www.nextgenscience.org

Nix, T. (2010). *Providing outreach to families of youth with disabilities from culturally and linguistically diverse backgrounds by working with cultural groups and community organizations.* Unpublished dissertation, Lawrence: University of Kansas.

Noonan, P.M., & Morningstar, M.E. (2012). Effective strategies for interagency collaboration. *Handbook of adolescent transition for youth with disabilities* (pp. 312–328).

Noonan, P.M., Morningstar, M.E., & Clark, G. (2009). *Transition assessment: The big picture.* Lawrence, KS: University of Kansas, Department of Special Education. Retrieved from www.transitioncoalition.org

Noonan, P.M., Morningstar, M.E., & Erickson, A.G. (2008). Improving interagency collaboration effective strategies used by high-performing local districts and communities. *Career Development for Exceptional Individuals, 31*(3), 132–143.

O'Brien, J. & O'Brien, C.L. (2000). *The origins of person-centered planning. A community of practice perspective.* Retrieved from http://delawareebse.pbworks.com/f/The+Origin+of+Person+Centered+Planning.pdf

Odom, S.L., Thompson, J.L., Hedges, S., Boyd, B.A., Dykstra, J. R., Duda, M.A., & Bord, A. (2014). Technology-aided interventions and instruction for adolescents with autism spectrum disorder. *Journal of Autism and Developmental Disorders, 45*(12), 1–15.

Office of Disability Employment Policy. (n.d.). *Skills to pay the bills: Mastering soft skills for employment success.* Washington, DC: Department of Labor. Retrieved from www.dol.gov/odep/topics/youth/softskills

Office of Disability Policy. (2007). *Essential Skills for Getting a Job.* Retrieved from: www.dol.gov/odep/documents/EssentialSkillsforGettingaJob.doc

O'Leary, E. (2005, January). *Overview, comments and recommended action for transition services: Individuals with Disabilities Education Improvement Act of 2004.* Unpublished white paper. (Available from Ed O'Leary, eoleary@rap.midco.net)

OSEP Technical Assistance Center on Positive Behavioral Interventions and Supports. (2017). *Positive behavioral interventions & supports.* Retrieved from www.pbis.org

Otten, K., & Tuttle, J. (2011). *How to reach and teach children with challenging behavior: Practical, ready to use interventions that work.* San Francisco, CA: Jossey-Bass.

Pianta, R.C., La Paro, K.M., & Hamre, B.K. (2008). *The classroom assessment scoring system: Manual K-3.* Baltimore, MD: Paul H. Brookes Publishing Co.

Povenmire-Kirk, T., Diegelmann, K., Crump, K., Schnorr, C., Test, D., Flowers, C., & Aspel, N. (2015). Implementing CIRCLES: A new model for interagency collaboration in transition planning. *Journal of Vocational Rehabilitation, 42*(1), 51–65.

Rebora, A. (2010, April). Responding to RTI. *Education Week Teacher Professional Development Sourcebook, 3*(2). Retrieved from www.edweek.org/tsb/articles/2010/04/12/02allington.h03.html?qs=allington

Reed, D., & Vaughn, S. (2010). Reading interventions for older students. In T.A. Glover & S. Vaughn (Eds.), *The promise of response to intervention: Evaluating current science and practice* (pp. 143–186). New York, NY: Guilford Press.

Reinke, W.M., Lewis-Palmer, T., & Martin, E. (2007). The effect of visual performance feedback on teacher use of behavior-specific praise. *Behavior Modification, 31*(3), 247–263.

Repetto, J., McGorray, S., Wang, H., Podmostko, M., Andrews, W.D., Lubbers, J., & Gritz, S. (2011). The high school experience: What students with and without disabilities report as they leave school. *Career Development for Exceptional Individuals, 34*(3), 142–152.

Reynolds, C.R., & Kamphaus, R.W. (2015). *BASC-3: Behavior assessment system for children.* San Antonio, TX: Pearson.

Roberts, M.M, Murphy, A., Dolce, J., Spagnolo, A., Gill, K., Lu, W., & Librera, L. (2010). A study of the impact of social support development on job acquisition and retention among people with psychiatric disabilities. *Journal of Vocational Rehabilitation, 33*(3), 203–207.

Rojewski, J.W. (2002). Career assessment for adolescents with mild disabilities: Critical concerns for transition planning. *Career Development for Exceptional Individuals, 25*(1), 73–94.

Rowe, D.A., Alverson, C.Y., Unruh, D.K., Fowler, C.H., Kellems, R., & Test, D.W. (2015). A Delphi study to operationalize evidence-based predictors in secondary transition. *Career Development and Transition for Exceptional Individuals 8*(2), 113–126, Online First. doi:10.1177/2165143414526429

Ryndak, D.L., Alper, S., Hughes, C., & McDonnell, J. (2012). Documenting impact of educational contexts on long-term outcomes for students with significant disabilities. *Education and Training in Autism and Developmental Disabilities, 47*(2), 127–138.

Salend, S.J., & Duhaney, L.M. (2011). Historical and philosophical changes in the education of students with exceptionalities. *Advances in Special Education, 21,* 1–20. doi:10.1108/S0270-4013(2011)0000021004

Sanford, C., Newman, L., Wagner, M., Cameto, R., Knokey, A.M., & Shaver, D. (2011). *The post-high school outcomes of young adults with disabilities up to 6 years after high school.* Key findings from the National Longitudinal Transition Study-2 (NLTS2) (NCSER 2011-3004). Menlo Park, CA: SRI International. Retrieved from www.nlts2.org/nlts2/reports/2011_09/nlts2_report_2011_09_complete.pdf

Sargent, L.R., Perner, D., & Cook, T. (2012). *Social skills for students with autism spectrum disorders* (Vol. 1). Arlington, VA: Council for Exceptional Children.

Satir, V. (1972). *Peoplemaking.* Palo Alto, CA: Science and Behavior Books.

Sebring, P.B., Allensworth, E., Bryk, A.S., Easton, J.Q., & Luppescu, S. (2006). *The essential supports for school improvement.* Research Report. Consortium on Chicago School Research.

Shaw, S.F., Madaus, J.W., & Dukes, L.L. (2010). *Preparing students with disabilities for college success: A practical guide to transition planning.* Baltimore, MD: Paul H. Brookes Publishing Co.

Shogren, K.A., Palmer, S.B., Wehmeyer, M.L., Williams-Diehm, K., & Little, T.D. (2011). Effect of intervention with the self-determined learning model of instruction on access and goal attainment. *Remedial and Special Education, 33*(5), 320–330. doi:10.1177/0741932511410072

Shogren, K.A., Wehmeyer, M.L., Palmer, S.B., Rifenbark, G.G., & Little, T.D. (2013). Relationships between self-determination and postschool outcomes for youth with disabilities. *The Journal of Special Education.* Advance online publication. doi:10.1177/0022466913489733

Simonsen, M., Stuart, C., Luecking, R., & Certo, N.J. (2013). Collaboration among school and post-school agencies for seamless transition. *The Road Ahead: Transition to Adult Life for Persons with Disabilities, 34,* 137.

Sinclair, M.F., Christenson, S.L., & Thurlow, M.L. (2005). Promoting school completion of urban secondary youth with emotional or behavioral disabilities. *Exceptional Children, 71*(4), 465–482.

Sitlington, P., Neubert, D.A., & Leconte, P.J. (1997). Transition assessment: The position of the Division on Career Development and Transition. *Career Development for Exceptional Individuals, 20*(1), 69–79.

Smith, S. (2002, August). Applying cognitive-behavioral techniques to social skills instruction. ED469279. *ERIC/OSEP Digest.* Arlington, VA: ERIC Clearinghouse on Disabilities and Gifted Education. Retrieved November 9, 2015 from www.ericdigests.org/2003-3/skills.htm

Snyder, E.P., & Shapiro, E. (1997). Teaching students with emotional/behavioral disorders the skills to participate in the development of their own IEPs. *Behavioral Disorders, 22*(4), 246–259.

Snyder, T.D., & Dillow, S.A. (2012). *Digest of education statistics 2011.* National Center for Education Statistics.

Solberg, V.S., Wills, J., & Osman, D. (2012). *Promoting quality individualized plans: A "how to guide" focused on the high school years.* Washington, DC: National Collaborative on Workforce and Disability for Youth, Institute for Educational Leadership.

Stodden, R.A., & Leake, D.W. (1994). Getting to the core of transition: A re-assessment of old wine in new bottles. *Career Development for Exceptional Individuals, 17*(1), 65–76.

Strawhun, J., O'Connor, A., Norris, L., & Peterson, R.L. (2014, September). *Social skills instruction.* Lincoln, NE: University of Nebraska, Student Engagement Project. Retrieved November 9, 2015 from http://k12engagement.unl.edu/social-skills

Technology-Related Assistance for Individuals with Disabilities Act. (1988). PL100-407, §140.25.

Test, D.W., Fowler, C.H., Richter, S.M., White, J., Mazzotti, V., Walker, A.R., & Kortering, L. (2009). Evidence-based practices in secondary transition. *Career Development for Exceptional Individuals, 32*(2), 115–128. doi:10.1177/0885728809336859

Test, D.W., Fowler, C.H., & Scroggins, L.C. (2011). *Tool for tiered interventions and secondary transition planning for students with disabilities: 101.* Charlotte, NC: National Secondary Transition Technical Assistance Center, University of North Carolina at Charlotte, College of Education, Special Education & Child Development.

Test, D.W., Mason, C., Hughes, C., Konrad, M., Neale, M., & Wood, W.M. (2004). Student involvement in individualized education program meetings. *Exceptional Children, 70*(4), 391–412.

Test, D.W., Mazzotti, V.L., Mustian, A.L., Fowler, C.H., Kortering, L., & Kohler, P. (2009). Evidence-based secondary transition predictors for improving postschool outcomes for students with disabilities. *Career Development for Exceptional Individuals, 32*(3), 160–181. doi:10.1177/0885728809346960

Test, D.W., & Neale, M. (2004). Using the "self-advocacy strategy" to increase middle graders' IEP participation. *Journal of Behavioral Education, 13*(2), 135–145.

Thapa, A., Cohen, J., Guffey, S., & Higgins-D'Alessandro, A., (2013). A review of school climate research. *Review of Educational Research, 83*(3), 357–385. doi:103102/0034654313483907

Therriault, S.B., Heppen, J., O'Cummings, M., Fryer, L., & Johnson, A. (2010). *Early warning system implementation guide: For use with the national high school center's early warning system tool v2.0.* Washington, DC: American Institutes for Research, National High School Center.

Thoma, C. A., & Getzel, E. E. (2005). Self-determination is what it's all about: What post-secondary student with disabilities tell us are important considerations for success. *Education and Training in Mental Retardation and Developmental Disabilities, 40*(3), 35–48.

Thoma, C.A., & Tamura, R. (2013). *Demystifying transition assessment.* Baltimore, MD: Paul H. Brookes Publishing Co.

Todd, T., & Reid, G. (2006). Increasing physical activity in individuals with autism. *Focus on Autism and Other Developmental Disabilities, 21*(3), 167–176.

Trainor, A.A. (2007). Person-centered planning in two culturally distinct communities responding to divergent needs and preferences. *Career Development for Exceptional Individuals, 30*(2), 92–103.

Trainor, A.A., Morningstar, M.E., Murray, A., & Kim, H. (2013). Social capital during the postsecondary transition for young adults with high incidence disabilities. *Prevention Researcher, 20*(2), 7–10.

Transition Coalition. (n.d.) *Transition planning process flow chart.* Lawrence: University of Kansas.

Turnbull, A., & Morningstar, M.E. (1993). Family and professional interaction. In M. Snell, (Ed.), *Instruction of students with severe disabilities* (4th ed.) (pp. 31–60). Upper Saddle River, NJ: Merrill-Prentice Hall.

Turnbull & Turnbull (2001) Families, professionals, and exceptionality: Collaborating for empowerment. Upper Saddle River, NJ: Pearson Prentice Hall.

Turnbull, A., Turnbull, H.R., Erwin, E., Soodak, L., & Shogren, K. (2011). *Families, professionals, and exceptionality: Positive outcomes through partnerships and trust.* Upper Saddle River, NJ: Pearson Prentice Hall.

Turnbull, A., Turnbull, R., Wehmeyer, M.L., & Shogren, K.A. (2013). *Exceptional lives: Special education in today's schools* (7th ed.). Upper Saddle River, NJ: Pearson Prentice Hall.

U.S. Department of Commerce. (2013, May). *Current population survey (CPS), October, 1967 through 2012.* Washington, DC: Census Bureau. Retrieved from http://nces.ed.gov/programs/digest/d13/tables/dt13_219.70.asp

U.S. Department of Education. (2010). *Blueprint for reform.* Retrieved from http://www2ed.gov/policy/elsec/leg/blueprint/index.html

U.S. Department of Education. (2011). *Individuals with Disabilities Education Act (IDEA) resource website.* Retrieved from http://idea.ed.gov

Utah State University, Academic Success Center. *Estimating my weekly study hours worksheet.* Logan, UT: Utah State University. Retrieved from www.usu.edu/asc

Van Ruesen, A.K., Bos, C.S., Schumaker, J.B., & Deshler, D.D. (1994). *The self-advocacy strategy for education and transition planning.* Lawrence, KS: Edge Enterprises.

Villa, R.A., Thousand, J.S., & Nevin, A.I. (2013). *A guide to co-teaching: New lessons and strategies to facilitate student learning.* Thousand Oaks, CA: Corwin Press.

Virginia Department of Behavioral Health and Developmental Services. (2009*). Person-centered planning advanced training.* Retrieved from www.dbhds.virginia.gov/ODS-PersonCenteredPractices.htm

Virginia Department of Education Self-Determination Project (2005). *Good day plan.* Virginia: Department of Education. Retrieved from www.imdetermined.org/quick_links/good_day_plan

Virginia Department of Education Self-Determination Project. (2005). *I'm determined one pager.* Virginia: Department of Education. Retrieved from www.imdetermined.org/quick_links/one_pager

Wagner, M., Kutash, K., Duchnowski, A.J., Epstein, M.H., & Sumi, W.C. (2005). The children and youth we serve: A national picture of the characteristics of students with emotional disturbances receiving special education. *Journal of Emotional and Behavioral Disorders, 13*(2), 79–96.

Wagner, M., & Newman, L. (2012). Longitudinal transition outcomes for youth with emotional disturbance. *Psychiatric Rehabilitation Journal, 35,* 199–208.

Wagner, M., Newman, L., Cameto, R., Levine, P, & Garza, N. (2006). *An overview of findings from wave 2 of the National Longitudinal Transition Study-2 (NLTS2).* Retrieved from www.nlts2.org/reports/2006_08/nlts2_report_2006_08_complete.pdf

Wagner, M., Newman, L., D'Arnico, R., Jay, E.O., Butler-Nalin, P., & Marder, C. (1991). *Youth with disabilities: How are they doing?* Menlo Park, CA: SRI International.

Walker, A., & Bartholomew, A. (2012). Student development: Employment skills. In D.W. Test (Ed.), *Evidence-based instructional strategies for transition* (pp. 79–95). Baltimore, MD: Paul H. Brookes Publishing Co.

Walker, A.R., Kortering, L., Fowler, C.H., Rowe, D.A., & Bethune, L. (2013). *Age-appropriate transition assessment guide* (2nd ed.). National Secondary Transition Technical Assistance Center: University of North Carolina, Charlotte.

Walker, A.R., Richter, S., Uphold, N.M., & Test, D.W. (2010). Review of the literature on community-based instruction across grade levels. *Education and Training in Autism and Developmental Disabilities, 45*(2), 242–267.

Wehman, P., Inge, K.J., Revell, W.G., & Brooke, V.A. (2007). Supported employment and workplace supports. In P. Wehman, K.J. Inge, W.G. Revell, & V.A. Brooke (Eds.), *Real work for real pay: Inclusive employment for people with disabilities.* Baltimore, MD: Paul H. Brookes Publishing Co.

Wehman, P., Brooke, V.A., & Revell, W.G. (2007). Inclusive employment: Rolling back segregation of people with disabilities. In P. Wehman, K.J. Inge, W.G. Revell, & V.A. Brooke (Eds.), *Real work for real pay: Inclusive employment for people with disabilities.* Baltimore, MD: Paul H. Brookes Publishing Co.

Wehman, P., Brooks-Lane, N., Brooke, V.A., & Turner, E. (2007). Self-advocacy for supported employment and resource ownership. In P. Wehman, K.J. Inge, W.G. Revell, & V.A. Brooke (Eds.), *Real work for real pay: Inclusive employment for people with disabilities.* Baltimore, MD: Paul H. Brookes Publishing Co.

Wehman, P., & Kregel, J. (2012). *Functional curriculum for elementary, middle, and secondary age students with special needs.* Austin, TX: PRO-ED.

Wehmeyer, M.L. (2005). Self-determination and individuals with severe disabilities: Re-examining meanings and misinterpretations. *Research and Practice for Persons with Severe Disabilities, 30*(3), 113–120.

Wehmeyer, M.L., Agran, M., & Hughes, C. (2000). A national survey of teachers' promotion of self-determination and student-directed learning. *The Journal of Special Education, 34*(2), 58–68.

Wehmeyer, M.L., Agran, M., Palmer, S., & Mithaug, D. (1999). *A teacher's guide to implementing the Self-Determined Learning Model of Instruction.* Lawrence, KS: Beach Center on Disability.

Wehmeyer, M.L., & Field, S.L. (2007). *Self-determination: Instructional and assessment strategies.* Thousand Oaks, CA: Corwin Press.

Wehmeyer, M.L., & Kelcher, K. (1995). *The Arc's self-determination scale.* Silver Springs, MD: The Arc of the United States.

Wehmeyer, M.L., Lawrence, M., Garner, N., Soukup, J., & Palmer, K. (2004). *Whose future is it anyway? A student-directed transition planning process* (2nd ed.). Lawrence, KS: Beach Center on Disability.

Wehmeyer, M.L., Morningstar, M., & Husted, D. (1999). *Family involvement in transition planning and implementation.* Austin, TX: PRO-ED.

Wehmeyer, M.L., & Palmer, S.B. (2003). Adult outcomes for students with cognitive disabilities three years after high school: The impact of self-determination. *Education and Training in Development Disabilities, 38*(2), 131–144.

Wehmeyer, M.L., Palmer, S.B., Lee, Y., Williams-Diehm, K., & Shogren, K.A. (2011). A randomized-trial evaluation of the effect of Whose Future is it Anyway? on self-determination. *Career Development for Exceptional Individuals, 34*(1), 45–56.

Wehmeyer, M.L., & Schwartz, M. (1997). Self-determination and positive adult outcomes: A follow-up study of youth with mental retardation or learning disabilities. *Exceptional Children, 63*(2), 245–255.

Wehmeyer, M.L., Shogren, K.A., Palmer, S.B., Williams-Diehm, K.L., Little, T.D., & Boulton, A. (2012). The impact of the self-determined learning model of instruction on student self-determination. *Exceptional Children, 78*(2), 135–153.

White, J., & Weiner, J.S. (2004). Influence of least restrictive environment and community based training on integrated employment outcomes for transitioning students with severe disabilities. *Journal of Vocational Rehabilitation, 21,* 149–156.

Wilkins, J., & Huckabee, S. (2014). *A literature map of dropout prevention interventions for students with disabilities.* Clemson, SC: National Dropout Prevention Center for Students with Disabilities, Clemson University. Retrieved from www.ndpc-sd.org/documents/wilkins-huckabee-lit-review.pdf

Will, M. (1983). *OSRS programming for the transition of youth with disabilities: Bridges from school to working life.* Washington, DC: U.S. Department of Education, Office of Special Education and Rehabilitative Services.

Winner, M.G. (2007a). *Thinking about you, thinking about me* (2nd ed.). San Jose, CA: Think Social Publishing.

Winner, M.G. (2007b). *Social behavior mapping: Connecting behavior, emotions and consequences across the day.* San Jose, CA: Think Social Publishing.

Wolf, L.E., Thierfield Brown, J., & Bork, R. (2009). *Students with Asperger Syndrome: A guide for college personnel.* Shawnee Mission, KS: Autism Asperger Publisher Company.

Wolfe, P.S., Boone, R.S., & Blanchett, W.J. (1998). Regular and special educators' perceptions of transition competencies. *Career Development for Exceptional Individuals, 21*(1), 87–106.

Wolgemuth, J.R., Cobb, R.B., & Dugan, J.J. (2007). *The effects of self-management interventions on academic outcomes for youth with disabilities.* Fort Collins, CO: Colorado State University.

Wolman, J.M., Campeau, P.L., DuBois, P.A., Mithaug, D.E., & Stolarski, V.S. (1994). *AIR self-determination scale and users guide.* Palo Alto, CA: American Institutes for Research.

Wraparound services and positive behavior support. (n.d.). In PBIS.org. Retrieved from www.pbis.org/school/tertiary-level/wraparound

Yazzie-Mintz, E. (2010). *Charting the path from engagement to achievement: A report on the 2009 High School Survey of Student Engagement.* Retrieved from http://ceep.indiana.edu/hssse/images/HSSSE_2010_Report.pdf

Zarrow Center for Learning Enrichment. (n.d). *Putting it all together: The summary of performance lesson. Student-directed transition planning.* Norman, OK: University of Oklahoma. Retrieved from www.ou.edu/content/education/centers-and-partnerships/zarrow/trasition-education-materials/student-directed-transition-planning/sdtp_home/summary-of-performance.html

Zarrow Center for Learning Enrichment. (n.d.). *The self-directed IEP.* Norman, OK: University of Oklahoma. Retrieved from www.ou.edu/education/centers-and-partnerships/zarrow/choicemaker-curriculum/self-directed-iep.html

# Index

Note: Page numbers followed by *f* indicate figures, *t* indicate tables.